Psychoanalysis as Science

Ernest R. Hilgard, Ph.D.
Lawrence S. Kubie, M.D.
E. Pumpian-Mindlin, M.D.

Psychoanalysis as Science

The Hixon Lectures on the Scientific
Status of Psychoanalysis

Edited by
E. Pumpian-Mindlin, M.D.

GREENWOOD PRESS, PUBLISHERS
WESTPORT, CONNECTICUT

These lectures were delivered at the California
Institute of Technology, Department of Biology,
Pasadena, California, March–May 1950, under the
sponsorship of the Hixon Fund Committee.

Editor's Preface

The Hixon Fund was established at the California Institute of Technology in 1938 through a grant from the estate of Frank P. Hixon. Its purpose was the furthering of such scientific endeavor as would increase the understanding of human behavior. In line with this purpose it has aided in many types of studies dealing with the application of biological and physiological principles to human behavior. These include studies such as the use of electroconvulsive therapy as a therapeutic agent in mental disorders, the efficacy of various treatments for battle fatigue and motion sickness, the distribution of electrical potentials in nerves, etc. In addition, the Hixon Fund has subsidized a series of symposia and lectures such as the recently published *Cerebral Mechanisms in Behavior* (1948)[1], the present series of lectures, a series of four lectures by Dr. G. Marmont of the University of Chicago on modern concepts of nerve transmission, and others.

Under the chairmanship of Professor A. van Harreveld, the Hixon Fund is administered by a committee which includes Professors G. W. Beadle, James Bonner, Henry Borsook, Max Delbrück, Linus Pauling, A. H. Sturtevant, and C. A. G. Wiersma.

In the fall of 1949 the Committee, after lengthy consideration, decided to sponsor the present series of lectures on psychoanalysis. This decision represented a departure from the general principles which had hitherto prevailed in its policy. In the preliminary deliberation of the Committee, Dr. Ruth S. Tolman and Dr. Ruth Valentine played a significant role in presenting the pertinent material so that it was finally decided to sponsor the present series.

The Committee was moved to undertake these lectures by the very fact that there was so much question in the minds of many regarding the scientific status of psychoanalysis. If through this series the controversy over the status of psychoanalysis as a science can be even partially clarified, perhaps some of the "sound and fury" surrounding psychoanalysis may be quieted and more dispassionate objective attitudes adopted. In any case, there exists no question as to the broad influence which psychoanalysis exerts in our society. Therefore, be it a science or not, it has to be reckoned with as a phenomenon in our present-day world.

The plan of this symposium was to present in a series of five lectures the scientific basis of psychoanalysis. Dr. Ernest R. Hilgard, then chairman of the Department of Psychology, at present Dean of the Graduate Division, Stanford University, former president of the American Psychological Association, gave the first two

[1] John Wiley & Sons, Inc., 1951.

lectures on the "Experimental Approaches to Psychoanalysis." Dr. Lawrence S. Kubie of New York, clinical professor of psychiatry at Yale University School of Medicine, faculty, New York Psychoanalytic Institute, member of the American Psychoanalytic Association, gave the next two on "Problems and Techniques of Validation in Psychoanalysis." The last lecture was presented by me, then clinical director, now chief of the Mental Hygiene Clinic of the Veterans Administration, Los Angeles, member of the American Psychoanalytic Association, on "The Position of Psychoanalysis in Relation to the Social and Biological Sciences."

At the conclusion of the lecture series the Hixon Fund Committee offered me the editorship of the series, a position which I felt honored to accept. It was my feeling that the lectures should appear in book form in much the same style as when they were originally presented, in order to preserve the atmosphere which surrounded them on the campus of the California Institute of Technology. Therefore, no attempt was made to force them into an artificial stylistic uniformity or to unify the approach, emphasis, or attitude of the individual authors.[2] I think that the results herein justify this decision. The individuality of each author is easily apparent, and yet areas of agreement with regard to certain fundamental propositions of psychoanalysis are quite evident.

It is my feeling that the Hixon Fund Committee manifested its foresight and wisdom in sponsoring this series of lectures. Certainly they were received by the audience of scientists with interest and thoughtfulness. I do not think that all the problems with regard to the status of psychoanalysis are solved in these lectures. However they certainly stimulated much discussion and thought among scientists who hitherto had felt unable to evaluate the scientific aspects of psychoanalysis properly. Among the social sciences psychoanalysis was one of the first to attempt to approach the human being as a total functioning whole. The very consideration of broad aspects of human behavior and thought creates problems for all of us (including the psychoanalysts themselves). All of us "normal" people tend to consider ourselves as integrated, functioning human beings. As such, we pride ourselves (each in his own particular way) on being "experts in human nature." It seems presumptuous to be told that not only are we not experts in judging and evaluating other people, but that, adding insult to injury, we do not even know everything about ourselves, our own attitudes, feelings, and behavior. Thus psychoanalysis encounters very basic difficulties in approaching its chosen field of endeavor from its chosen vantage point.

It is my hope that the reader who is not trained in psychoanalysis will find in this series of five lectures an attempt to discuss basic problems of observation,

---

[2] Bibliographical references for all the lectures are presented at the end of the book rather than after each lecture.

methodology, validation, and theory as they have been applied in psychoanalysis. In addition, I hope there has been a sufficient presentation of the raw data of psychoanalytic observation to enable him to form an independent and considered judgment of his own.

E. PUMPIAN-MINDLIN, M.D.

LOS ANGELES, CALIFORNIA
April 26, 1952

Contents

Psychoanalysis as Science

Experimental Approaches
to Psychoanalysis

I. PSYCHODYNAMICS

THE NAME OF SIGMUND FREUD stands out as one of the great names of the last hundred years. He belongs to the cultural history of our times, along with men like Darwin and Marx and Einstein. But he is a controversial figure, related to psychology more as Marx is related to economics than as Darwin is to biology or Einstein to physics. Although he has been without question a highly influential figure, psychologists are not uniformly grateful for what he has taught us. In approaching an interpretation of psychoanalysis we are entering into an arena of heated debate.

You have a right to know whether you are listening to a proponent of psychoanalytic theories, to an opponent, or to someone who considers himself nonpartisan. Curiously enough, it is difficult to give a straightforward answer, for it is something like defining your political position as right or left of center when there is no agreement as to where center lies. I am reminded of a story by the distinguished clergyman Harry Emerson Fosdick. A young man came to him, defiantly, saying: "I do not believe in God." Fosdick asked him what kind of a god he did not believe in. After the boy told him, Fosdick replied: "Neither do I believe in that kind of a god." This is an awkward way of saying that psychoanalysis, from my point of view, is not one thing toward which your attitude must be one either of acceptance or of rejection. My own position is that Freud and other psychoanalysts have hit upon enough reality so that there is much for us to learn from them, and, with some reworking, there will be a substantial body of scientific generalizations resulting. I say "resulting" rather than "remaining" for I do not care whether we end up believing that Freud was a scientist or a romanticist. If eventually we are able to make science out of materials that he called strongly to our attention, then we shall owe him that historical debt, whatever the verdict may be about his own formulations.

In these two lectures, I am to deal with efforts to test some of the teachings of psychoanalysis, and not with an appraisal of the results of full-fledged psychoanalytic treatment. This obviously has its limitations, for the complete story of psychoanalysis can be told only in the reconstruction of individual biographies, painstakingly (and somewhat painfully) revealed in hour after hour on the psychoanalytic couch. Much that I report may seem trivial compared with the richness of such individual biographies, but it is always one of the tasks of science to make its problems bite-size, so that they can be worked upon with the instruments that the scientist has at his disposal. In this lecture I propose to discuss what have come to be called "psychodynamics," that is, some of the principles of development, motivation, and conduct that are part of the fabric of psychoanalytic theory. In the second lecture I shall discuss principles of psychotherapy—not the appraisal of full-scale analysis, but the conjectures about the turning points in a patient's progress that can be selected for separate study.

THE CONSEQUENCES OF INFANTILE FRUSTRATION

The importance of early childhood is one of the most familiar teachings of psychoanalysis. We hear a great deal about sucking and toilet-training as important background factors in the formation of later personality or character structure. These early experiences of the child are said to result in a secure individual, provided the needs they represent are appropriately gratified. Such a child will take the hurdles of growing up in stride. If, however, the needs are met in such a way as to induce frustration, the consequent insecurity and anxiety will hound the individual throughout his life.

Here, then, are some generalizations that can be restated more precisely and subjected to investigation. I shall delve into the growing literature only at one or two points, in order to show what is involved in trying to experiment in these fields.

The Need to Suck, and Consequences of Its Frustration

One generalization that takes shape is that the infant has a *need to suck*, as well as to receive nourishment. If this is true, it may be inferred that if the infant is fed too rapidly it will have to fulfill its quota of sucking by sucking its thumb, or the bedclothes, or some convenient nipple substitute.

David Levy some years ago studied this problem by selecting a litter of six puppies, and dividing them into three pairs (25). One pair remained at the mother's breast. The two other pairs were fed by bottle. The "long-feeders" had a small hole in the bottle's nipple, and after feeding sucked as long as they wished on a nipple-covered finger. The "short-feeders" received their milk through a large-holed bottle and did not have the nipple-covered finger to suck upon. The results agreed in general with the theory. That is, the short-feeders as compared with the long-feeders did much more sucking between meals on each others' bodies, on rubber balls, and other objects, and were more responsive to sucking tests with the experimenter's finger between meals. The breast-fed dogs did the least body- and finger-sucking. These results with dogs were in line with results Levy had earlier reported for human infants (26). More recently, a group of workers including pediatricians and psychologists have studied the consequences of feeding human infants from a cup, beginning at birth. Only preliminary reports are available, but the suggestion comes out that the need to suck may be an acquired one (7). For infants who have not learned to suck it appears that not to suck is not frustrating. If these results are confirmed, the generalizations about the need to suck will have to be somewhat modified. It might then be stated that the sucking experience is one in which a need to suck may be learned, and, when the need has been acquired, unless appropriately gratified, it may produce the behavior characteristic of frustration. Perhaps this points out what I mean when I say that the final generalization need not be the original psychoanalytic one in order for psychoanalysis to have been of service. It is useful if it provides a first approximation to the generalization, and thus defines the field of inquiry.

In addition to the immediate consequences of frustration, resulting, in the case of frustrated sucking, in such substitutive behavior as thumb-sucking, the theory goes on to assume that there are more remote consequences. Even though there is a period that is symptom-free, perhaps when a new crisis develops, say at adolescence, the consequences of infantile insecurity may again manifest themselves.

Hoarding as a Consequence of Infantile Frustration

We may try to state a more precise theorem about this. If through frustration in infancy food has been the occasion for anxiety, there will be a tendency to overanxiety about food in adulthood, manifested, for example, in a tendency to hoard excessive amounts of food. This is perhaps illustrated by the American housewife who felt so threatened by the shortages during the war. According to this theory, her anxiety would be explained by feeding difficulties associated with the child-rearing practices of the last generation.

An experiment was performed with that favorite animal of the psychological laboratory—the white rat (21). Litter mates provided control groups. One group of young rats was fed consistently, after weaning always having enough food and water present to satisfy hunger and thirst. The second group suffered feeding frustration and deprivation through irregular feeding. While fed enough to maintain growth, there was great inconsistency in feeding, so that the animals were occasionally without food for long stretches. It is presumed that we here have an analogue of infantile frustration. After this differential treatment, the groups were again fed alike for some weeks and appeared to behave alike. The test of the remote consequences of infantile frustration came when, in late adolescence or early maturity, both groups of rats were subjected to irregular feeding, the one group for the first time, the other reinstating a childhood experience. Following this period of frustration, both groups were tested in an apparatus permitting food hoarding. An alleyway from the living cage led to a food supply at its end. The rats that had been frustrated in infancy hoarded over twice as many food pellets as the rats that in infancy had developed a secure feeling about food. The experiment has since been repeated several times with modifications. The later results are, in general, consonant with the earlier ones (28).

We are primarily interested in man, and when we make use of studies with animals we are seeking to exhibit in comparative fashion some of the principles believed to apply to human behavior. In the end, however, it will always be necessary to validate the principles through observations of man himself. The principle that early food frustration may lead to later hoarding behavior, as shown in the animal studies, has been interpreted as applying to some primitive human societies. Some of the observations have been summarized as follows by Hunt (21):

Tribes using relatively similar practices in nursing, weaning, toilet training, etc., appear to have similar typical personalities even though the geographical circumstances in which they live might appear to dictate different types of personalities. The Arapesh of New Guinea are generous, co-operative, and peaceful, in spite of the fact that they live on unfertile mountainous land and seldom have ample food. The Pitchentera of Central Australia are generous, often fatally optimistic, and do not hoard food, even though they live in a land of frequent famine. From the anthropological reports, it appears that both of these tribes are accustomed to provide infants with frequent and affectionate nursing. Crying is answered with immediate suckling. Weaning is late; and, among the Pitchentera at least, little attention is paid to toilet habits, and children are not expected to be clean. On the other hand, the Normanby Islanders, although they live where food is abundant, are dominated by a desire to collect large stores of food. They are competitive, and frequently quarrelsome. Their children, however, are nursed briefly and without affection. The Mundugumor, a people of the same race as the Arapesh, who live on the fertile lowlands of New Guinea, are arrogant, aggressive, impatient, and quarrelsome in the extreme. These Mundugumor nurse their children standing up for very brief periods, treat crying with slaps, and not infrequently permit their children to die from neglect.

Interesting as such parallel histories of development are, two important precautions need to be stated. First, there are many cultures in which the relationship between infant handling and adult behavior does not conform at all neatly to the hypothesis (29). Second, children are influenced throughout life by the adults with whom they live, so that adult behavior cannot be attributed solely to training in infancy. Children who grow up in a friendly culture (or in a quarrelsome one) continue to learn what is expected of them as they grow up. It would be instructive to see what would happen to an Arapesh child adopted into a Mundugumor household beyond the age of infancy. Would the child grow up aggressive like the Mundugumor or peace loving like the Arapesh? His adult personality would provide a better test of the influence of the early years than it would were he to grow up among the same people who provided his environment in infancy.

Our own society shows reflections of food anxiety, typified by the hoarding behavior during the war, or by the carrying over of home-canned fruit from one season to the next by a thrifty housewife. If our infant handling is now becoming more permissive and less frustrating to the child, we would have to predict, according to the hypothesis under discussion, that the next generation would be less threatened were it again necessary to institute rationing of food.

DEFENSE MECHANISMS

Let us turn now to defense mechanisms. The defense mechanisms were those features of psychoanalytic theory first domesticated by academic psychology, so that now every student of elementary psychology knows about rationalization and projection and compensation and sublimation. How long a list of mechanisms he knows depends upon who his teacher is and which textbook he reads. He may know a great many of them, however, without knowing anything about their origin in psychoanalytic theory.

The specific mechanisms lend themselves readily to experimental study. The studies have been ably reviewed by Sears (32, 35) and the mechanisms given extended treatment in recent books by Symonds (38, 39). These treatments are by academic psychologists. Among the psychoanalytic discussions, that by Anna Freud (12), "The Ego and the Mechanisms of Defense," is perhaps the best single source. I shall characterize a few studies briefly, chiefly to give an over-all picture of the kind of thing being done in the laboratory.

1. *Repression*. There is abundant clinical evidence for repression as a mechanism of defense. Perhaps the most convincing evidence to the outsider is that from amnesia, when a person loses his personal memories, often to recover them later without relearning. Amnesias show that memories may be unavailable even though they are not really lost.

Experimental studies of repression have been directed very largely to one problem: the selective forgetting of the unpleasant as compared with the pleasant. Most of these studies have made the mistake of confusing the pleasantness or unpleasantness of *subject matter* with the pleasantness or unpleasantness of *recalling* it. In a list of words containing the words quinine and sugar, for example, the mere fact that quinine is bitter and sugar sweet has little relevance to Freud's theory. Yet many experiments have been done to determine whether the word quinine would be forgotten more readily than the word sugar. More sophisticated experiments seek to find items out of the personal biography that arouse anxiety when they are recalled. It is such items that should undergo repression, according to the theory (31, 35).

Despite the crudity of the experiments, nearly all of them have shown that pleasant items or experiences are more readily recalled than unpleasant ones, and that memories that reduce self-esteem are recalled with greater difficulty than those that enhance self-esteem. Thus the experimental results in general agree with psychoanalytic theory, though few of the experiments have been very helpful in moving us forward in our understanding of the phenomena. In the next lecture I shall describe one somewhat more satisfactory experiment in which repression is produced and then relieved. The study of repression remains a promising field of experimentation.

2. *Projection.* One form of the mechanism of projection is that of attributing to others unpleasant traits in ourselves that we would prefer to deny. Sears (33) had a group of college fraternity men rate each other on several traits. By comparing self-ratings with the ratings of others, projection could be ascertained. Those who lacked insight into their own traits, for such an undesirable trait as stinginess, tended to assign higher stinginess scores to other students than those students assigned to each other. This accords with the theory of seeing our weaknesses in others. Frenkel-Brunswik (11) in a somewhat related study found a tendency to convert our own traits to the opposite; that is, a subject might say, "Above all else, I am kind," when others are likely to rate him as unkind.

3. *Regression.* The tendency, under frustrating circumstances, to return to an earlier or more primitive mode of behavior is known as regression. The question arises whether or not this is an actual age regression, that is, a return to one's own earlier years, or merely a primitivization, that is, a turning to less mature ways of responding, though not necessarily ways closely related to his own personal biography. An adult, in anger, might engage in a fist fight even though he had not engaged in such fights as a child. That would be primitivization without age regression.

Following frustration, children often act like children a year or two younger than they, whether judged by the kind of play they engage in or by their scores on intelligence tests. Results such as these are best interpreted as primitivization.

In one such experiment (3) children of kindergarten age were permitted to play first in a room of part-toys. They filled in the gaps imaginatively, drawing tracks for the train to run on, or using paper as the water in which to sail a boat. Then they were shown into a larger playroom, where richer material could be found. There was a real track for the train, a real pond for the boat. The frustrating experience was provided by withdrawing the child from the larger room to the original one, though the larger one now remained visible through a wire screen. Under these circumstances the constructiveness of play deteriorated. Drawings became scribbles. Toys previously acceptable now were rejected, sometimes thrown or jumped on. Quantitative treatment of the observations showed that the children who experienced frustration acted, on the average, more than a year younger after the frustration than before.

In another experiment (24) a prize was offered to the child who succeeded in solving a problem that looked easy but was actually baffling. The problem was to remove a ball from a wastebasket that was out of reach. Few properties were provided. A toy dog on a leash had to be used as a tool to bounce the ball out of the basket. Even when the appropriate method was chosen, the success was partly a matter of good fortune. Half the boys who participated in the experiment left gleefully with their prizes, half left disappointed. The boys were tested with intelligence test items from the Stanford-Binet both before and after the experimental success or failure. Those who experienced failure showed a significant drop in tested mental age following the frustrating episode.

The regression in both of these experiments suggests behavior of younger children, but not necessarily behavior dating back to an earlier period in the individual biography of the frustrated child.

There have been a number of experiments on regression under hypnosis in which the individual is told to act as he did at a given age. Here the second conception of regression, as a real return to early life, is under investigation. A recent report (40) uses as the test of the success of true age regression the ability to recall the day of the week on which the child's birthday occurred at ages ten, seven, and four. In the waking state, the subjects are quite unable to recall childhood birthdays, but under hypnotic regression the reported success is remarkable. Of fifty subjects aged twenty to twenty-four, forty-one were able to give entirely accurate statements of their birthdays and the day of the week on which Christmas fell for the three years in which they were four, seven, and ten years old. The hypnotist, of course, is able to check the calendar to verify the true birthday and Christmas Day.

Hypnosis is a very promising method for the study of psychodynamics, but its results have to be interpreted with extreme caution. This is not a matter of questioning the reality of hypnosis, for the phenomena are now quite generally accepted by psychologists. The problems are those of experimental control. Hypnotic subjects are unusually co-operative, and they may even practice outside the laboratory what they expect the hypnotist to demand of them. One striking case was provided by a subject who showed monocular blindness under hypnotic suggestion. The usual methods of showing the presence of vision in the blind eye by the use of misleading lens systems failed to break through the monocular blindness. The experimenter was even able to plot the blind spot of the seeing eye while both eyes were open, a feat quite impossible for those who see normally with both eyes. Only the persistent skepticism of the experimenter led finally, under deep hypnosis, to the patient's admission that she had practiced plotting her blind spot at home so that she knew its outline and could simulate one-eyed plotting while both eyes were open. Her monocular blindness, that stood up test after test, was an unconscious expression of her desire to do what the experimenter wanted her to do (30).

In experiments on hypnosis it is always necessary to select those subjects who are hypnotizable, and then they are usually brought back for successive sessions. Because there is incomplete control of what goes on between sessions, every precaution has to be taken lest the subjects' co-operation be mistaken for unusual ability under hypnosis. With proper precautions, hypnosis offers an unusually favorable method for the study of the mechanisms, of which regression is but one.

4. *Aggression*. In the foregoing discussion, illustrations have been given of approaches to repression, projection, and regression. One final illustration will suffice to complete these examples of avenues of approach to the study of the mechanisms. This final line of investigation is that concerned with aggression as a consequence of frustration. The hypothesis that aggression is a typical consequence of frustration was brought strongly to psychologists' attention by a book from the Yale Institute of Human Relations entitled *Frustration and Aggression* (8). In this, many instances were collected from the laboratory and from social and political behavior, giving support to the hypothesis.

The problems of *displaced* aggression are particularly pertinent because they illustrate the nature of the irrational derivatives of our impulses. When it is impossible to locate the source of frustration, or when the source is not vulnerable to our attack, then aggression is directed to some convenient substitute, some innocent bystander, some scapegoat. This is known as displaced aggression. Some of the studies from the University of California at Berkeley have been pointing out the extent to which anti-Semitism among college students represents such displaced hostility (2).

As a laboratory illustration of the mechanism of displacement I wish to call attention to some experiments by Neal Miller with white rats (27). Rats were taught to fight each other in order to obtain release from electric shock. Two rats were placed in a small compartment with a floor consisting of a grid that could be electrified. The current was turned off if they struck each other. By the ordinary methods of trial and error they soon learned this, and so began to strike each other when placed in the compartment.

A rubber doll standing in the corner of the apparatus—the innocent bystander—was ignored so long as the other rat (the direct object of learned aggression) was present. When a rat found himself alone in the apparatus, however, and the mounting current began to make him uneasy, he turned his attack upon the available scapegoat—the rubber doll (Fig. 1, opposite page 22). Miller goes on in the experiment to determine the nature of the object toward which aggression is likely to be displaced. Thus his experiment goes beyond a mere demonstration of displaced aggression to some clarification of its operation. The purpose of experimentation is to extend knowledge, not merely to illustrate what we already know.

THE THEORY OF DREAMS

No other single book so well characterizes what is unique in psychoanalysis as Freud's *Interpretation of Dreams* (14). Here we find the problems of repression, the active unconscious, the significance of motivation, plus the variety of distortions, symbols, and condensations that make psychoanalytic theory at once so fascinating and so perplexing. Psychologists have generally quoted the distinction between the manifest and latent content of a dream, and then let it go at that (19). The fascinating problems of what Freud called the "dream work," by which the latent content is transformed into manifest content, are surely problems of general psychology, but as psychologists we have found no very good ways of going about their investigation. Unfortunately, during the era of behaviorism, dreams were thought too "subjective" for investigation. Now that we have outgrown the taboos of the earlier behaviorism, we are again ready to face genuine psychological problems, whether or not they appear to be subjective.

One of the most fruitful approaches to the study of dreams is by hypnosis. Dreams can be suggested, and the subject can remember what he has just dreamed. In a recent film produced by Dr. Lester F. Beck, entitled *Unconscious Motivation*, a young man and a young woman are both hypnotized at once. Both are told of a childhood incident involving disobedience and parental disapproval. With this somewhat common motivational background, both are told that they will dream, and then, following the dreams, they tell their dreams to each other. The similarities and differences between the dreams are interesting. The girl dreams of being at some sort of carnival, whirling around on a disk, but unable to get off. The feeling tone is that of the general anxiety that the induced memory has created, while the disk itself comes to be interpreted as symbolizing one of the stolen pennies that entered the story. The boy dreams of being caught in a woods, with trees bending over him as though to overpower him. As he runs to escape, he is delayed by picking up pebbles, also interpreted later on as representing the stolen pennies. The anxiety is incorporated in different manner in both dreams, and the pennies enter in distorted forms. We here get a glimpse of the process of transformation from a latent content that we know to a manifest content that appears in the actual dreams. One of the tasks of psychoanalysis is that of reversing the history, and inferring the latent content from the manifest.

One of the studies on hypnotic dream production is that by Klein (23). Klein hypnotized his subjects and instructed them to dream and then immediately report the dream. He presented sharply defined stimuli to the subjects, such as sounds, cold touch, the touch of cotton, and loss of support of the head. The presented stimulus invariably influenced the dream content, but the stimulus often appeared in disguise. In some instances the stimulus, such as a sounding bell, did not come until the end of the dream content, the rest of the content seeming to have been worked out to explain it. This is familiar in such dreams as going to a fire and then hearing the fire engine—all while the alarm clock is ringing. This rapid dreaming is not so mysterious when we realize that a great many experiences may be condensed into a few images (41). This is as true in waking fantasy as in dreams. Let us engage in a little experiment together. Imagine a picture of a mountain climber approaching the top of a mountain peak. Now think up a story of what went before, what he is thinking now, and what is about to happen. You may conjure up the preparation for climbing, perhaps years of anticipation, the hazards in mountain climbing, a happy or unhappy ending. This sketch comes quickly, because much of it comes ready made from the past. If you were to tell it to me or to write it down, it would take much longer than the time since I raised the question to the present. There have been about one hundred words since I mentioned the mountain climber. You will have to judge for yourself how richly your own fantasies ran along during this quite brief time.

Other experiments have shown, in agreement with Freud, that dreams incorporate a good deal of manifest content from the preceding day as well as stimuli present during the time of dreaming. But they also draw in many items from the past, even from early childhood.

Ella Sharpe uses the following figure to dramatize the condensation in dreams of items from earlier life (37):

Suppose that a hundred small objects made of different materials lie on a table. If a magnet is drawn through them in all directions every article made of iron will be picked up by the magnet. So one may think of any dynamic unconscious interest as a magnet which will gather together out of the whole reservoir of past and present experiences just those particular ones that are pertinent to the magnet. Such experiences would extend from present-day situations to infancy if it were possible to find them.

Here is a bold idea, one familiar within psychoanalytic practice, but at the same time one difficult to bring into the laboratory.

An aspect of dreams possible of experimental study is that of dream symbols. There are said to be some universal symbols, and, in addition, symbols arising out of individual experience. The snake as a symbol of sex is such a universal symbol. A dream symbol depending upon a pun, such as a kitten standing for a sister named Catherine who is called Kitty, would be an individual symbol. Farber and Fisher (9) proposed that if there are universal symbols, then under appropriate circumstances subjects naïve about psychoanalytic theory ought to be able to interpret them. Because under hypnosis some of the inhibitions of waking life are removed, it was conjectured that subjects under hypnosis might be able to interpret dreams.

The experiment was done with volunteer students, aged eighteen to twenty-one, recruited from college classes. All were naïve about psychology and about dream theory, and they were instructed not to read about the subject during the course of the experiment.

Dream translation was remarkably successful under hypnosis for those few (five of twenty subjects) who were able to do it at all. For example, an eighteen-year-old girl was told under hypnosis: "Dreams have meaning. Now that you are asleep you will be better able to understand them. A girl dreamed that she was packing her trunk when a big snake crawled into it. She was terrified and ran out of the room. What do you think the dream means?" Almost before the question was finished, the subject blushed, hesitated a second, then said, "Well, I guess she was afraid of being seduced. The snake would be the man's sex organ and the trunk hers."

In an interesting variation, one subject dreamt under hypnosis and the other interpreted her dream. We have here a two-way translation, from latent to manifest content, then from manifest to latent. It was suggested to one subject under hypnosis that as a child she had wet the bed and been severely reprimanded by her mother. In response she dreamed of falling into a pond of water and being scolded by her mother. This dream was then related to a second girl, under hypnosis, who was ignorant of the origin of the dream. Without any hesitation the second subject said, "Oh, that girl must have wet the bed!" She thus recovered the instruction that had produced the dream.

It might be supposed that the authors would have been satisfied that they had supported the orthodox theory of dream symbols. Instead, however, they go to some pains to show how the hypnotic relationship may have been interpreted as in some sense a sexual one, hence influencing the dreams in the direction of sexual interpretations. Subjects, for example, interpret dreams differently for a familiar hypnotist than for a strange one. Classical psychoanalysis interprets the transference situation as essentially a sexual one. It may be that this interpersonal relationship accounts also for the sexual emphasis in dream interpretations within the analytic period.

These hypnotic experiments, interesting as they are, point to the extremely hazardous nature of psychodynamic interpretations, a point recently emphasized by Brenman (5). This should not discourage further experimentation, but it should warn those interested in psychoanalytic theory that *factionalism* based upon theoretical interpretations represents a premature freezing of viewpoints, while there remain so many unknowns in psychodynamics.

PSYCHOSEXUAL DEVELOPMENT

Inherent in the importance attributed by psychoanalysis to early childhood is the notion of the continuity of development. Let me illustrate. We have already seen how frustrated sucking may give rise to thumb-sucking. Perhaps thumb-sucking may later turn into cigarette smoking. Some smokers may be classified as suckers, some as biters. Pipe smokers are more apt to be biters, although they may be either suckers or biters. The point is that what smoking means to the individual could be traced back, if we were able to untangle the threads, to something beginning in infancy.

This general principle of continuity has, however, some more universal characteristics attributed to it, so that all individuals are said to progress through several stages in the course of normal development. There may be arrested development at one or another of these stages, in which case we find some sort of personality distortion. The classical formulation of the stages of psychosexual or libidinal development is that of Abraham (1). The six stages are, in order: (1) Early oral (sucking) stage, (2) late oral-sadistic (cannibalistic) stage, (3) early anal-sadistic stage, (4) late anal-sadistic stage, (5) early genital (phallic) stage, and (6) final genital stage. Corresponding to each of these stages there are corresponding developments of object love, and the various types of neurotic or psychotic disease are said to be related to dominant points of fixation when the normal transition from one stage to the next has failed to occur.

An experimental approach to this theory is a large order. I am going to refer to three experiments, merely to point out that we are not completely helpless when it comes to trying to get data that are relevant.

The Anal Character

One kind of personality syndrome recognized by Freud (13) was the so-called anal character. This term characterizes the individual who carries into adult life some of the problems of anal stages earlier referred to. The traits that are said to represent such a character are those of *stinginess, obstinacy,* and *orderliness*. A remote, but nevertheless legitimate, test of the theory is provided by a determination whether or not these three traits do, in fact, go together as a cluster. Such a test was made by Sears (33, 35) as part of the experiment cited earlier. Ratings were made of each other by thirty-seven men living together in college fraternities. Ratings were made on a seven-point scale, so that it was possible to obtain an average rating for each of the men on each of the traits of stinginess, obstinacy, and orderliness. The reliabilities of the pooled ratings were found to be statistically satisfactory by correlating the ratings made by half of the raters with those made by the other half, the reliabilities being represented by coefficients of correlation of .85 for stinginess, .93 for obstinacy, and .96 for orderliness. What this means is that there was substantial agreement by the raters as to the position of each of the men on each of the traits. Now the test of the theory comes in finding a correspondence among the traits. The correlations between the pairs of traits were found to be as follows:

Stinginess and orderliness ...... $+.39$
Stinginess and obstinacy .... $+.37$
Obstinacy and orderliness ...... $+.36$

The correlations, while low, are all positive and in the expected direction. The results are all the more convincing when it is pointed out that orderliness is considered a desirable trait and stinginess and obstinacy undesirable traits. This was demonstrated within the experiment by a popularity rating. Popularity correlated *negatively* with stinginess and obstinacy, but slightly *positively* with orderliness. Despite this attenuating factor in ratings, the three traits hang together. As Sears has pointed out, the mere fact of this trait cluster would not necessarily make it dependent upon anal eroticism, although earlier data by Hamilton (18) make it plausible that there is such a connection. Out of a group of a hundred married men and women, Hamilton found that thirty-five men and twenty-four women recalled some form of anal eroticism in childhood. These men and women, as adults, showed a higher frequency of reported stinginess or extravagance than the non-anal ones, showed more frequently reported fetishism, more concern for clothes, more sadism and masochism. These differences are all in line with the theory of the anal character.

The Oral Character

In the discussion of the need to suck, it was suggested that adult personality might be influenced by food frustration in infancy. Such frustration is a result not only of the prevailing practices within a culture but of the specific handling of the individual child. It has been conjectured that there is an oral character, which, like the anal character, reflects residues from early experiences. A test of the oral character, somewhat along the lines of Sears's test of the anal character, has been made by Goldman (17). On the basis of self-ratings of one hundred fifteen young adults, she selected twenty extreme cases representing the orally satisfied and orally unsatisfied. The trait clusters of these extreme groups corresponded roughly to the theoretical expectations from the theory of oral character formation. Her study has been criticized for the paucity of detail in the published account (34), but it serves to provide an additional illustration of the possibility of making empirical approaches to the complex principles derived from psychoanalytic thinking.

The Blacky Test

The third experiment bearing upon the theory of libidinal stages provides another illustration as to how we may find ways of putting psychoanalytic conjectures to a test. I refer to a monograph by Blum (4), entitled "A Study of the Psychoanalytic Theory of Psychosexual Development." This was a Ph.D. dissertation in clinical psychology done at Stanford.

The task that Blum set himself was to find an experiment conceived within the framework of psychoanalytic theory, and yet designed so that it would not bias the results in such a manner as to enforce confirmation of the theory. He hit upon a projective test, whereby, through processes of thinly veiled identification, adult individuals might reveal their own psychosexual histories as represented in their present attitudes.

The test consists of twelve cartoon drawings or caricatures depicting the adventures of a dog named Blacky. The cast of characters includes Blacky, Mama, Papa, and Tippy (a sibling figure of unspecified age and sex). The first cartoon introduces the characters, and the rest portray either stages in libidinal development or object relationships characteristic of the stages. When the test is presented to a male, Blacky is described as the "son"; when presented to a female, Blacky is described as the "daughter." The author of the test defends his choice of dog characters because of the greater freedom of personal expression as contrasted with human figures which would be "too close to home." He points out that the canine medium, thanks to Walt Disney cartoons and comic strips, still preserves sufficient reality so that subjects can identify themselves quite fully with the cartoon figures and project their innermost feelings.

The rather playful way in which Blacky's problems are depicted can be told best by describing a few of the pictures.

After the introductory cartoon that gives the cast of characters, the next is designed to exhibit oral eroticism. Blacky, who is almost too big, is shown nursing his (or her) mother.

Here is a response to this picture that would be scored as showing strong oral eroticism in the adult subject whose statement this is:

Blacky has just discovered the delightful nectar that Mama can supply—it is an endless supply and she is enjoying it. She doesn't know where it is coming from, but she doesn't care. Mama is pacific throughout it all—she doesn't particularly like this business of supplying milk, but she is resigned to it. It is a pretty day and they are both calm and happy.

A later cartoon depicts the problem of castration anxiety in males and penis envy in females by displacing the problem to that of the sibling Tippy standing blindfolded before a chopping block, with a knife threatening his (or her) tail. Blacky is shown watching this threatening attack on his sibling's tail.

That the intended effect is produced in the responses of at least some of the subjects is shown in this spontaneous account by one of the young women given the test.

Blacky's curiosity has been aroused about the opposite sex and she decides to look closely at Tippy's sex organs when he is not aware that she is looking at him. Tippy's tail is going to be cut off and Blacky watches interestedly.

In this particular case, the subject went back and revised the story, striking out the material on the curiosity about sex organs. The full story is, of course, more revealing than the expurgated version, that now became simply: "Tippy's tail is going to be cut off and Blacky watches interestedly."

The cartoon showing positive identification is of Blacky making an assertive gesture toward a toy dog (Fig. 2, opposite page 23). Here is a representative protocol:

"Now listen you, you little pooch, when I bark, you jump, do you get that?" Blacky feels very superior to this little dog. He is making believe that he is the boss, or maybe pretending to be his father talking to him in a superior tone.

Although in clinical practice the test is administered individually, a group form worked satisfactorily for experimental purposes. The subjects were given the following instructions:

What we have here is a bunch of cartoons, like you see in the funny papers, except that there are no words. We'll show them to you one cartoon at a time and the idea is for you to make up a little story about each one—just tell what is happening in the picture, why it's happening, and so on. Since this is a sort of test of how good your imagination can be, try to write vividly about how the characters feel. You will have two minutes for each story, which means about one or two paragraphs on each cartoon. It is desirable to write as much as possible within the time limit.

Following the spontaneous account, the subject was asked a few questions, chiefly of the multiple-choice type. Because in a projective test of this sort, it is possible to go off in several directions, the fixed-alternative questions assure that each subject gives some replies in a common context. This corrupts the replies to some extent through restricting spontaneity, but makes the statistical handling of the data much easier. It is an inevitable paradox of quantitative methods in science that some of the richness of the original experience has to be lost in order to improve the precision of the findings.

Before turning to some of the data obtained through the use of the Blacky test, we may well ask to what extent we are here dealing with a scientific experiment. If all we come out with are some data illustrative of psychoanalytic ways of thinking, that is not enough. Other criteria of science must be met. Let me suggest two ways in which this investigation justifies its classification as an experiment.

1. One feature of an experiment is that observations are made under conditions specified by the experimenter and, to some extent, controlled by him.

In this experiment those to participate were selected from a general college population, so that the results are applicable to such a population, and not merely to those who for whatever reason seek psychoanalytic treatment. Furthermore, their responses were obtained under the standard conditions of the Blacky test. The element of control is present.

2. A second feature of an experiment is that there is in it some design, so that the data obtained can be made to bear crucially upon some hypothesis. Such design involves both theory about the events under study and an understanding of the logic of proof. The theory about the events under study in this experiment is classical psychoanalytic theory, especially as developed by Abraham and later by Fenichel. The logic of proof in this case requires a little further discussion.

Because the projective test was designed to draw out information based on the theory of libidinal stages, it introduced a bias in favor of finding such stages. Thus the evidence from the study is not much good for showing that adults sometimes talk about the satisfactions of the nursing experience, or that they talk about mutilation threats, or that they identify with parents. The pictures themselves give such strong suggestions that the data are corrupted by the theory. I am not here denying the validity of the experiment. I merely point out that we have to be careful about noting what it *can* and what it *cannot* prove. These limitations are present in all experiments. I may point out, as an aside, that these limitations are much more difficult to surmount when clinical case studies are interpreted. In the Blacky test we know the extent of the suggestions given by the pictures; in the psychoanalytic interview we seldom know the extent of the suggestions given by the analyst's interpretations.

The design of the experiment allowed for independent study of two sets of hypotheses arising from the theory of libidinal development. That is, evidence bearing upon these hypotheses was not biased by the experimental arrangements; evidence could either agree with or refute the predictions from the hypotheses.

We may turn now to some of the data. The first hypothesis to be tested has to do with the differences in libidinal development of men and of women. The matter is too complex to go into here in any detail, but the main point is that boys and girls are said to differ in the ways in which they progress through the stages of libidinal development, and in the residues that remain from each of the stages as they grow older. As one illustration, Fenichel says that, in normal development, the relationship of women to their mothers is more frequently ambivalent than is that of most men to their fathers (10). This assertion can be tested within the Blacky test by studying the identification of men and women with parental figures. If the assertion is correct, the ambivalence represented in women's replies to the cards should exceed that represented by men's replies to the cards. The usual statistical tests can be applied to ascertain whether or not the differences found are in excess of differences that might arise by choice.

Behind the ambivalence toward the mother is said to lie disappointment in the mother because of experiences associated with weaning, toilet-training, and the birth of siblings, as well as the disappointment over the lack of a penis, for which the mother is held responsible. Freud links the girl's hostility directly to oral frustration (15):

The [girl's] complaint against the mother that harks back furthest is that she has given the child too little milk, which is taken as indicating lack of love.

One of the pictures of the Blacky test that tests oral sadism, a consequence of oral frustration, is that in which Blacky is shown chewing Mama's collar.

One of the questions asked following the spontaneous account of this picture was as follows:

What will Blacky do next with Mama's collar?
1. Get tired of it and leave it on the ground.
2. Return it to Mama.
3. Angrily chew it to shreds.

Confronted with these alternatives, more females than males chose the sadistic alternative (Angrily chew it to shreds). This finding is then in agreement with the theoretical expectation that more females than males will retain oral-sadistic tendencies.

Perhaps this is enough to show how the test is used in the study of sex differences. Even though the dog chewing Mama's collar strongly suggests oral sadism, there is no bias in favor of more replies in the sadistic direction by women than by men. The presence of oral sadism is suggested, but its *relative intensity* in men and in women is a matter of *data*. Following this general pattern of analysis, it was found possible to select from theoretical sources seven areas in which specific sex differences ought to be found. For two additional areas, reasonably good conjectures could be made as to what psychoanalytic theory would predict.

A number of addition areas could have been studied with the aid of the test, but psychoanalytic theory is itself too unclear in the treatment of sex differences for any firm predictions to be stated and then tested. Of the nine areas in which conjectures could be made, results from the test were consonant with the theory in eight. That is, in each of these eight areas replies by men differed from replies by women in a statistically satisfactory manner in the direction predicted from theory.

The one area of disagreement is a matter of some interest. The superego figure, represented as a personified conscience in the Blacky test, is more often seen as a mother figure by the women, and as a father figure by the men. According to Fenichel, the male superego should have been decisive for both sexes. The author of the monograph under discussion says that this departure from Fenichel's stated opinion may very possibly be a reflection of the increasing influence of the mother in American life, in contrast to the patriarchal European society in which psychoanalysis grew up. On the whole, the agreement between the test results and the theory is rather striking. A score of eight hits out of nine tries is a very good one.

The second set of hypotheses put to test in this experiment was concerned with the interrelationships between stages of development. Thus those who show developmental disturbances at one level should show them at others. Such interrelationships can be demonstrated by correlation coefficients. For example, Fenichel says: "Guilt feeling not only has an oral character in general but an oral-sadistic character in particular" (10). We can infer, then, that there will be some correspondence between *oral-sadistic* responses to the dog chewing the collar and recognized *guilt feelings* in relation to the superego figure of the later cartoon. The inference can be tested by correlating the scores of the responses to the two pictures.

How successful was the test in detecting interrelationships predicted by the theory? Fourteen significant correlations were obtained related to inter-correlational statements or inferences from the writings of Freud and Fenichel. In *every case* these correlations were in the direction predicted from theory; that is, they showed significant positive correspondence when the theory demanded that, and significant negative relationship when the theory demanded that.

The real productiveness of an experimental approach of this kind rests not only in its support (or refutation) of previously stated psychoanalytic principles, but in its discovery of correlations not anticipated by earlier theory. Because it was Blum's purpose to test classical theory, he did not elaborate the additional possibilities within his data. Those possibilities exist, however, so that contribution in line with the fundamental purpose of science, to discover new truth, is not excluded.

I have devoted so much time to this one experiment because I believe it illustrates the possibility of experimentation closely related to psychoanalytic concepts kept in their context. In some respects it is more satisfactory than the earlier experiments with animals and human subjects that isolate one generalization at a time. The experiment has a number of difficulties inherent in such experimentation, difficulties that its author is the first to acknowledge. One source of awkwardness so far as interpretation is concerned is the large number of nonsignificant correlations that were discarded. For the purposes of preliminary experimentation, the author used as tests of theory only correlations that were significantly negative or significantly positive. A tighter experiment has to interpret its nonsignificant correlations as well as its significant ones. Let us not rush off, then, believing that this experiment has proved the psychoanalytic theory of libidinal development beyond all doubt. I believe that it has demonstrated the plausibility of many relationships stressed by classical psychoanalysts. It has not, of course, shown how these relationships are caused, and it has nothing to say about the relative influences of biology and of culture. Hence many of the controversies among contemporary psychoanalysts cannot be resolved by an appeal to these data. At the same time, the "caustic critic" of psychoanalysis is here confronted by many correspondences between data and theory, which at least invite his inspection.

EXPERIMENTAL PSYCHODYNAMICS

We have made a fairly hasty acquaintance with what is by now a substantial literature in a field that may be described as experimental psychodynamics. I prefer to call it that rather than experimental psychoanalysis because it is not necessary to confine the experiments to the confirmation or disproof of psychoanalytic concepts. The basic problem is to make good science in the field opened up by psychoanalysis.

The possibilities before us are numerous. I wish, by way of summary, to call attention to a few of them.

I wish to note first of all that the experiments reported in this lecture were all concerned with normal individuals, whether animals, children, or adults. It is not necessary to confine the study of psychoanalytic concepts to the neurotic people who present themselves for treatment. Freud, of course, set the stage for the study of normal people in his observations on the psychopathology of everyday life (16).

A second observation is that all of the studies reported were carried out without the use of the psychoanalytic method, as defined by what goes on within psychoanalytic therapy. Of the methods used, two, however, are analogous to psychoanalysis. One of these is hypnosis. While hypnosis was rejected as a method by Freud early in his career, the state of *rapport* in hypnosis has

Fig. 1.—Displaced aggression in the rat. The rat has been taught to strike the other rat, in order to gain relief from electric shock. When the other rat is absent, the animal directs his aggression to the doll—the innocent bystander (27). By permission of N. E. Miller and the American Psychological Association.

Fig. 2.—Blacky. This picture of Blacky illustrates identification because Blacky acts as a parent toward the toy. Courtesy of G. S. Blum. (Reproduced by permission of The Psychological Corporation.)

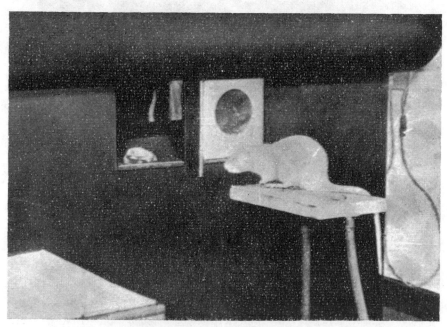

Fig. 3.—Abnormal fixation in the rat. Despite the fact that the rat sees the food in the open window, when he jumps he will jump at the circle, strike his nose, and fall into the net below. By permission from *Frustration, the Study of Behavior Without a Goal*, by N. R. F. Maier. Copyright 1949 by McGraw-Hill Book Co., Inc.

affiliations with *transference* in psychoanalysis. A sophisticated use of hypnosis is likely to prove one of the most revealing methods for testing psychoanalytic principles. The second method is that of the projective test, illustrated by the Blacky experiment. The associations with such pictures have much in common with free associations within the analytic hour. The relationships established within short experimental periods may be superficial, but their careful study may tell us a good deal about the more penetrating consequences of a long-continued psychoanalysis.

The usefulness of animal subjects in studies of psychodynamics is subject to question. Animals have the advantage that we may completely control their culture, as we cannot for human subjects. Their social relationships are free of language, and hence tell us how far social responses are language-free. Despite lack of language, animal subjects exhibit many social responses resembling what we call shame and guilt. We may, in studying them, see many familiar mechanisms at work, without the elaborate disguises of which the human animal is capable. But for the very reason that animals lack language, we miss in animal studies one of the most significant features of human psychology. Anyone who has watched a skilled demonstration of hypnosis cannot fail to be impressed by the magic of words over human conduct. At a signal, amnesias can be created and broken, the environment can be perceived in distorted ways, either through insensitivities to things present or through hallucinations of things not present. Such behavior, if present in animals, is hard to get at, and is surely less rich than in man.

The human infant is in many ways our best source of data on the dynamics of development. We have the choice of experimental studies done with groups of infants given differential treatment, or of intensive studies of a few infants. Such studies must, of course, be guided by good theories. Our theories may tell us that we have to study the parents as carefully as the children. This has been one source of neglect in some of the earlier studies of child development. Sex differences among boys and girls, for example, cannot be understood unless we know what the parents expect of their sons and daughters. Anatomical and hormonal differences are important, but insufficient to explain the individual. Furthermore, our theories tell us what events in the life of the individual are critical, so that we know how to direct our observations. Often a very full descriptive record of a child will fail to record exactly how the birth of a new brother or sister was received, just what happened when thumb-sucking was given up, how absence of the father from home affected conduct, and so on. Among the countless events in a child's life, only a few can be recorded. Unless there is some theory about crucial events, the most significant features of the developmental life may be missed. Guided by good theory, the observation of child development is likely to prove to be one of our richest sources of psychological data.

The topics of psychodynamics are not side issues for psychology. They lie at the very heart of psychological subject matter, for we cannot understand motivation, learning and forgetting, perceiving, personality development, or social behavior until we understand the issues of psychodynamics. The renewed interest in the concept of the self in contemporary psychology (20) stems in part from the concern of psychoanalysis to understand the role of self-knowledge, and to understand the devices of self-deception. The tasks of psychodynamics cannot be left solely to those specialists within psychology and psychiatry concerned with treating the mentally or emotionally disturbed. They are tasks that belong to all of psychological science.

II. PSYCHOTHERAPY

Psychoanalysis is primarily a way of treating people who are emotionally disturbed. It is a medical psychology. To study it as a system of psychological principles, as we did in the last lecture, is in some sense to put the cart before the horse. My reasons for choosing this order are not difficult to state. It is somewhat easier to do experiments on psychodynamic generalizations than it is on psychotherapy. The subject worked on does not have to be ill, and the experimenter does not have to possess therapeutic skills. But were we to stop with experiments on psychodynamics, we would have a very incomplete picture of psychoanalysis.

THE METHOD OF PSYCHOANALYSIS

It is important that we agree as to what we are talking about when we mention psychotherapy. The dictionary meaning is easy enough. We are talking about cure by psychological means, as contrasted with cure by surgery, or by drugs, or by other forms of physical or medicinal treatment. When we speak of psychotherapy we usually mean a cure by way of conversations between the patient and the therapist, but it is not quite as easy as that. Psychotherapy may be caricatured as a talking cure, if you will, so long as we know that this is a caricature. Psychoanalysts sometimes distinguish between psychoanalysis and psychotherapy, meaning by the former the full-scale long-time analysis, by the latter, shorter methods of therapy. The shorter methods make use of psychodynamic principles but do not employ complete psychoanalytic technique. Thus, if we follow this distinction, most child guidance clinics use psychotherapy, but the children and parents who go there for treatment do not get psychoanalyzed.

I do not intend to enter here into the professional problems of conducting a psychoanalysis, or into controversy as to just where psychotherapy ends and psychoanalysis begins. I am using the word psychotherapy as a classificatory word for the process of achieving changes in emotional adjustment by psychological means. I am interested in what we have found out, and what we can find out, about how the changes in the patient take place, so that these changes, and the control of them, may become part of established psychological science.

The general conduct of a psychoanalysis has become familiar to the public through the motion picture, through cartoons in the weekly magazines, and even in the comic strip of the daily newspaper, with the usual distortions that these media produce. Let me describe what psychoanalysis is actually like. The analyst usually begins by getting something of the personal biography of the patient, after the manner of a social worker's case history. The patient sits up and talks as he would to any physician. The analyst may have better interviewing methods, but there is little that is distinctive about the early sessions. There may be several sessions before the patient takes to the couch, before the typical free association method is used. Then the patient is taught to follow, as well as he is able, *the basic rule*: to say everything that enters his mind, without selection. This is much harder than it sounds, even for patients who are eager to co-operate with the analyst. As Fenichel puts it, "Even the patient who tries to adhere to the basic rule fails to tell many things because he considers them too unimportant, too stupid, too indiscreet, and so on. There are many who never learn to apply the basic rule because their fear of losing control is too great, and before they can give expression to anything they must examine it to see exactly what it is" (6). In fact, the whole lifetime has been spent learning to be tactful, to achieve self-control, to avoid outbursts of emotion, to do what is proper rather than what is impulsive. This all has to be unlearned for successful free association.

What free association aims at is the bringing to awareness of impulses and thoughts of which the person is not aware. Because these impulses are active, but out of awareness, they are called unconscious. It is necessary to break through resistances in order to bring them to awareness. The role of the psychoanalyst is, essentially, to help the patient break down these resistances, so that he may face his disguised motives and hidden thoughts frankly, and then come to grips in realistic manner with whatever problems or conflicts are then brought into view.

The activity of the analyst is directed skillfully at this task of helping the patient eliminate resistances. He does this in part by pointing out to the patient the consequences of his resistances: the times of silence when his mind seems to go blank, forgetting what he intended to say, perhaps forgetting to show up at an appointment, drifting into superficial associations, or giving glib interpretations of his own. The analyst not only calls attention to signs of resistance, but he also interprets the patient's associations in such a way as to facilitate further associations.

Fenichel defines interpretation as "helping something unconscious to become conscious by naming it at the moment it is striving to break through" (6). If this is accepted, then the first interpretations are necessarily fairly "shallow" ones, the "deeper" interpretations waiting until the patient is ready for them.

The deeper interpretations are the ones we often think of in characterizing psychoanalysis, but very much of the time in an actual psychoanalysis is spent in rather matter-of-fact discussion of attitudes toward other people and toward oneself as they show themselves in daily life, without recourse to universal symbols, references to libidinal stages, and so on. Not all psychoanalysts agree on just how interpretations should be made, or when they should be made, and it is my guess that those who think they do agree may actually behave quite differently when conducting analyses of their patients. This is one reason why it is difficult to study psychoanalytic therapy, and a reason, also, why there are so many schisms within psychoanalytic societies.

Another aspect of the psychoanalytic therapy goes by the name of "transference." Transference refers to the tendency for the patient to make of the analyst an object of his motivational or emotional attachments. It is too simple to say that the patient falls in love with the analyst. Sometimes he makes of the analyst a loved parent, sometimes a hated parent; sometimes the analyst substitutes for a brother or sister, or for the boss at the office. The patient unconsciously assigns roles to the analyst of the important people in the patient's own life. Part of the task of the analyst is to handle the transference. The word "handle" is easily spoken, but this handling of the transference is said to be the most difficult part of the analyst's art.

The psychoanalytic interview is a social one, an interpersonal one, with two people involved. The analyst is a person, too, and he reacts to the adoration and abuse of the patient he is analyzing. He is a good analyst to the extent that he understands himself well enough so that he preserves his role in the analytic situation, and does not himself become involved, as his patient is, in what is called countertransference, that is, using the patient as an outlet for his own emotions. If the patient's exploits become the occasion for the analyst's fantasy life, then the analyst gets preoccupied with his own free associations and cannot listen attentively to his patient. The discipline of learning to listen, and only to listen, is considered by Frieda Fromm-Reichmann (7) to be the essence of the analyst's problem.

I have gone this much into detail here because the public does not always understand why psychoanalysts insist that they must themselves be analyzed. The reason is that they could not otherwise handle the problems of transference with the kind of detachment that is necessary if the patient is to be helped. The reason is not that they must have a laying on of hands or special indoctrination in order to transmit the faith held by their therapist. If it works that way, as it occasionally does, then the training analysis has been unsuccessful in achieving its aim (as it undoubtedly is in some instances). To make the blanket charge that psychoanalysis is unscientific because the method requires that the analyst himself be analyzed is unwarranted, although this charge is commonly made (12). There is a danger that analysts become too doctrinaire. If you ask an analyst about his theoretical position, he may reply by telling you under whom he had his analysis. There are parallels in other sciences as well. A biologist's or a physicist's work often reflects the master under whom the scientist studied. There is need for caution in both instances. To cite but one example from the field of physiology: the word "inhibition" suggests an entirely different set of phenomena to those who studied under Sherrington from what it suggests to those who studied under Pavlov. Because there is danger of indoctrination does not mean that there are not ways of avoiding that danger. For example, psychoanalysts profit greatly from doing control analyses under more than one training analyst, representing somewhat divergent viewpoints. Postdoctoral fellows in the natural sciences often prefer to work in laboratories at a different place from the one in which they received their training, in order to break their provincialism. It may be that a personal analysis is as essential to conducting a psychoanalysis as learning calculus is to becoming an engineer. The problem then becomes how to achieve the gains and avoid the pitfalls.

Very often there is within the midst of psychoanalysis a state in which the patient is more disturbed than he was before entering treatment. Those unfriendly to psychoanalysis occasionally use this as an indication of its therapeutic ineffectiveness (11). Two comments can be made here. First, what appears to others to be disturbance may not be "neurotic" at all. Some individuals are excessively kind to other people, at great cost to themselves. If they suddenly express their feelings more openly, they may become less pleasant to live with or to work with, because they can no longer be exploited. The troublesome child may be a healthier child than the child who is too "good."

If a person changes, new social adjustments are required, and some that were in equilibrium now get out of focus. This is the first observation regarding apparent disturbance in the midst of analysis. The second comment is that the disturbance in the midst of analysis may be a genuinely neurotic one, an aggravation of the typical transference. That is, the substitution of the analyst for other figures emotionally important to the patient may produce an emotional crisis, in which the patient actually acts more irrationally than before treatment. If this crisis is well handled, the patient emerges the better for it. Although some analysts believe that such crises are inevitable in an analysis, other analysts attempt to ward them off by such devices as less frequent therapeutic sessions when transference problems become too hard to handle (1, 2, 5, 6, 10). In any case, the fact that an aggravated transference neurosis may occur does not invalidate the therapeutic usefulness of psychoanalytic technique.

Three words often crop up in discussion of what is taking place as the patient improves. These are "abreaction," "insight," and "working through." "Abreaction" refers to a living again of an earlier emotion, in a kind of emotional catharsis—literally getting some of the dammed-up emotion out of the system. The therapeutic need is that described by the poet:

> Home they brought her warrior dead.
> She nor wept nor uttered cry.
> All her maidens watching said:
> "She must weep or she will die."
>
> —TENNYSON, *The Princess*

"Insight" refers to seeing clearly what motives are at work, what the nature of the problem is, so that instinctual conflicts, as psychoanalysts call them, are recognized for what they are. Insight is not limited to the recovery of dramatic incidents in early childhood that were later repressed. Sometimes such insights do occur, and sometimes they are associated with relief of symptoms. But neither a single flood of emotion in abreaction nor a single occasion of surprised insight relieves the patient of his symptoms. He requires, instead, the process of "working through," that is, facing again and again the same old conflicts and finding himself reacting in the same old ways to them, until eventually the slow processes of re-education manifest themselves and he reacts more nearly in accordance with the objective demands of the situation and less in accordance with distortions that his private needs create.

It is chiefly because the process of working through takes so long that psychoanalysis takes so long. The psychoanalyst often has the basic insights into the patient's problems quite early in treatment, but the patient is unready for them and could not understand the analyst if he were to insist upon confronting him with these interpretations. I have sometimes likened an analysis to the process of learning to play the piano. It is not enough to know what a good performance is and to wish to give one. The process has to be learned. The learner may know all about musical notation and may have manual skill and musical appreciation. But there is no short cut. Even with a good teacher the lessons must continue week after week before the player can achieve the kind of spontaneous performance he wishes to achieve. We do not begrudge this time, because we believe that the end is worth it. What the analyst is attempting to do is far more complex than what the piano teacher is attempting to do. The skilled management of a life is more difficult than the skilled management of a keyboard.

It must be clear by this time that laboratory experimentation that preserves anything like the richness of a psychoanalysis will be very difficult indeed, if not, perhaps, impossible.

THE PRODUCTION AND CURE OF NEUROTIC DISTURBANCES IN ANIMALS

With this background, we may well wonder whether there is any profit in attempting to study psychotherapy using animal subjects. Surely they will not free-associate, develop resistances, and improve through the careful handling of the transference. What meaning can abreaction, insight, and working through have for them?

As a matter of fact, the outlook is not so bleak as might be supposed, and a number of studies have been concerned with the induction of neuroses in animals and with the therapy of these artificially induced neuroses.

Pavlov, the distinguished Russian physiologist whose name is associated with the work on conditioned reflexes in dogs, spent the last years of his life attempting to relate his work on conditioned reflexes to problems of psychopathology. His translator boldly (and somewhat inappropriately) entitled the last volume of his lectures *Conditioned Reflexes and Psychiatry* (19).

An experimental neurosis was created in Pavlov's laboratory as early as 1914. A dog was trained to salivate when a luminous circle was projected on a screen. After the conditioned response was well established, a discrimination was obtained between the circle and an ellipse with a ratio between the semi-axes of 2:1. The discrimination was acquired fairly quickly. The shape of the ellipse was then approximated by stages to that of the circle, and the discrimination training continued. Finally an ellipse with a ratio of the semi-axes of 9:8

was reached. At this point the discrimination not only did not improve but in three weeks of training it became worse.

At the same time the whole behavior of the animal underwent an abrupt change. The hitherto quiet dog began to squeal in its stand, kept wriggling about, tore off with its teeth the apparatus for mechanical stimulation of the skin, and bit through the tubes connecting the animal's room with the observer, a behavior which never before happened. On being taken into the experimental room the dog now barked violently, which was also contrary to its usual custom; in short it presented all the symptoms of a condition of acute neurosis (18).

This creation of neurosis by conflict arising out of difficult discrimination certainly has its parallels in some of the problems of neurotic indecision in man. In man, however, the problems leading to conflict are essentially social, so that the evidence from conditioned reflex studies is tangential at best. Pavlov conducted some minor experiments in therapy, using chiefly bromides and caffeine. His interpretations of mental disease are in terms of his theory of excitation and inhibition, together with a rather naïve typology. Were it not for Pavlov's eminence in other fields, his studies and interpretations here would have received little attention. Some popularizers have made bizarre claims for the efficacy of conditioned reflex methods. Direct use of these methods is merely a form of suggestive therapy—a type of therapy that has long been efficacious in removing certain types of symptoms, especially those of hysterical origin.

The most successful methods of curing animal neuroses—even in laboratories using conditioned reflex methods—have gone beyond simple conditioning.

One of the laboratories carrying on extensive experiments has been that of Liddell at Cornell. I shall cite some of the experiments from his laboratory (3).

One of the dogs studied in this laboratory was cured of neurosis by reducing the conflict through easing the discrimination that the animal was forced to make. While this places the cure in the context of the conditioned discrimination method, the cure may be interpreted as psychotherapy based on the principle of "working through." Working through means facing the neurotic conflict first in reduced form, so that the conflictual situation is less threatening than it was.

The chief method of therapy used with neurotic sheep (the animal most studied in the Cornell laboratory) was the "rest cure," that is, a long period of time out in the pasture without any confrontation by the stimuli through which the neurosis had been generated. I suppose that the rest cure has been, historically, one of the chief methods of psychotherapy with man. When a patient is sick, the first thing we think of is bed rest. The results with sheep that were simply turned out to pasture were notably unsuccessful. Although there was occasionally some beneficial result, that is, some reduction in symptoms, the symptoms continued even after very long periods of rest.

The only sheep that was cured by a method analogous to psychotherapeutic treatment was Sheep D, observed over a period of twelve years. This would be nearly a record, even for psychoanalytic therapy (though the therapy itself did not take that long). The sheep was desensitized to the disturbing stimuli through a combination of extinction and transference therapy. Extinction consists in presenting all stimuli but never giving the electric shock which had been associated with these stimuli in the course of training through which the neurosis developed. The sheep is a social animal. It is necessary, in order to do conditioned reflex experiments with the sheep, to have another "social sheep" tethered in the laboratory. Only then can the normal experimental animal be made to stand quietly on the experimental table. This neurotic sheep apparently made some therapeutic use of the transference to the experimenter. When a new experimenter came along and showed affection for the sheep in the form of "coddling," it began to improve. I suppose we might say that this sheep was cured by a supportive therapy, during which there was a process of working through. This is somewhat loose talk, but I am inclined to believe that there are some psychological realities beneath the analogies I am suggesting.

A more direct attempt to parallel psychoanalytic concepts while curing animal neurosis was made by Masserman (14). Dr. Masserman is himself a trained psychoanalyst as well as an experimental physiologist.

The cat, which is the subject of the experiment, learns to lift the lid of a food box at a signal (sound or light). After the response is well learned, an air blast is introduced at the moment the lid of the food box is raised. While the air blast is harmless, it is apparently fear-inspiring and produces a strong conflict between the positive response to food based on hunger and the withdrawal response based on fear. An experimental neurosis results, with chronic "anxiety" in and out of the experimental situation, "phobic" responses, and other neurotic manifestations. The cat may refuse to eat, it may lose interest in mice, or may put its head into the food box without eating.

Masserman studied six types of psychotherapy. These were:

1. *Rest away from the experimental situation.* Recovery was very unstable.
2. *Alleviation of hunger outside the experimental situation.* Less hungry animals showed less marked symptoms when again in the conflict situa-

tion. The conflict was evidently reduced by this reduction in one of the motivational components.

3. *"Reassurance" and "suggestion" ("transference")*. Hand feeding and care by the experimenter proved beneficial.

4. *Forced solution through environmental manipulation.* When the animal was mechanically forced into the presence of the food box containing highly attractive food seasoned with catnip, inhibitions were overcome, and compulsive eating ensued.

5. *Social imitation.* A cat with normal eating responses was placed in the cage with the neurotic animal. The neurotic animal gradually joined in response with the normal one, but the method did not prove very efficient.

6. *Working through.* Cats were taught to control the signal that released the lid of the food box. The control was a simple foot switch, at a distance from the box. Because the signal could then be made to appear when the animal was "ready," it learned to overcome its conflict, despite the continued presence of the air blast.

Of the two most successful methods—working through, and forced solution—the first is analogous to psychoanalytic therapy, the second to various other forms of social therapy.

The parallel between psychotherapy with cats and with human patients is thus described by Masserman (15):

A neurotic animal becomes exceedingly dependent upon the experimenter for protection and care. If this trust is not violated, the latter may retrain the animal by gentle steps: first, to take the food from his hand, next to accept food in the apparatus, then to open the box while the experimenter merely hovers protectively, and finally to work the switch and feed without special encouragement from the therapist. During its rehabilitation the animal masters not only its immediate conflicts but also its generalized inhibitions, phobias, compulsions, and other neurotic reactions. This process may be likened to the familiar phenomenon of "transference" in clinical psychotherapy. The neurotic patient transfers his dependent relationship to the therapist, who then utilizes this dependence to guide and support the patient as the latter re-examines his conflictual desires and fears, recognizes his previous misinterpretations of reality and essays new ways of living until he is sufficiently successful and confident to proceed on his own.

The usefulness of experiments like Masserman's for the study of the dynamics of behavior is well illustrated by some experiments of his on alcohol. Neurotic cats often can face their problems more readily if they have taken a little bracer. Given a choice of plain milk or milk and alcohol, they prefer the drink that has been spiked. But after psychotherapy, when their neurotic conflicts have been reduced, they prefer the plain milk to the alcoholic milk.

It is through alcohol that they seem to seek a needed escape while they are neurotic, but it is no longer desired when they are well (16). This should please the moralists among us.

Possibly there may be a preferred animal for the study of psychotherapy, just as there are preferred animals useful in other scientific investigations. The salivary glands of Drosophila are almost ideal for the study of heredity; the ear of the guinea pig appears to be God's gift to researchers on audition. Possibly some animals have the ideal nervous system for studying neurosis and psychotherapy. So far we have been introduced to experiments on dogs and sheep and cats. The cat is the least sociable of these animals, but even it is capable of transference relationships, if we follow Masserman.

The lowly white rat also enters the picture of neurotic behavior and attempted therapy. Two major forms of behavior abnormality have been studied in the rat. With one of these, epileptiform convulsions, we need not be concerned. These seizures are produced by the high tones accompanying an air blast, jangling keys, or similar stimuli. The second form of abnormality consists of stereotyped behavior as a consequence of frustration. This stereotyped behavior has been designated "abnormal fixation" by Maier (13), who has experimented most extensively with it.

Rats placed in a discrimination situation normally learn to discriminate between a positive and a negative card by being rewarded for the positive choice and punished for the negative choice. The apparatus consists of a jumping stand, facing two windows covered by the stimulus cards. The rat is forced to jump by an air blast. If he jumps to the positive card, the card falls over, and the rat lands on a feeding platform where he receives the food reward. If he jumps to the negative card, he bumps his nose and falls into a net (Fig. 3, opposite page 23).

If the situation is an insoluble one, so that each card results half the time in reward and half the time in punishment, the animal may adopt a stereotyped response, usually choosing one of the windows, say the right-hand one. Now the experimenter makes the situation solvable, correct response being rewarded, incorrect punished. But once response has become fixated, the rat behaves like a fanatic, and does not change to the other window even though it is left open, with food in plain sight, and even though he is punished every time that he jumps to the right. He may continue to take punishment for several hundred consecutive trials. Here we have an analogy to types of compulsive behavior that psychoanalysts have reported as extremely difficult to treat. Some human symptoms that are familiar are nail biting, stuttering, arithmetic and reading difficulties. These habits are often very resistant to change, especially if the subjects have been punished or teased. The ritualistic behavior resists change through the ordinary operation of punishment.

In the case of these rats, a relatively simple therapy described as "guidance" proves helpful. The experimenter gently directs the rat to the open window by interposing his hand when the rat is about to make his stereotyped jump. Once the old pattern is broken, and the guided response leads to reward, the animal makes rapid progress in learning what is now expected.

It is a mistake to brush aside the experiments on animal neurosis on a priori grounds, because man has more developed symbolic capacities than they. A genuine comparative method always verifies the results obtained with lower animals through studies of man, but where to look and what to try may very well be suggested by the animal studies. The primates represent an unusually favorable opportunity to study one of man's near relatives, under circumstances in which a complete life history can be obtained. The first chimpanzee born to the colony in the Yerkes Laboratory of Primate Biology, a female named Alpha, spontaneously developed highly neurotic behavior as an adult. With sudden onset, she developed extreme symptoms in which a food phobia oscillated with unusual aggression toward the experimenter. It is interesting that this first reported case of neurotic disease in an adult chimpanzee should have developed in one who spent her first year of life raised by human parents! Another reported case of neurotic behavior differs from this one in that the picture concerning this second chimpanzee was that of general instability and depression, without sudden onset, but continuous with discordant behavior from the earliest years. Hebb, the author of the report on these animals (8), believes these spontaneous neuroses to be very different from laboratory-produced ones and is not inclined to give a psychogenic interpretation. The paper is commented on, however, by O. H. Mowrer, who sees many possibilities for a psychoanalytic account of the events leading up to the neurotic symptoms. Chimpanzees have also served as subjects for experiments on morphine addiction, in which much of the behavior is like that of the human addict (24). The second of the two neurotic chimpanzees referred to in the foregoing account had served briefly in the experiments on morphine addiction, but her difficulties cannot be attributed to this fact. On the contrary, she was chosen for those experiments precisely because she was already an animal unsuitable for breeding purposes.

The possibility of psychosomatic studies on these animals is a genuine one. One familiar psychosomatic symptom is the readiness with which their bowels become watery whenever they show emotional excitement—an observation which anyone who experiments with them soon makes. Gorillas have been less studied than chimpanzees, but in a recent conversation with Dr. Yerkes, who was working with the infant gorillas at San Diego, I had the distinct impression that he thought the gorilla reacted much more "subjectively" to its state of bodily health and comfort than the chimpanzee. It is as though a stomach-ache is a more depressing experience to a gorilla than to a chimpanzee. If we are wise enough to make the most of naturalistic observations, we may find some clues that will help us to design better experiments.

EXPERIMENTAL STUDIES OF PSYCHOTHERAPY WITH HUMAN SUBJECTS

Whatever may be the situation with respect to animals below man, our primary interest in therapy is in the treatment of human illness, so that experiments that study therapeutic principles directly with human subjects have a cogency that experiments with animals can never have.

One kind of venture is that which seeks to evaluate the relative success of different kinds of therapy without any experimental control of the therapy itself. Such investigations are important, but the scientific generalizations from them are bound to be meager. They may tell what kind of patient ought to go to what kind of physician, but then we would still have to ask why one is more successful than the other. We might find, for example, that Alcoholics Anonymous did more than psychoanalysts for alcoholics. But this would be only a start in further inquiry. Today we are concerned with what goes on within psychotherapy, not with what kind of therapeutic arrangements are to be recommended in the community.

I wish to give one illustration of the kind of data that can be obtained from therapeutic sessions that deal with the course of treatments of real people who come to a psychotherapist for help. Sometimes scientists use data that they create for experimental purposes; sometimes they turn available data to scientific use. This first illustration is the kind of situation in which available data are turned to scientific account. I refer to some studies of short psychotherapy made by Carl Rogers and his students in the counseling center at the University of Chicago (20, 23). To those of us oriented in the field of contemporary clinical psychology, it may seem somewhat surprising that I bring Rogers into a discussion of psychoanalysis, for he is, in some sense, an enemy, or at least a competitor. But a person in trouble who is being counseled is not concerned about the theory that is being used on him. He is burdened by his troubles, and if he finds relief and we discover how, the principles are important ones, no matter who his therapist is. In some sense, Rogers' antagonism to psychoanalysis produces interviews that reveal better than psychoanalysis itself some of the principles about which analysts speak.

Rogers' method, known as nondirective therapy, consists in a supportive therapy based primarily upon the permissiveness of the therapist. An effort is made to avoid getting embroiled in transference, and interpretations are at a minimum. The therapist listens attentively and reflects the feeling in the assertions of the patient, avoiding evaluations or judgments of his own. What then happens during successive sessions?

Rogers and his students have systematically recorded what is said in their interviews, using the modern electromagnetic records. Secretaries are taught to transcribe the "mm's" and "ah's" and to note the lengths of rest pauses. Hence it is possible to make detailed content analyses of the interviews to give quantitative answers to some questions about what goes on. It is said, for example, that in the early interviews the patient commonly restates his problem, returning over and over again to the same point of difficulty, but after he has been in the situation awhile he gradually achieves insight, and these occasions of insight are signs of therapeutic progress. By carefully coding what is happening in the interviews we may ascertain whether or not this march of events does in fact go forward. In Figure 4 are plotted the average results of ten cases for whom there were from three to nine interviews each. When the records are divided into fifths, we see that the statement and restatement of the problem decreases relative to the increase in statements revealing insight and understanding.

One can imagine a real experimental design superimposed upon a process of this sort. For example, at some stage the therapist might deliberately introduce interpretations of the kind carefully avoided in the nondirective method. If the height of the line showing statements of insight and understanding increased, by this criterion the interpretation would be shown to be helpful; if the line were to taper off, it would show that the interpretations slowed up the progress.

One of the chief advantages of Rogers' method for purposes of research on psychotherapy is that it provides a highly disciplined interview technique, with minimum active participation by the therapist. Hence other methods might well use it as a control method, noting how the other methods accelerate or slow up progress. Fortunately, the consequences of Rogers' nondirective method are generally benign, so that no harm would be done in using it as a reference method.

A start has been made in the direction of comparing two methods in a very ingenious experiment by Keet (9). I wish to describe his experiment in some detail because it serves as a useful model of experimental design in this difficult field. If its results are substantiated by others, I believe that the experiment will prove to be something of a landmark.

Thirty normal subjects participated in this experiment designed to compare the effectiveness of two counseling techniques in overcoming a conflict symptomatized by the inability to recall a word just memorized. Through a cleverly devised method, the subject learned a list of six words, including a critical word to which he had shown emotional responses in a word association test.

The word association test was the one made familiar by Jung. A list of one hundred words is read off to the subject, one word at a time. The subject is instructed to reply as promptly as possible with the first word that he thinks of. The experimenter notes the word, and records the time of response with a stop watch. The list is gone through a second time. Emotional conflict is shown

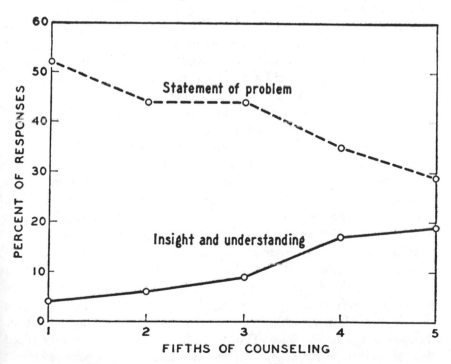

Fig. 4.—Changes taking place during brief psychotherapy. Statements by the patient during the psychotherapeutic sessions are recorded electromagnetically, transcribed, and coded. Restatements of the problem occur with less relative frequency, while statements of insight and understanding increase. Replotted from data presented by Seeman (1949).

in a number of ways, according to what have come to be known as "complex indicators." These include far-fetched responses, failure to respond, repeating back the stimulus word, repeating an earlier response, and so on. In this experiment two complex-indicators were chosen. First, those words were selected for which responses were changed from the first to the second reading. Second, among these words, that one was chosen for the purpose of the experiment that had the longest reaction time. By this strictly objective method, a critical family of three words was selected, one stimulus word and the two words given as responses to it on the two trials. In the example to which we are about to turn the set of key words was "nasty—messy—mean." That is, to the word "nasty" the subject had replied "messy" after a delay on the first trial, and then on the second trial had replied "mean," but also after a delay.

The critical stimulus word was then imbedded in a list including five neutral words. Subjects experienced no difficulty in learning and remembering this list of six words. But now a new list of six words was memorized, producing some interference with recall of the first list. We experimental psychologists have a fancy expression for this interference. We call it retroactive inhibition. When the effort was made to recall the first list, twenty-five of the thirty subjects forgot the critical word but remembered the remaining five neutral words. We here see the activity of a moderate repression. The emotionally loaded word is forgotten when conditions for recall are made slightly more difficult, even though the word was freely recalled in the process of memorizing the list of six words. Subjects felt very annoyed that they could not recall this word that was "right on the tip of the tongue."

This "microneurosis" provided an opportunity for short therapy, the success of the therapy to be judged, first of all, by the recovery of the forgotten word. Two therapeutic techniques were compared. One of these, called the "expressive technique," was permissive, and allowed expression of feeling. It was very close to Rogers' nondirective technique. As used in this experiment it was unsuccessful. It failed in all thirteen of the cases with whom it was used. That is, none of the thirteen recovered the forgotten word during the therapeutic session. The second technique, called the "interpretive technique," had all the features of the first, but added the more active interpretive comments of the therapist at appropriate times. Thus to the insights of the client were added those of the therapist, at, of course, a "shallow" level from the point of view of psychoanalysis. But the method deviates from the Rogers method in the direction of the psychoanalytic method. The method was highly successful. Eleven of twelve subjects met the first criterion of therapeutic success: that is, they recalled the forgotten word within the therapeutic session.

The question we wish to ask is this: Just how did interpretation help to bring about the recall of the forgotten word? The author Keet suggests that through interpretation his subjects were freer to use normal associative processes. Then the affective experience that determined the failure to recall came into awareness. Once the affective experience was in awareness, the conflict over recall could be resolved, because the subject was able to recall the circumstances under which the critical word was forgotten.

I wish to present a verbatim account of one of Keet's interpretive therapeutic sessions, to illustrate the nature of his interpretations and provide evidence that will permit us to judge whether or not the consequences are as he describes them.

The subject, a young married woman, replied to the word "nasty" first with the word "messy," then with the word "mean." Because both of the replies were long delayed, the word "nasty" was chosen as the critical word in the memory experiment. She first memorized the following list of six words: green, make, ask, nasty, paper, sad. This she did without difficulty. Then she learned another list of six words. The memory method used was somewhat unusual, but I am not going to take the time to give the details. After the memorization of the second list she was asked to recall the first. It is at this point that the therapeutic interview took place.

EXPERIMENTER: Now please repeat the first set of key words.

SUBJECT (*confidently*): Green, make, ask, paper, sad. (*A pause followed with the experimenter looking inquiringly at the subject.*) Wait a minute, there were six and I have only five. That's silly. Of course there were six. I should be able to remember the sixth one. Let me see. Green, make, ask, sad, paper. No, that's wrong. Paper comes before sad. That's right, isn't it?

E: You want me to help you. [This is a characteristic Rogers nondirective response.]

S: If you would only tell me that, then I would perhaps remember the missing word. (*Pause.*) It's annoying. . . . It's funny. . . . I know it was in the fourth place, wasn't it?

E: Try to work it out by yourself, by . . .

S: I see you want me to recall the word by myself.

E: That would be more satisfying, wouldn't it?

S: Sure. I mean it is always nice to solve a little problem. It's quite an easy job remembering six words after you've said them several times. (*She moves in the chair and gives vent to little sounds of annoyance . . . a considerable pause.*)

E: You are quite annoyed with yourself.

S: Yes, I am, why should I be so stupid. . . . Green, make, ask, blank, paper, sad . . . sad, paper, blank, ask. Oh, that will be no use. (*She tries again, counting on fingers and apparently saying the words silently. Makes exclamations of annoyance.*) Is it bread? No, it isn't. That's in the second lot. . . . *Is it bread?*

E: We agreed that it would perhaps be better if you tried to remember it yourself.

S: I am too annoyed to think clearly. All sorts of words pop into my mind. Is is all right if I say them?

E: You are free to go about it any way you please.

S: Well, the last set was water, long, try, bread . . . er . . . er . . . bird, wasn't it?

E: You do want help, don't you?

S (*laughs heartily*): Yes, I'm all mixed up. If I could get certainty on the last list it might help me to remember.

E: You feel confused.

S (*laughs*): Yes, all mixed up and disturbed. It's funny that I can remember the last list and not the first one. One word in the first one: blank, blank, blank. That's no good. I shall have to give up.

E: You are quite free to do that, you know.

Up to this point the interview has followed the general pattern of the expressive technique. The experimenter has been permissive, has recognized the subject's feeling, but has not interpreted. The permissiveness of the experimenter's last response ("You are quite free . . .") releases a good deal of expressed emotion in the next response. This is the kind of therapeutic consequence claimed for the nondirective method. The first response classified as an interpretation follows this release of feeling by the subject.

S: That's a relief. You think me very stupid, don't you? (*Laughs.*) I suppose I am, really. I should be able to recall the word. It is most exasperating. I feel quite angry with you, sitting there smug and self-satisfied. Could you do it? I mean have you tried it on yourself? (*She laughs when she sees the experimenter smiling.*) Oh, is the word "green"? That doesn't seem to ring quite true. I am sure it is not "green." I went overseas once and got quite seasick . . . turned green . . . (*pause*).

[Now note that the experimenter departs from the nondirective method to offer a simple interpretation.]

E: Perhaps there is something about the word itself. . . . You may have had some experience, or something like that. . . .

S: I often used to feel sick when I got angry. I did a moment ago. Just the faintest feeling in my stomach when I felt a bit angry with you. I was very seasick when I went to Europe. Turned pasty and green. . . . I was all alone . . . the youngest in a swimming team. Pasty. (*Pause.*)

[You will notice the similarity between the word "pasty" and the word she is trying to recall which is "nasty." The experimenter stays with the problem of her feelings, however.]

E: You say you feel a little nauseated when you are angry.

S: Yes, whenever my sister and I quarreled and I got very angry I was nauseated. Once I even got sick and vomited. I didn't like the mess. This is not so bad nowadays. Only when I try to hold my irritation back, then I get it. I always thought my sister was stronger than I am. We used to have real fights sometimes. (*Laughs.*) I don't feel so confused any more. Do you think the blank, blank word . . . (*laughs*). I can't remember it yet. Can it have something to do with my quarreling with my sister? My father liked her very much more than he did me. (*Pause.*)

E: Maybe. And perhaps it is connected with some more recent experience.

[These interpretations by the experimenter may seem to be very trivial, but their importance lies in their timing. He had noted in the subject's hesitation at this point something that might be interpreted as a thought near to expression. Her response proves the correctness of his hunch.]

S: You mean with my husband. . . . Oh, that just slipped out. (*Laughs.*) Now I have said it, I might as well tell you we had a quarrel the other day—a rather bitter one. (*Pause.*) I still think he was very mean. (*With some vindictiveness.*) When people get nasty like that I get very angry. I mean nasty. Of course, that is the word. "Nasty." Well, I never. How do you like that! Do you really think this has something to do with my quarrel with my husband? It is very funny.

The success of the cases in which there were these rather simple interpretative intrusions as contrasted with those in which interpretations were avoided gives clarity to the manner in which such interpretations help penetrate a thin veil of resistance. The element of surprise at what she discovers is, by the way, characteristic of the insights that come in psychotherapy.

But I am not yet through talking about this experiment. So far we have seen one therapeutic result: the recall of a word that had undergone repression within the experiment.

The experimenter was not satisfied with this, for that would be mere symptom alleviation. Therapy must go deeper than that. Now, he asked, did the therapy here go any deeper, or, to put it another way, can any generalization or spread of its results be detected?

The second cycle of the experiment was almost a repeat of the first, by again introducing the learning of a list, the learning of a second list, and then the attempted recall of the first. But this time one of the response words in the critical set was used. The subject who said to "nasty" first "messy" and then "mean" is now asked to learn a list in which the first response word ("messy") is included. The conjecture is as follows. If the therapy really released some of the emotion or produced some insight connected with the disturbing set of key words, then the repressive tendencies should have been weakened. Hence those whose therapy was unsuccessful should repress the new word, while those whose therapy was successful should be able to recall the word without trouble. The conjecture was completely substantiated. Those who forgot and never recovered the original stimulus word in the first part of the experiment *also* forgot the response word in the second part of the experiment; those who forgot, but later recovered the stimulus word, had no trouble in recalling the response word in the second cycle of the experiment.

If we take the experiment at its face value it is a beautiful epitome of much that is said to go on within psychoanalysis. I have no reason to doubt the experimental findings, except that psychologists are brought up to be skeptics, and I shall not rest happy until someone repeats and confirms the experiment. Whether or not the results in a repetition turn out as decisive as Keet's results, I believe he has set a very useful pattern for further work.

There are several very good features to Keet's experimental design. (1) In the first place, the subjects are selected from the general population for the purposes of the experiment. They are not people who come to a physician because they believe themselves to be sick. (2) In the second place, a symptom is produced under laboratory conditions, so that an element of control is introduced. (3) In the third place, the methods of therapy used are clearly delineated, and criteria of therapeutic success operationally defined. (4) Fourth, all of this is superimposed upon a recognition that a laboratory neurosis is necessarily connected with the biography of the individual. The word association test in this experiment provides a bridge to the real person, so that the experiment does not take place in a psychological vacuum. The importance of this is readily recognized when you recall the highly personal and individual material that comes out even in this very brief psychotherapeutic session.

Now we are ready for summing up and for a few comments on the prospects for the future.

PSYCHOLOGICAL SCIENCE AND PSYCHOANALYSIS

In the last lecture I dealt with experimental attempts to study psychodynamic principles in experiments with animals, children, and adults. In this lecture I have dealt with the induction and therapy of neuroses in animals and human subjects. The main points that I have been emphasizing are that it is possible to experiment in this field and that we already have a considerable body of experimental results.

We may well ask what this all adds up to. Several statements are in order:

1. For one thing, it has been possible to parallel many psychoanalytic phenomena in the laboratory. When this is done, the correspondence between predictions according to psychoanalytic theory and what is found is on the whole very satisfactory. Even a fairly unfriendly statement of the case, as that by Sears in his reviews of the literature (21, 22), time after time finds the agree-

ment between the fact and theory, even though the author prefers to disparage the importance of the evidence.

2. A second point needs to be made. If experiments supporting psychoanalytic interpretations are any good, they ought to *advance* our understanding, not merely *confirm* or *deny* the theories that someone has stated. This is really what worries Sears. So many of the experiments give merely trivial illustrations of what psychoanalysts have demonstrated to their own satisfaction in clinical work. Such illustrations may be useful as propaganda, or in giving psychoanalysis a fair hearing, but they do not really do much for science unless there is some fertility in them. Only a few of the experiments that I have reported serve this constructive role, but these few set useful patterns for the future.

In the first lecture I mentioned Miller's experiment (17) on displaced aggression as one that added some lawfulness with respect to the kind of object that could serve as the substitute for the primary object of aggression. Blum's experiment with Blacky uncovered relationships not clearly enunciated in theoretical writings about psychoanalysis, thus opening the door to advances in theory.

Today I pointed out how the content analysis of Rogers and his students might be used to produce new knowledge about the course of improvement under psychotherapy. Finally, Keet's experiment suggests that we may be able to produce and cure mild neuroses in the laboratory, thus making possible precise comparisons of different methods.

3. A third point is that experimental work thus far bears most directly only on the most superficial aspects of psychoanalytic theory, while many of its deeper problems are scarcely touched. I do not worry much about this, however, for if we are able to design experiments appropriate to the more superficial aspects, we can move on to deeper stages. Some of the experiments with hypnosis, for example, seem to me to come close to penetrating some of the deeper questions, such as the sexual significance of the transference relationship and its influence upon dreams.

We must be careful not to be trapped by the word "deeper," when we think of psychoanalysis as a "depth" psychology. Two meanings are possible. An impulse or emotionally loaded experience may be deeply repressed, possibly because it is connected with something from very early childhood. This is the usual meaning of deeper. But there is another meaning. Something is deeply important for the individual if it is in some sense central or nuclear, heavily freighted with emotion. Classical theory says that these two senses correspond—the nuclear conflicts are those from early childhood, and deeply repressed. But we may find that what is deeply important for therapeutic purposes is that which arouses depth of feeling in the present, regardless of its relative importance at some remote time. Depth is a metaphor, and we need to know the realities to which it refers.

There is no doubt but that psychological science will be advanced further, as it has already been advanced, by taking cognizance of the teachings of psychoanalysis. This would be true even though psychoanalysis were to disappear in the process.

But how about psychoanalysis itself? What are its prospects as a science?

In a trenchantly critical, albeit friendly, review of the possibilities for a scientific psychoanalysis, Ellis (4) notes a number of "dangers," that is, features tending to delay the development of a truly scientific psychoanalysis. His main points are that psychoanalysts seem to prefer defending an accepted theory to an impartial examination of evidence, and they move too quickly to a complete and final explanation of events, when, in the present state of psychological knowledge, more modest claims would be both more fitting and more becoming. Anyone who tries to give an honest appraisal of psychoanalysis as a science must be ready to admit that as it is stated it is mostly very bad science, that the bulk of the articles in its journals cannot be defended as research publications at all. Having said this, I am prepared to reassert that there is much to be learned from these writings. The task of making a science of the observations and relationships may, however, fall to others than the psychoanalysts themselves.

If psychoanalysts are themselves to make a science of their knowledge, they must be prepared to follow some of the standard rules of science. Ellis lists thirty-eight suggestions, although many of them overlap. Half of his statements warn against accepting speculative theories uncritically: making a god of some one psychoanalytic authority, letting one's own prejudices stand in the way of accepting contradictory evidence, falling into mysticism and obscurantism, seeking "complete" explanations. The other half restate the ordinary principles of science: hypotheses tentatively proposed and subject to empirical test, control experiments, objectively recorded data, experiments on subjects other than patients under treatment, a search for contradictory as well as for confirmatory evidence, repetition of observations by independent investigators, and so on. It must not be implied that psychoanalysts themselves have not been concerned about these matters. Some suggested research problems and procedures will be discussed in the lectures by Dr. Kubie that follow.

Whatever the psychoanalysts do about research, the obligation is clearly upon experimental, physiological, and clinical psychologists to take seriously the field of psychodynamics, and to conduct investigations either independently or in collaboration with psychoanalysts. It is a tribute to Freud and his psychoanalytic followers that the problems faced by psychologists in their laboratories have been enormously enriched by the questions the analysts have taught us to ask.

——————— LAWRENCE S. KUBIE ———————

Problems and Techniques of Psychoanalytic Validation and Progress

I

INTRODUCTION

IN MARCH OF 1950, Professor Hilgard presented before this same audience two lectures which summarized some of the recent experimental tests of the validity of certain aspects of psychoanalytic theory and technique. His first lecture dealt with theories of unconscious psychodynamics, the second with problems in psychotherapy. In order to avoid duplicating Professor Hilgard's lectures I asked him to send me his manuscript. This he kindly did, thus making it possible for me to approach our subject with a complementary purpose. Professor Hilgard's aim was to show that it is possible to confirm certain psychoanalytic concepts and techniques under controlled laboratory conditions. Mine will be rather to indicate where we need help from the exact sciences in making our own concepts more precise and in the development of new qualitative and quantitative instruments. We shall see that special technical difficulties must be overcome, and we shall discuss the organization which is needed to further such research. In other words, my lectures will attempt to suggest areas and objectives of future co-ordinated interdisciplinary studies. You will learn that I am no optimist about the difficulties which such studies must overcome.

I approach this subject from the point of view of one who for twenty-odd years has been spending about ten hours a day in a process which is at once perplexing, confusing, enormously stimulating, exciting, and provocative. Many times during these years I have had an intimation that something of enormous value lay just beyond my vision, outlined hazily in the accumulating data on human life. Consequently, for about fifteen of these twenty years I have from time to time attempted to investigate various components in the psychoanalytic process. I cannot refrain from expressing my hope that this series of lectures may point the way to the more systematic researches in this field which are long overdue, and may even help indirectly to stimulate the organization of adequately staffed and financed institutes for research in

46

psychoanalytic psychology. I hope that someday you will meet here to consider the results of active investigations and not merely the nature, the objectives, and the conditions of future investigations.

I should not want this distinguished audience to gather the misapprehension that this is the first time that problems of validation and of experimental control have been considered by analysts (8, 9, 10, 16, 17, 25, 28, 41, 43, 46, 48, 52, 54, 55, 56, 65, 66, 76, 77), nor the first time that a program of basic research has been planned. On the contrary, both have been discussed many times, but these deliberations have not borne fruit. I should be guilty of gross ingratitude if I failed to express to you my appreciation of the heartening significance of this occasion to me as an analyst. Not only is it an undeserved personal honor but also a challenge to address so distinguished a group of friendly but skeptical scientific colleagues from other disciplines. In undertaking the assignment I am heartened by the hope that the occasion may conceivably mark a change in the climate of science, a turning point in what has heretofore been a losing struggle to integrate psychoanalysis with its more precise siblings. Please do not misunderstand me. I do not say this with any unspoken anticipation that such a development could come as a direct and immediate consequence of these lectures. My optimism is for the future, through the gradual and indirect influence of such a series of lectures as these on the men who make the policies of foundations and of medical schools and universities. Thus I confess that I cannot help looking over your shoulders hopefully toward these statesmen of science.

In the course of the subsequent lectures we shall repeatedly come up against a certain group of problems in varied forms. We shall find that our consistent working assumption is that our problem is to understand the interrelationships between conscious and unconscious forces in psychological affairs and how they interact on each other. In other words, we shall want to know both how unconscious forces influence conscious processes and how conscious processes in turn influence unconscious levels of psychological organization. When it comes to the question of how psychological processes go off the rails, e.g., the so-called neurotic process, we shall want to know what starts it, what keeps it going, what resolves it, the laws which determine its transformations and its multiple manifestations, and what determines their many secondary consequences on a patient's life. This will lead to a consideration of certain difficult questions, such as what the primary ingredients of the neurotic process are, and what its secondary and tertiary manifestations are, and how we can differentiate these.

Certain of these complex and basic issues have not been solved nor even satisfactorily formulated by analysts themselves. This lack of clarity within analysis is one of the major obstacles to a clarification of its relationship to the other sciences. We shall have to deal with these questions as best we can within the framework of existing concepts. Where the confusion of analytic theory is still too great, a consideration of interdisciplinary integration will have to be postponed.

FROM THE VIEWPOINT OF THE QUANTITATIVE SCIENCES, WHAT IS PSYCHOANALYSIS?

I want to begin by outlining a few basic facts about psychoanalysis, so as to establish grounds of mutual understanding. I believe that it is fair to ask you to use these statements as our working hypotheses throughout the succeeding discussion. (There is no clearer or more succinct summary of certain aspects of what follows than in the recent book by B. D. Lewin, *The Psychoanalysis of Elation* [57].)

The Significance of the Symbolic Process

The symbolic process will occupy a central position in this story. The human being is capable of two kinds of symbolizing processes. One gives him the ability to make condensed abstractions of concrete experience and to contemplate them and act on them and communicate them to others in the form of psychological processes of which he is aware. These constitute his conscious purposes, his conscious feelings, and his conscious thoughts, which he expresses deliberately by means of acts, gestures, facial expressions, sounds, words, and the written symbols of words. Accompanying these, however, is a running fugue of muscular, vascular, and glandular changes, some voluntary and some involuntary, of which he has variable degrees of conscious knowledge and control. At the same time there is another symbolic process, by means of which in disguised and denatured forms man gives partial expression to psychological processes of which he is not only unaware, but also unable to become aware, by any simple process of direct self-inspecion. The first is the symbolic process of self-expression through some form of language and action; the second might best be called the symbolic process of self-deception. The neurotic process is made possible by this peculiarly human capacity to represent our psychological processes in symbolic forms and then to deceive ourselves through symbols which express in disguised forms some fragment of what goes on inside us. To avoid misunderstanding, let me point out at once that the formal "symbol" of the dream is merely a special and indeed somewhat minor manifestation of this second type of symbolic process.

In the developing infant and child, these two symbolizing processes have a common origin; and the ability to represent internal experiences in symbolic forms is the *sine qua non* both of speech and of the neurosis. We have wholly inadequate information as to the extent to which either symbolic process is significantly possible among animals lower than man. Consequently, we do not know whether the so-called "experimental neurosis" of laboratory animals is identical with the human neurotic process itself, or whether it is equivalent only to the emotional disturbances which are the inevitable concomitants of human neuroses. It is clear, of course, that stormy and protracted emotional disturbances can be induced deliberately in laboratory animals, disturbances which are comparable to the emotional disturbances which frequently accompany human neuroses; but such emotional disturbances are not identical with the neurotic process itself. (Dr. Howard Liddell in a personal communication subscribes to this cautious reservation; also see Reference 59.)

Early in life, then, a fateful split occurs between symbolic processes in which the symbol represents internal psychological tensions of which we are conscious, and symbols which represent psychological tensions which which we have already repressed and of which thereafter we are unable to become conscious through simple self-examination. Indeed the essential difference between speech and the neurosis resides in this fact, namely, that in speech the relationship of the symbol to internal tension is easily accessible to consciousness, whereas it is inaccessible to consciousness in the neurosis. Thus the distortion of the symbolic process which we call the neurosis can best be described as follows: (1) Psychological tensions accumulate which we are unable to discharge unaltered, because of the influence of a mixture of conscious and unconscious guilts and fears. (2) At the same time this mixture of conscious and unconscious, self-critical and self-protective mechanisms operates automatically in such a way as to render unconscious these psychological tensions which are unacceptable, a process which is called "repression." (3) The precise nature of the energetic processes which underlie psychological states remains undetermined, but, whatever their nature, those energetic processes which had been associated with conscious psychological states before their repression became dissociated from these states after repression, yet continue to exercise a powerful influence upon our thoughts, feelings, and behavior. Consequently, all these psychic acts are a symbolic language for the expression of mixtures of energetic processes, some of them having their origins in conscious and some in unconscious psychological processes.

In short, the neurosis requires: (*a*) the ability to *repress* those processes which are born of unacceptable conflicts, (*b*) the dissociation of energetic processes from the repressed tensions, and (c) the ability to represent these tensions in symbolic psychological acts which conceal their sources. Experience has shown that in every moment of life everything we do represents an algebraic summation of many psychological processes, of some of which we are conscious and of others unconscious. Psychoanalysis is the first attempt to understand and explain human behavior in terms of the confluent influence of such conscious and unconscious processes. Without unconscious processes and their symbolic representation there could be no neurosis.

Elsewhere I have summarized this as follows (35, p. 1):

(1) In every man there are psychological processes of which he is unconscious as well as those of which he is conscious. (2) At every moment of life the unconscious processes play an important contributory role in determining much of our behavior. (3) Where they play a dominant role, the resulting behavior can neither be understood nor influenced materially without first altering the underlying unconscious psychological processes. (4) In order to do this, it is necessary to find out what they are. (5) This requires the use of special techniques, among which the pioneer and still the most important is psychoanalysis. (6) The purpose of this technique is to overcome the internal obstacles which interfere with the emergence of unconscious processes into consciousness. (7) At the same time, the technique aims to modify the disturbing and sometimes destructive influence of the unconscious processes as they are brought into consciousness. (8) Therefore in therapy, in prevention, and in education, the inclusive goal of psychoanalysis is to broaden the domain of conscious control in human life and to shrink that darker empire in which unconscious forces play a dominant role.

In short, what brought analysis into existence, and what brings men to analysis, is the fact that so large a share of what we do is dominated by psychological forces of which we are unable to become conscious without the aid of some special psychological instrument.

Again, to avoid any possible misunderstanding, I would remind this audience that there is another kind of unaware psychological process which is important for all normal symbolic creative thinking, whether artistic or scientific. This kind of unawareness arises in a quite different manner and has characteristics and effects which are wholly different from the unconscious processes which form the kernel of the neurosis. It arises automatically through the process of learning by repetition, in the course of which many intermediate steps are fused into a simple unit. The original intervening steps remain accessible, however, to conscious, retrospective self-inspection. They are on what William James called "the fringe of consciousness," which is essentially equivalent to what Freud had in mind when he used such terms as "preconscious" or "subconscious," as opposed to the dynamically charged, repressed, and organized "unconscious." It is this fusion of intermediate steps which makes possible those intuitive leaps in art and science by means of which the creative process sometimes dons seven-league boots. Other than to warn against this confusion, in these lectures I will not have to deal further with this economizing intuitive function of our psychological apparatus.

All that I have said thus far, if viewed from the point of view of research, can be boiled down to two central, technical problems: (1) How can we appraise with qualitative and quantitative precision the relationships between conscious and unconscious levels of symbolic activity, when these operate concurrently and interact on each other continuously? (2) How can we impart this understanding to patients? Every important scientific problem about analysis is an effort to answer one or the other of these two questions. The challenge of these lectures is to consider how the nature of these relationships and processes can be explored in experiments which are designed to isolate individual components out of the complex interweaving currents of psychological experience which make up the daily life of every human being.

In the design of any such experiments, it must be kept clearly in mind that the spectrum of psychological events is always continuous, with concrete experience at one pole, dreamed experience at the other, and waking fantasy in between (Fig. 1). Furthermore, in every psychological experience all three of these components are always present in varied combinations. There is no event so purely factual that it is not interwoven with some quality of fantasy and dream, just as there is no dreamed experience which does not draw some of its material from the concrete data of daily life, i.e., from the residues of recent experience. Therefore, the differences between these two types of psychological experience (actual events, fantasies, and dreams) are relative rather

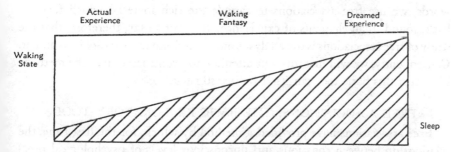

FIG. 1.—Note that the diagram is drawn so as to indicate that there are dreamlike and fantastic components in every real experience and reality elements in every dream, with every possible admixture between. The variations in relative proportions is a matter of fundamental importance, as will be seen in later discussions.

than absolute. Consequently, it is impossible to conceive of an inclusive investigation of a single moment of behavior, much less of personality as a whole, which did not cover the whole range of the spectrum—man's factual life history, his waking fantasies, and his dreams. We shall also see that the relative roles of conscious and unconscious processes vary at different points along the spectrum. In this connection, it is significant that we know more about the ways in which unconscious processes influence and shape our conscious processes, rather than the other way around. Indeed this is one of the basic limitations of our knowledge of the dynamics of the psychotherapeutic process in general.

The clinical appraisal of the interplay of conscious and unconscious psychological forces in human affairs depends in no small part upon a study of discrepancies: discrepancies between conscious purposes and actual behavior, between conscious purposes and aberrant fantasy, between conscious purposes and the highly charged symbols of the dream, between reality and the affective state. Where the patient is himself aware of these intimate details of his own life, he finds both the frank contemplation of them and their revelation extremely painful. Consequently, the ability of the analyst to elicit such information depends in part upon the sensitivity and accuracy with which the analyst understands and uses his rapport with the patient so as to facilitate the patient's ability to communicate with him. Where, as is largely true, the patient is unaware even of gross discrepancies, our understanding of the interaction of conscious and unconscious processes depends predominantly on the skillful use of what we call free associations. Transference material, the discrepant historical data, and the intricacies of fantasy and dream are all subjected to minute exploration by observing and interpreting the significance of the sequences which occur in the patient's free associations to them. In other words, we use free associations to sample the rich material which forms a background to all elements of experience. It is fair to say, therefore, that the study of free associations is the analyst's most searching exploratory instrument. Consequently, we will first turn our attention to a consideration of the methods by which this basic tool can itself be investigated.

FREE ASSOCIATIONS: THE BASIC EXPLORATORY TOOL

Free associations have provided a method by which, for the first time, the relationship between conscious and unconscious levels of psychological processes can be studied systematically. Consequently, over the last fifty years in one form or another free association has proved to be an essential tool in the exploratory phase of any form of psychotherapy which attempts to bring to light the unconscious levels of psychological integration. The technique of free associations is a fundamental exploratory instrument because it is our only approximation to a psychological Gallup poll, i.e., to a method of gathering relatively random samples of psychological activity. When a patient talks to me in the way I am addressing this audience, he uses continuously and automatically an unconscious process of picking and choosing among multiple simultaneous psychological processes, eliminating irrelevancies as he selects special thoughts and ideas to present in words. This is essential for the communication of ideas, but the articulate result is far from providing a full or true picture of the totality of what has been going on in the speaker's head at the time. When, as in analysis, our task is to try to understand *all* that is going on, then we must ask a speaker not to present such a selected or weighted sample but to give us instead as random a sample as he can of all of the psychological processes which are accessible to him. In essence, this is the critical significance of free association in the exploration of our mental processes.

It is important that in this context the word "free" should not be misunderstood. If the word carried the empty philosophical implication that free associations were exempt from the directing influence of physiological and psychological forces, the term would of course be a misnomer. However, the term is not so misused. It implies freedom only from conscious and deliberate interference with the spontaneity of the stream of thought itself, freedom that is from conscious selection and rejection among the elements of that stream.

I can well imagine that at this point many of you may be saying: "This is all well and good. Doubtless a technique as fundamental as free associations should itself be thoroughly explored for its own sake; but how and why does it clarify the relationship of varying levels and states of psychological awareness, and what has all of this to do anyhow with the more precise exploration of psychoanalytic theory?" These are legitimate and indeed helpful questions, the answering of which will take us on a considerable detour.

1. In the first place free associations are the basic and spontaneous *modus operandi* of the mental apparatus. I have previously formulated this in the following words (35, pp. 45-47):

> It is not always realized that free association is the natural process by which the mind of the artist and scientist creates. Free associations enable the psychological process to roam through the mental highways and byways, unhampered by conscious restrictions, gathering up ideas and impressions, putting them together in varying combinations, until new relationships and new patterns come into view. Both in science and in the arts, free association is an essential tool in the process of creative search. Subsequent logical scrutiny subjects the new patterns to a necessary secondary process of retrospective checking and testing. In analysis the free

associations are provided by the patient; the logical scrutiny by the analyst. . . . There are two psychological levels of linkages, one conscious and the other unconscious. If we allow ourselves consciously to pick and choose from among the thoughts which come freely to mind, it becomes almost impossible to study the influence of unconscious forces on the stream of psychological events. If, on the other hand, all conscious choices are eliminated, then the unconscious influences come into view. Free associations, therefore, provide a key to the unconscious, indeed the major key we now possess.

Consequently, in all states of consciousness "free" or unselected linkages provide the most direct lead to an understanding of the psychological content of the psychic apparatus at any particular moment and under any special physiological and psychological circumstances.

2. Secondly, from the earliest stages in the development of the symbolic process of language, its symbols represent abstractions of concrete experience. At the start, however, the ability to represent concepts by the verbal currency which we call words is far from precise. Indeed, on the contrary, early verbal representatives even of experiences which differ widely may have broad areas of overlap. This was once described in the following terms (30):

Since the child's world begins inevitably with his body, and since the force which instigates the child to expand his knowledge is always the pressure of bodily desires, and since every new fact of experience which enters into psychic life can make its entrance only by relating itself to that which is already present, it follows that every new fact apperceived by the child must somehow relate itself to bodily things. . . . If this represents with any degree of fidelity the process of expanding knowledge, it must also represent the process of expanding speech. This means that there is at first a long period in which concepts are vague, broad, and overlapping; and that with advancing years these concepts become discrete and distinct. . . . Therefore it is not surprising to find that in sleep, in a state of semi-dozing, and in delirium, we drop back from the topmost levels of language development at which all concepts are completely separate from one another to lower levels of imagery in which ideas and their related feelings fuse, interact, and overlap. It is also clear then that some of the energy infusing speech must at all times derive not from the top levels alone but from deeper, broader, more inclusive meanings.

3. During sleep, therefore, in states of hypnagogic reverie, and under toxic, hypnoidal, drugged, or other "twilight" conditions, our thinking processes, or more specifically our powers of abstraction and of symbolic representation, revert automatically to this important earlier phase in the development of language. Consequently, any method of inducing any one of these altered states of consciousness in a limited and controllable fashion may give us bridges between the various levels of psychological function.

4. Since repression and regression both involve either a generalized or circumscribed alteration in the state of consciousness, all psychological processes which take place under the influence of such forces make some use of the type of symbolic abstractions which are equally characteristic of the language of early childhood and of dreams.

5. Therefore, states of "twilight" consciousness, whether spontaneous or induced, provide an opportunity to explore directly the interrelation of conscious and unconscious processes at different levels. Sometimes this makes it possible to translate the one into the other directly and unequivocally. Illustrative examples of this will be given.

6. The most objective approach, therefore, to a study of the interrelation of conscious and unconscious processes is through the study of "free" associations as produced in altered and controlled states of consciousness, the alterations being induced by many and varied devices, the controls maintained by various conditions (Kubie, 44, 45; Kubie and Margolin, 51, 52, 53, 63). I would emphasize that here again the tool which will give us the least weighted sampling of psychological processes for the investigation of the interaction of levels of consciousness is a precise and meticulous study of free associations.

7. One of the special advantages of such studies is the fact that in such induced twilight states (or as we have called them elsewhere "states of induced and controlled dissociation," Reference 45) the relationships between conscious and unconscious levels of behavior are, in large part, self-translating. As a result no seemingly arbitrary and far-fetched interpretations need be employed. On the contrary, under these circumstances symbolic productions tend to be self-translating, and complex transference relationships become transparent. Consequently, these states are useful both for the validation of past concepts and theories and for research on the frontiers.

During the war, in the treatment of combat-precipitated neuroses, a beginning was made toward a study of the influence of induced and controlled dissociated states on free associations. Such investigations require more systematic control than was possible under the pressure of wartime work. Perhaps the most illuminating and provocative observations made under wartime conditions were those reported by Spiegel, Shor, and Fishman (80). Under hypnosis these workers induced in a soldier a return to a series of earlier ages in his own life. At each of these artificial childhood ages and while under hypnosis the subject was put through a battery of psychological tests (psychometric, word association, language, Rorschach, figure drawings, handwriting, Bender-Gestalt, etc.). On each he performed as though he actually were the imposed age. In essence this was an experimental demonstration of the fact that a part of us tends to remain forever whatever we have been in the past. It is as though we age by laying down successive personality layers surrounding but not altering what we have been before, much as a tree lays down new rings year by year. Such work requires precise corroboration and a search for the range of human variability. Furthermore, no one as yet has studied the influence of such hypnotically induced chronological regressions on free associations themselves. Later I shall describe the complex technical equipment and the specially trained and experienced personnel which such studies as these require.

Indeed it is unfortunate that except for a few preliminary studies of free association (such as those of Carl Rogers, which Professor Hilgard described in his second lecture) this fundamental technique has never been subjected to objective investigation. Rogers' surveys have been sufficient, however, to indicate that qualitative and quantitative analyses of automatic recordings of the stream of free associations will prove fruitful. Furthermore, their value will be greatly enhanced when the process of free associations and its products are studied in a setting into which it is possible to introduce both physiological and psychological variables which will influence also the state of consciousness of the subject. Unpublished data indicate that these variables result in changes in the pattern and speed of speech and ideation, changes in the rhythm of recurring topics, changes in distractibility and in verbal symbolic distortions, and in other formal aspects of the stream. (Thus belatedly Mrs. Dalloway comes into her scientific heritage.)

There is further suggestive evidence that the variations in patterns of free associations which arise under these controlled conditions are important in the exploration of emotional states (elation, depression, rage, and anxiety), whether conscious or unconscious, and for a clarification of some of the fundamental differences between affective and schizophrenic processes. There are further hints that free associations, when recorded and analyzed in this precise fashion, constitute a direct and sensitive projective technique, perhaps the only one which is always accessible and which can be repeated indefinitely without distortion by learning or repetition. Therefore, it may be that patterns of free association, when obtained under standardized conditions, will provide us with something for which the investigator of psychotherapy has long been seeking, namely an individualized base line, or "thinking-profile," an individual psychological norm against which to estimate the influence of internal and external forces of all kinds, both psychotherapeutic and psychonoxious. Indeed much of the current data suggests that the most sensitive and precise qualitative and quantitative indicator of the psychological effects of any maneuver is the changes which it introduces into a base line of free associative material as standardized for any individual subject. Consequently such a base line when determined for different states of consciousness will constitute a point of departure for many fundamental studies as well as for an estimate of the therapeutic and/or noxious influence of specific procedures.

Many physiological changes can induce reversible alterations in states of consciousness. Among these are variations in oxidation and reduction potentials, in carbohydrate metabolism, in hydration and dehydration, in salt and water balance, in bile salt metabolism. In addition, there are certain direct effects from different kinds of electrical currents, certain changes induced by changes in body temperature, and, of course, the influences of a wide variety of drugs. In addition we know that, although there is a high degree of individual variability in all such reactions, there are certain drugs and certain pathological conditions (such as some types of jaundice) which are regularly accompanied by depression; there are others which tend to induce elation, while others cause transient anxiety and anger. Some of these physiological variables are known to alter some of the basic physiological constants of the body, such as the characteristics of the electrical change which accompanies the central transmission of the nervous impulse, the duration of the synaptic delay, the duration of the refractory phase, etc. Correlations should be sought between such changes and the varied patterns of free associations. These studies will provide a foundation for interpretations of the significance of changes in free associations in response to such psychological and analytical forces as interpretations, specific types of transference relationships (when expressed, suppresed, or repressed), suggestion, hypnosis, hypnotically induced chronological regressions, and the like.

In all such work it is essential to remember that free associations are possible only when the relationship between the subject and the observer is correctly understood and properly used. This is equally true whether the observer is an analyst in a therapeutic relationship or an experimenter in a situation designed for research alone. In either situation both the conscious and the unconscious components of the relationship will influence free associations profoundly, facilitating them, blocking them, and steering them, as a consequence of the interplay of conscious and unconscious elements in the relationship and the way in which these are interpreted. This is the aspect of the analytic procedure which is known as the "analysis of the transference." It requires objective quantitative study, both in itself and with respect to its influence on free associations. Mention of this is relevant here primarily because it must be considered carefully in every experimental procedure. Furthermore it suggests that for comparative purposes it may be necessary to study free associations as they are produced in solitude, as a base line for comparison with free associations as they are produced in the presence of others. At this point, therefore, let me describe further the phenomena of transference and countertransference as we meet them in therapeutic situations.

TRANSFERENCE FORCES

The production and communication of free associations are continuously dependent in part upon conscious and unconscious aspects of the relationship between the analyst and the patient.   Therefore as we consider the experimental validation and extension of analytic theories and techniques, we must take time to consider what is done about this relationship in analysis. Furthermore, this is relevant to the more general scientific problems which we are discussing, because any experiment must duplicate in the laboratory the essence of this aspect of the clinical relationship. Otherwise, no matter how illuminating in other directions the experiment may be, it will not illuminate fully the analytic process itself.

What then are the ingredients of the analytical process which have most to do with these essential transference forces? Foremost is the fact that the analyst is a stranger to the patient. At the start of his work with any patient, except as a name he is an unknown figure; and to the best of his ability the analyst will remain as unknown as possible throughout the course of treatment. A number of purposes are served by maintaining "the analytic incognito" in this way: (*a*) By keeping clear of personal involvements, the analyst avoids making emotional demands which would serve his own needs rather than the patient's. Such demands, both conscious and unconscious, become unavoidable if the two become "friends," precisely as occurs in any two-way human relationship. (*b*) By keeping out of the picture, and by remaining as inconspicuous and as unobtrusive as possible, the analyst further lessens the danger of confusing the patient by intruding any fluctuating moods and tensions of his own, thereby reducing by just so much the complicating influence of exogenous variables. In any experimental procedure it is a sound principle to have only one source of variables; and to the extent to which this is achieved in analysis, variations in the patient's moods and needs and associative material will represent the patient's unconscious, apart from the analyst's. (*c*) In analysis, therefore, as in any scientific process, the goal is to maintain from day to day as constant an external milieu as is attainable, so that variables will enter the picture through only one avenue. In the analytic situation this should be the patient's conscious and unconscious needs, and not the analyst's. The conscientious protection of the analytic incognito contributes greatly to this. (*d*) Most critical, however, is the fact that, as long as the analytic incognito is preserved, any feelings which the patient experiences about the analyst will be predominantly projections of the patient's conscious and unconscious fantasies. It is in this way that the misty and unknown figure of the analyst can serve as a sample drawn from the grab bag of all humanity, as a blank slate on whom the patient can project those feelings which unconsciously he tends to generate about all mankind. For example, if the analyst remains inconspicuous, a patient can react to a male analyst as though he were a woman, to a young woman analyst as though she were an old man, etc. It is the clarification and interpretation of precisely this sort of unconscious distortion which enables the two to discover together how the patient's unconscious needs and fantasies can distort his relationships to any human being. In other words, by remaining as far as possible a dummy in a store window on whom the patient drapes his fantasies, the analyst becomes a screen on which the patient projects the shadows out of his own past (Kubie, 35, chaps. viii and xxi). The analyst cannot serve these uncovering purposes if he presents himself to the patient as a real human being, with tastes and interests and hobbies and children and vanities and moods and standards and ideals, to which the patient must in some measure adapt. (*e*) Finally, the preservation of the analytic incognito helps to protect the patient from enslavement to yet another newly imposed parental image.

The analysis of these transplanted and consequently inappropriate feelings constitutes what is called "the analysis of the transference." Let me illustrate this by an example which I have already published (35, pp. 58–59), and which may illustrate the whole problem:

A man came for help who was poor, homely, sick, and in desperate need. Analysis was started at once; but it was many months before the risk of suicide and of complete mental disintegration had been averted. Because the patient's illness had destroyed his business and rendered him penniless, he was treated for nothing. For this the patient was sincerely grateful; yet in spite of his gratitude, day after day he exploded at the analyst with furious bitterness, resentment, hostility, and fear. The violence of his feelings toward the analyst is hard to describe, yet for a long time its cause remained obscure. The analyst knew only that the patient had had equally violent and equally unprovoked emotional storms in many other relationships. Then one day the patient related a dream, which suddenly brought back to his mind something that he had forgotten. On the occasion of the patient's first visit, as the analyst had entered the waiting room with his hand outstretched to greet the patient, and before a word had been spoken by either, the patient suddenly thought, "He has an impediment in his speech." This fantasy had been repressed at once, not to be recalled until several months later during the stormy course of his analysis, when it recurred to him in association to his dream. Further associations brought to light the fact that the most important person in the early years of this patient had been an uncle, who had alternated between effusive affection for the patient and stormy anger against him. This uncle, long dead, had in fact suffered from the impediment in his speech which the patient had momentarily attributed to the analyst. From this and other data it became clear that even before he had entered the analyst's office, the patient had been prepared unwittingly to identify the analyst with his uncle; and it was this unconscious anticipation which had led him to imagine that the analyst suffered from the uncle's speech defect, then to repress this notion, and finally to feel toward the analyst the violent fear and hate which as a small child he had felt toward his uncle. This chain of associations led to the uncovering of the fact that similar feelings had been transplanted into the patient's relationships to his wife's father and brother, to friends and teachers in school and college, to his business associates, and even to his own sons. Thus the clarification of the source of these transferred feelings threw light on one of the roots of this man's illness and eliminated one of the disruptive forces in his life, making possible a spontaneous improvement in all of his human relationships. This is an example of what psychoanalysis means by "the analysis of the transference."

In this instance hostile feelings, rather than affection for the analyst, were the transplanted and distorting force which had to be analyzed. Yet these hostile feelings were bedded deep in an unconscious loving dependence, which had long been hidden beneath the hate and fear of his dead uncle. It is clear that such unconscious and transplanted affects would influence equally any experimental procedure in which two human beings participate. The challenge to our fellow scientists is to help us develop methods which will do more than make manifest these concealed forces which distort human relationships. The analytic process, strictly practiced, achieves this much; and the interpretation of free association provides working hypotheses concerning the nature of these concealed forces. What are lacking are instruments of precision for their qualitative and quantitative evaluation.

Sometimes in states of altered consciousness which are induced by various pharmacological and physiological and psychological maneuvers, certain ingredients out of the conglomerate mass of unconscious transference forces are given an opportunity to express themselves, by translating themselves into self-evident conscious terms. I will quote a few examples of this which have already been published (Kubie and Margolin, 53, p. 149, *et seq.*):

1. A man in his early forties, in the course of a fairly lengthy period of analytic treatment, had never been able to feel for his mother anything except mingled intolerance, scorn, and impatience, tempered occasionally by indulgence. Under sodium pentothal he began to say in a little boy's voice, "I want my mama, I want my mama, I want my mama." As he emerged from the influence of the drug he called the therapist "mama" and for a long time subsequently in the analysis treated him as though he were in fact his mother. . . .

2. A young woman in a hypnagogic reverie induced without drugs, identified one of us with an American Indian who had played an important role in the fantasies of her childhood; and the other of us with her grandfather who was the storm center of the most violent early experiences of her life. . . .

3. A young Italian, the youngest of a large family of seven brothers who for many years had made him the slave of the family, resisted all forms of treatment. In analysis he could not talk. The attempts of several hypnotists to hypnotize him had failed in spite of his urgent and persistent plea for hypnotic treatment. Under nitrous oxide the identification between the therapist and the oppressive parental and fraternal figures was completely exposed, with facilitation of his production of material. After a subsequent period of sleep, a cathartic discharge occurred of the pent-up bitterness and rage with which he had been struggling throughout his life. . . .

4. A meticulously courteous man in his late thirties was so rigidly formalistic in his relationships as to make it difficult to ascertain any of his real feelings. Internally he dealt with fear, jealousy and rivalry towards all men. Under nitrous oxide he let down his barrier of formality, treated us as though we were childhood playmates, whose seduction of him was crucial in the evolution of his neurosis. When he was under gas, we became "youse guys" to him. . . .

Although all of this is somewhat elementary, I emphasize it both because it is so often misunderstood, overlooked, or forgotten, even by some who call themselves analysts, and even more because unconscious transference forces operate in the relationship between a researcher and his subject and must, therefore, be understood by the investigator and included in his thinking if he is not to make gross misinterpretations of his own data. Furthermore, precise studies of the transference relationship between subjects and experimenters will throw additional light on the relationship between patient and analyst.

In this connection, many questions present themselves: Should the analyst (or experimenter) be in the same room as the patient (or subject)? Should he be hidden? Should his voice be artificially distorted? Should his comments be in writing or spoken? To raise these questions about variations in such simple elements of procedure may sound forced and unnatural, indeed almost a burlesque. Yet their influence on the relationship can either facilitate or obstruct the free production of conscious and unconscious material, and, to that extent, they are fundamental for the study of more complex issues.

Moreover, they lead us to a consideration of the ultimate question: Why does there have to be an analyst at all? What would happen if the patient were to produce his material in absolute solitude? An objective inquiry into this issue will require mechanical recordings, because when a patient produces associations freely, without picking and choosing, without rejecting, without ordering his thoughts by subject matter, logic, or chronologies, he will not be able to remember either the content or sequence of his material or his concomitant feelings. So there would be no checks on the tricks which his emotions would play on his memory, and introspective studies without automatic records would be worthless. Furthermore, such records are needed to show us how we actually look and sound and feel and behave. No one knows the look and sound of his own anger quite as his family and children know it. Similarly, as with the analyst and patient, the experimenter and subject must often be unaware of their own feelings and conduct in the experimental situation. Now that it is possible to record not merely the verbal productions but also intonations, gestures, expressions, and color changes, we are able to study all that we have done and said, and also how we have said and done it. Through the re-examination of such recordings of material produced under varied circumstances, it would be possible for any individual to study the discrepancies between conscious intent and unconscious attitudes as betrayed by actual behavior.

The "varied circumstances" referred to above would include absolute solitude, the presence of silent observers, the active participation of analysts, and altered states of consciousness. Among other variables to be tested would be the effect of the sex of the investigator, of the number of observers present, of having both a man and a woman analyst present together, and of analytic work in groups.

The effects of facing an auditory and visual image of one's own psychological activity has never been examined systematically. We do not know if it would be therapeutic or noxious, and whether it would by-pass the resistances to insight or increase them. Many considerations suggest that it would put certain psychoanalytic assumptions to searching tests. Here again the initial focus of the inquiry would be on the influence of these technical maneuvers on the patient's spontaneous and free production of material from conscious and unconscious levels of his personality. However, even if an individual could analyze himself by such a retrospective scrutiny of recordings of his own free associations and free activities, something vital would be omitted. It is one thing to face the truth about oneself alone, knowing that no other human being will ever hear it from you or with you. It is quite another thing to face the same truth under the eyes of another human being, however permissive and friendly. It would seem probable that it is only in the presence of others that the patient's conscious and unconscious "transference" attitudes to others can be worked out, but we have no right to assume that this is so without further tests. In analysis, we have always taken it for granted that everything must be worked out in the presence of another human being. It is quite possible, however, that certain types of insight may be gained more readily if a patient works out part of his material alone and part of it with somebody else. It is also possible that there may be some types of personalities which cannot be analyzed in the presence of another individual, others who may require a two-stage operation, i.e., a preliminary analytic process done in solitude before they can produce free associations in the presence of anyone else. At all events the influence of these and other ways of varying the transference situation can now be explored systematically by studying their influence on the patterns of recorded free associations. A systematic exploration of all such variations might bring to light information which is not now accessible. These suggestions are made to illustrate the sort of research I have in mind, and also because clinical and experimental experiences suggest that such studies would be rewarding.

In these introductory sections I have pointed to two areas of basic technical research: first, the study of the exploratory value of free associations under varying physiological, pharmacological, and psychological influences; and, second, the specific influence on free associations of varying the transference forces which are operative in analysis. Bearing in mind these preliminary considerations concerning fundamental procedures, let us turn next to the critical question of the investigation of the interaction of conscious and unconscious processes.

THE DIRECT MANIFESTATIONS OF THE INFLUENCE OF UNCONSCIOUS ON CONSCIOUS PSYCHOLOGICAL PROCESSES

I selected for initial discussion the study of the process and products of free associations, because this is our fundamental exploratory and fact-gathering implement. Next in importance came the closely related problems of transference and countertransference, because of their direct influence on free associations. As was explained, the facilitation of free associations requires precise attention to the operation of conscious and unconscious transference forces, as manifested in and highlighted by the relationship to the analyst. This brings us to the conclusion that, whether research is designed to test and validate old hypotheses or to break new ground, the laws which govern free associations and transference phenomena must be understood and obeyed as meticulously in investigative work as in therapy. Consequently, the experimentalist must be sophisticated in his understanding and use of these techniques; and the experimental situation must be designed in such a way as to render free associations and transference relationships accessible to observation, record, and control. Because these precautions are so rarely observed in research work, it was worth while to restate this principle here.

In this area the goal of experimental work, as of therapy, is to clarify the relationship between conscious and unconscious levels of psychological functioning. In therapy this is done by setting up a cumulative series of translations of the one into the other. These translations (or "interpretations") are in essence working hypotheses which we gradually confirm, correct, or discard on the basis of the patient's subsequent free associations. Ideally our interpretations are based primarily on the patient's own free associations to his thoughts and feelings, to his activities, to his fantasies, and to his dreams. Much of the legitimate doubt about analysis centers around the validity of the process of interpretation in general, and of specific interpretations in particular. The next chapter will be devoted to a discussion of the problems of validation of specific interpretations. Before discussing this problem, however, a basic principle should be established concerning the function of experimental validation in science in general.

It is important that any experimentalist should first make himself thoroughly familiar with phenomena as these occur in nature, ascertaining what can be proved with the unaided eye and ear before deciding what to subject to experimental verification. Otherwise, investigators may use complex methods to prove something which needs no such proving, precisely because it is on the surface for all to observe, either during the naïve phases of childhood or in the facts of illness which are familiar to the clinician. For such data, validation in the laboratory is redundant, except in so far as it may induce reluctant human beings to accept some of the less agreeable and less flattering facts of human life. This is of educational value but not a scientific necessity. Unfortunately, however, people tend to cling to their fears of the implications of many human facts and consequently blind themselves to the significance of experiences which are available to every young parent. I would add one further and obvious qualification; namely, that the refinement and precision of data which the laboratory provides are never superfluous. My argument is solely against the uselessness of making pallid facsimiles in the laboratory of data which are already manifest in nature, merely to get around the human reluctance to look human nature in the eye. This comment is relevant to no small part of the experimental work that has been documented by Sears (76, 77), some of which was referred to by Professor Hilgard. Many of these laboratory charades are pedestrian and limited demonstrations of things which have been proved over and over again in real life. This is another reason why men who are going to experiment in this field should first become sophisticated as to what nature itself can tell them. Experimental facilities should not be wasted on issues which are already clearly proved, and to which human bias alone continues to blind us. The experimentalist should rather take up where the naturalist leaves off. He may ask the naturalist to guide him on a field trip, so that he can satisfy himself concerning the observations which the naturalist has made and has brought to him for investigation. It is not his duty or responsibility, however, to prove in the laboratory the existence of data which the naturalist reports to him. Much controversy about the empirical data of analysis has arisen because people have refused to look at facts which are clearly observable in the analytic situation. These parallel the controversies which arose over Van Loewenhock's microscope among men who had never used it yet who refused to believe in the reality of what he reported. Similarly there are many who have refused to look through the microscope of analysis, or to create a relationship with a child or an adult which would make it possible for that child or adult to express his fantasies undistorted by conscious restrictions. Such self-imposed blindness is usually expressed in terms of critical skepticism and as a demand for experimental proofs where simple objective observation would make this superfluous. Therefore, I want to introduce my discussion of the validation of interpretations by describing experiences in which no interpretation was needed, i.e., in which the relationships between various psychological levels were so transparent that they translated themselves spontaneously, and without requiring any act of interpretation. The illustrations to be given will be drawn from adults and from children, from the dreams of naïve people who knew nothing about theories of dream interpretation, and from studies under hypnosis. Because these experiences were self-translating and without arbitrary interpretations, they are equivalent to carefully controlled laboratory experiments. Yet their value is subject to one basic limitation to which I will refer after I have presented the examples themselves.

1. One hot summer night I arrived at the Grand Central Station in New York and asked a taxicab driver to take me to my home on East Eighty-first Street. On Eighty-first Street the traffic is westbound only. Quite correctly, therefore, we were traveling up Madison Avenue, which runs just east of my home. In the lower Sixties, however, the driver suddenly started to swing over to Fifth Avenue, which lies to the west of my home. This would have brought him into Eight-first Street against its one-way traffic, a cardinal crime in any cabby's book, so I called out to him, "Hey, where are you going? I asked you to take me to 7 East Eighty-first Street. You will be turning into Eighty-first Street against the traffic." He instantly straightened out his cab and answered in a puzzled and reflective fashion, "That's right. . . . That's right. . . . I

heard you say Eighty-first Street all right. . . . But here I've been thinking Eighty-second Street all the time. . . . What do you think I was doing that for?" I was amused at his asking a question out of *The Psychopathology of Everyday Life* (21), and answered jokingly, "I don't know. Maybe you don't like odd numbers." The driver jammed on his brakes in the middle of traffic, turned to me with his eyes popping from his head, and said, "Jeez', how did you know! I've been betting on 'em all afternoon, and lost my shirt." Then he proceeded to tell me that he had been playing the races in a bookie shop all afternoon, betting consistently on the odd positions at the post, and losing on every race. He chattered along about his wife, his children, his compulsion to bet on the "little giddyaps," as he called them, and what his wife would do to him when he reached home. It became evident that the association between an odd-numbered street and the odd-numbered gates at the race track had been too much for him. Until he became aware of this connection, he had to treat my odd-numbered street as though it were even. I said nothing, but I thought to myself what an uncanny fellow Freud had been. Here in a nutshell are the operations of unconscious repression, resistance, a symptomatic act of unconscious denial of guilt, an unconscious symbolic undoing of a misspent day, and more besides. Let us ask ourselves, however, what are the technical steps by which we would set out to prove that any specific interpretation of this little episode would be both *adequate* and *uniquely necessary*. The effort to answer this question will be deferred, however, until the next section.

2. A more banal illustration of the psychopathology of everyday life occurs so constantly that it passes almost unnoticed. Who of us has not been angered in a situation in which he could not express his anger, only to take it out on the elevator man, or the telephone girl, or his wife or children. You have undoubtedly heard of this under the title of "displacement" of affect. This daily occurrence, however, illustrates only the conscious or marginally conscious displacement of a transitory, acute, affective state, something which is equally easy to demonstrate either in the laboratory or in real life.

3. Of far greater importance to human life, but more difficult to demonstrate and to prove, is the unconscious displacement of *chronic unconscious affects and purposes*. A tragic and not infrequent example of this was the daughter of an alcoholic. Because she was deeply attached to her father, she had been deeply hurt by him. Unconsciously she blamed her mother for her father's drinking. Out of her unconscious need to ease this old hurt, she set out to salvage her father in effigy and to outdo her mother by marrying in succession three alcoholic men. The blindly automatic repetitiveness of this act plus her own free associations made the unconscious goals of her pattern

almost, if not wholly, self-evident, certainly more nearly self-evident than a single unfortunate marriage would have been. Again, however, we must ask ourselves: how are the adequacy and the unique necessity of an interpretation established?

4. Simpler evidence is available to anyone who will listen to the fantasies of children with sober and permissive respect, so as to create a relationship in which the child does not become abashed and shy and therefore secretive about his fantasies. It was not an analyst but Piaget, the careful Swiss-French psychologist, who said that the speech of childhood is a language of symbols (68). Yet we find it difficult to remember this until we have heard children speaking as though they had been reading the analytic textbooks. To obtain the kind of evidence which is about to be described, however, it is necessary to establish and maintain a special kind of relationship, whether we are dealing with an adult or with a child. Usually this requires the setting aside of many customary taboos (39).

a) Some years ago a three-year-old girl used to play a game with her father, a game that has been played by fathers and children since time began. She would leap from the floor while clinging to his hands, swing up to his shoulders, and then turn a backward somersault down to the floor again. One night, however, she varied the game by landing on his shoulders on her knees instead of her feet. This brought her genitals close to his face, and she deliberately pressed them forward against his chin. He drew back as slowly and unperturbedly as he could and looked up at her and smiled in silence. She looked down at him and said, "Would you like to see me naked?" He did a double-take, thought rapidly, sparred for time by smiling silently, and parried with the time-honored trickery of parents, "Would you like me to?" She answered at once, "Yes, but not when I'm asleep." Then she quickly slid down, hopped across the room, leaped up on a couch and said, "Come, let's play you are a snake." Was this an accidental coincidence, this use of the ancient phallic symbol of the snake from Eden's garden? Is this type of symbolism inherited? If so, then why in dreams has the airplane replaced the bird and the snake to so large an extent?

b) There was another little girl, an only child, who used to insist on wearing a large safety pin hanging from the front hem of her chemise. She would also put bits of pencil or of chalk inside the drawers of her dolls. She called these her penises. Many years later this girl, grown to be a beautiful young woman, passed through a phase of aggressive rejection of all men, and of rejection of feminine clothes almost to the point of transvestitism. Doubtless you have all heard of penis envy in girls. In this example it is self-translating not merely with respect to its immediate anatomic implications but also in its subtle later manifestations.

c) Then there was the four-year-old girl who said to her aunt, "Don't you know that daddies never marry their daughters?" When the aunt said, "Really, why not?" she answered, "Because their mommies won't let them."

d) This little girl is matched by the four-year-old boy who said that he did not want a penis, that he did not know why but that he thought he might be happier without one, that anyhow he wanted to grow up to be a lady and marry his daddy. Then he went on to a fantasy that his penis was a breast, that his urine was milk, that little birds came to nip it off for the sake of the milk, that a new penis would then grow again and that this was how little birds are fed. This was his slowly elaborated reaction to observing his mother nursing a new baby sister. Do we need to ask what it meant when subsequently he dreamed of birds and of cows and of wetting his bed?

e) Or take another boy of three who after the birth of a younger sister began to wet his bed, to stutter, and to show various other disturbances of behavior. This went on long enough to disturb his family, until the wise young mother sat beside him on his bed one evening and asked him gently, "Tommy, who wets his bed?" Tommy answered, "Babies." Then she asked, "Tommy, who has difficulty in speaking?" To this one he answered even more scornfully, "Babies, of course." Then, quietly, "Tommy, would you like to be a baby again?" The eager, bright-eyed, shining answer came, "Yes, but only for you and Daddy. Not if anyone else is around." You have heard of *regression*. Ordinarily this is a secret, unconscious process; but in this loving and permissive atmosphere it could become a conscious yearning, as this young mother provided her little boy with an opportunity first to talk out and then to live out the role of the infant he envied. She dressed him in baby clothes, including even a diaper, and allowed him to spend the day lying on his back in a crib, nursing from a bottle, and imitating the infant's noises. Whenever any visitor came to the home, however, he disappeared in a hurry, to resume the game as soon as the visitor had left. On about the fifth day, in the middle of the afternoon, he suddenly bounced out of the crib, dropped his bottle, and said in his own natural voice again, "Now, I'm through with that." Then he went on his way without further bed-wetting and without the stutter. Suppose that the same small boy had been punished, scolded, and humiliated instead! Would this not have roused in him an impotent rage with consequent terror and guilt, which in turn would have produced the repressions which would only have served to cause a *fixation* on the episode?

I could describe many such episodes, to illustrate the fecundity, fertility, and fantastic quality of the symbolic imagination of these early years. Let me add that these are not new in childhood. Children have not changed. Their feelings are as they have always been. The only novelty is the adults' efforts to create a relationship with children which makes it possible for them to communicate their yearnings and ideas and affects, without fear or shame or guilt, no matter how fantastic or "amoral" these may be. Only this is new; but this innovation marks a cultural revolution which is second to none in its ultimate significance to the human race.

I am tempted to tell you more stories, because I know that a few selected tales will leave you feeling that these must be exceptional rather than typical. To allay these doubts, however, you will have to create for yourself relationships with little children or with psychotics, which will make it possible for them to speak to you without fear or shame. Then if you will listen soberly and questioningly, not encouraging their fantasies but not discouraging them either, neither correcting them nor condescending to them with indulgent smiles, they will tell you spontaneously and without prompting many of the psychoanalytic interpretations which seem at first hearing to be far-fetched, fantastic, and improbable.

Since this occurs equally frequently in the children of people who know nothing about analysis and among the children of analysts, since it occurs among children of the illiterate as well as among the cultured, we must look upon this as a spontaneous occurrence in nature. Later in life these manifestations become disguised, with the result that at the age of twenty, it takes the complex processes of psychoanalysis to dig out of the depths what lay on the surface at three. Thus the spontaneous speech of childhood is the first laboratory of psychoanalytic validation. Indeed, until this rich mine of confirmatory material has been systematically assembled and studied, as a naturalist would study any phenomena in nature, efforts at experimental verification may even be said to be somewhat premature.

Those who want further documentation of such experiences can find it scattered through the literature of child analysis. A number of examples were described in articles published several years ago (30, 39).

5. Another natural source of objective and self-translating material is to be found in the dreams of naïve and immature patients who have never even heard of Freud. Out of many examples, I will select one which for many reasons is peculiarly convincing. This has been described in the article mentioned above (30):

Occasionally it falls to the lot of some observer to be presented with a ready-made experiment. In the observations on very young children this opportunity

comes not infrequently. As the years go on, however, with the sharper definition of thought, feeling, and concept, the opportunities become rare, and the
example which proves the case becomes correspondingly more valuable. Such
an opportunity occurred during the illness of a patient in the Henry Phipps
Psychiatric Clinic of the Johns Hopkins Hospital in 1921.

The patient was a gifted and attractive young woman of eighteen, in some
ways unusually naïve, and formally educated according to quite old-fashioned
ideas. She had literally never heard the name of Freud. Despite her conventional background, however, she had been subjected to certain very disturbing
influences through the fact that her father, an alcoholic, on rare occasions
had made erotic advances to his wife in the presence of the children, and
through the fact that her brother had manic-depressive spells in which he was
sexually exhibitionistic. The patient's illness was a mild depression, which
had been precipitated by her first proposal of marriage. Not long after her
admission to the hospital she had a nightmare which was as disturbing to
her as it was interesting to the physician. The dream was that she was walking
along a narrow street whose high, gray buildings converged at one end. Suddenly an airplane appeared overhead and began to shower her with bombs.
She repeated twice that it was a "funny-looking airplane." In the airplane was
a man whom she later recognized as her brother. In terror she ran up the nar-
rowing street, and finally hid in a box at the end of it—a box which she characterized as a "funny-looking box." The emphasis which she laid upon the
peculiar appearance of the airplane and the box led her physician to ask her
to draw them. She began by making a long oblong shaft from the upper right-
hand corner of the page. This, she said, was the fuselage of the airplane. Then
as she looked at it she said, "Oh, I know what was funny about it—the wings
were round," and she proceeded to draw two circles at the upper end of this
oblong. Then she added, "Oh, yes, the propeller was here in the rear," and she
made a blur of scribbled lines at the rear of the plane. When completed, the
drawing was an unmistakable erect phallus with testicles and pubic hair. The
patient's repressive mechanism was so strong, however, that her own drawing
excited no comments from her and no recognition. Nothing was said to her
except to ask her to draw the box. This she did in the lower left-hand corner
of the page, in the direction toward which the plane was pointing. She drew
a triangular box, then hesitated a moment, and said, "Oh yes, and up here at
the base was a funny little bit of a cover that didn't cover the whole box."
Again she failed to realize that she had drawn the vaginal orifice with a clitoris.
The completed picture is shown in the accompanying drawing. It is worth
stressing that when she had finished these drawings she still did not realize

their nature, but when shown the same drawings several months later without any intervening interpretation, she recognized them at once. Not only had she dreamed of sexual objects in this form but of sexual practices as an attack, a showering with bombs (semen), from which she retreated by going back inside a vagina—the box.

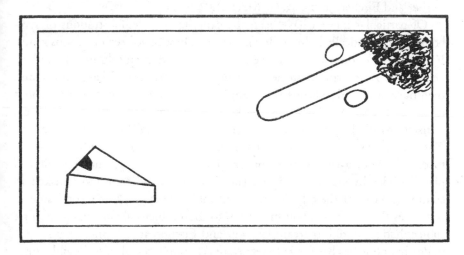

We can match this with many comparable experiences; e.g., the man who dreams of flying and who has an orgasm as his plane is rising from the ground; the little boy with a blinking tic who is troubled by sexual curiosity. After a discussion with his parents about the naturalness of such curiosity he dreams about an airplane in which he cannot tell the front from the back or the top from the bottom, a plane that is full of curious bulges and protuberances, and he wakens from the dream relaxed and peaceful, with his tic gone. Such examples could be multiplied indefinitely. Spontaneous self-translating symbols from the speech of a toddler who is just learning to talk, or from the dreams of the unsophisticate, are in a real sense experiments of nature.

6. Hypnosis has provided a bridge between the laboratory and the spontaneous events of nature. As such it has been a third source of self-translating data, which requires no interpretation. Through experiments with hypnosis it has been possible to demonstrate many of the laws which determine the influence of unconscious forces and their symbolic representation in human life. Of these experiments the simplest has been the use of posthypnotic suggestion to demonstrate the powerful and persistent operation of artificially implanted unconscious purposes and attitudes. These demonstrations go back to the earliest work with hypnosis. Recent studies are those of Erickson (9)

and Erickson and Hill (11) on repression, slips of the tongue, memory lapses, and, in general, the psychopathology of everyday life. More complex has been the experimental induction of stormy neurotic disturbances by the implantation under hypnosis of artificial conflicts, and their subsequent reliefs (Luria, 41, 60, etc.; Huston, Shakow, Erickson, 25; Brickner and Kubie, 49; Kubie, 32; Farber and Fischer, 16, 27, 43, 60, 64, etc.).

Of particular interest have been the experimental demonstrations of symbolism in hypnotically induced dreams (75). These have been of various kinds. For instance, under hypnosis naïve individuals have been told grossly and repellently erotic or sadistic stories as though they were actual happenings, and then have been told to forget these implanted experiences but to dream about them (61, 67, 70, 72). After they awoke, these dreams have proved to be direct translations of the suggested stories into conventional "Freudian symbols." The reverse has also been done. That is, under hypnosis a subject has been told to dream about a certain story or problem. Then another naïve subject is placed under hypnosis and is told the first subject's dream and is asked to comment on what the other's dream meant. Thereupon this second subject translates the dream symbolism back into the problem about which the first subject had been told to dream (Farber and Fischer, 16). Similarly, a subject under hypnosis has been able to translate accurately the almost illegible automatic writing of another patient under hypnosis, the two subjects being unknown to each other (Erickson and Kubie, 14).

These experiments are crucial in their significance, but many technical difficulties beset such work. Not all men are hynotizable. We do not yet know on what subtle factors hypnotizability depends. There remains a persistent difficulty in distinguishing with precision between hypnosis and sleep, or even between the hypnotic state and its simulation. There are qualitative and apparently quantitative differences that occur among various hypnotic subjects and hypnotic states. (This is usually referred to under the general term of the "depth of the trance" itself, a still unanalyzed descriptive concept.) Most workers with hypnosis are themselves so entranced by the subject that the protocols of their experiments have an almost evangelical quality which makes the critical worker uneasy. This is not true of all workers in the field (Brenman, Gill, *et al.*, 5, 6, 27).

7. Under drugs, as under hypnosis, there are many occasions when the interaction of various levels of psychological function becomes transparently clear, and "the anaesthetic revelation" of William James (26) becomes a tool of deeper psychological exploration.

Thus in recent studies (Kubie and Margolin, 53; Kubie, 45) examples were given of the direct and overt manifestations under drugs of transference relationships which had been completely masked and hidden in the normal waking state. Other examples were given of the automatic return of patients under drugs to the storm centers of their early conflicts, and also of the direct recovery under drugs of early memories which had hitherto been repressed and which had resisted months or even years of analytical investigation (Kubie, 44). In these studies, of special interest was the fact that the effective dose of any pharmacologic agent varied with the intensity of the emotional disturbance associated with the material with which the patient was dealing. Surgeons have long known that the amount of anesthesia required to put a patient to sleep for an operation varied with the severity of the patient's panic and his resistance to the anesthetic. This has recently been shown to be remarkably true for women in childbirth and for small children facing so-called minor surgery (such as a tonsillectomy). It is equally true in any experimental work which involves a deliberate alteration of the state of consciousness by the use of pharmacological agents, and it is true, of course, in any psychotherapeutic procedures under drugs. As has been indicated elsewhere (53), this probably parallels the well-known clinical fact that subclinical lesions of the central nervous system which do not give rise to any obvious neurological disturbances may in states of hypoglycemia suddenly show clear-cut and obvious clinical manifestations. In other words, it is as though the hypoglycemia affected first the integrations of the structurally disturbed area. In the same way the converse of this would seem to be true, namely, that "areas" which subserve unconscious conflicts which are highly charged resist the influence of sedatives and other pharmacologic agents more vigorously than do those nervous pathways which subserve less highly charged systems of conscious and unconscious purposes. An example of this is quoted by Kubie and Margolin (53, page 150):

A young soldier had been discussing his terror and unhappiness in battle experiences. He had reviewed this material several times until he felt much relieved. However, his symptoms were not wholly gone. On a subsequent occasion even larger doses of sodium pentothal failed to put him to sleep. As the injection was proceeding, he became restless, tense, worried, and anxious. His hand was cold, blue, and cyanotic. He kept saying, "It isn't going right. Have you made it up right? Is there anything wrong with the medicine. . . . ?It's making me sick. I think I'm going to vomit. You had better quit it, doc. Cut it out, I say. Leave me alone, I say. Leave me alone. What the hell is the matter with you? . . ." etc. This was interspersed with descriptions of his difficulties with his commanding officer, and he finally broke out into expressions of anger and resentment against this officer. In order to encourage the further discharge of his rage, and without anticipating in any way what was to come, the physician asked him, "What did you want to do to him?" Instead of answering, "Shoot him," which men not infrequently say under these circumstances, he suddenly said with cold, quiet, intense bitterness, "You know, castrate the son of a bitch." The physician was surprised and asked him to repeat it; but there was no reply. On looking up, the physician found that the young man's head had dropped on his shoulder. He was in a sound sleep, and his hand was warm and of normal color.

A further investigation of this whole episode while the patient was emerging from this sleep brought to light many extraordinarily interesting facts: the fact that he had gone into battle with a conscious terror of genital injury, and behind that the fact that he had been subjected to direct genital threats by a sadistic uncle early in life, an uncle who, furthermore, had married the patient's mother after his father's death. In this example, pharmacological agents clarified the interplay of remote and recent psychological experience, i.e., of the buried unconscious residues of early and current experiences with parallel fluctuations in the response to the drug itself. Another example is found in Bartemeier, Kubie, etc. (2, page 499):

One striking example was a young soldier from a tank destroyer unit. For the first few days, under increasing doses of insulin, he remained in a state of great emotional torment during both the day and night. After each session under insulin, he would be aware that he had had violent dreams, of which he could remember nothing. After the sixth such session, during which he had been particularly violent, he awoke peacefully and remembered a dream in which he was not in a tank destroyer but in a tank which had been hit and which was burning up. Out of this dream he awakened in a state of quiet calm, with mild depression.

Thus it seemed that in the hypoglycemic dreamlike experience he turned the tables on himself, and in suffering the death he had inflicted on others found at least some measure of peace.

THE VALIDATION OF INTERPRETATIONS

I have already indicated that analysis stands or falls by the validity of its specific interpretations in specific instances. In this respect, every sample given in the preceding section has had one essential limitation. Each has proved that certain types of interaction which psychoanalysis has described as occurring between conscious and unconscious processes *can* actually take place. Neither singly nor together, however, do they establish the validity of interpretations when applied to any specific psychological event. They show what kinds of interpretations can conceivably be true, but they do not show us which interpretations are both "adequate and uniquely necessary" in the special instance. They prove that it is possible for an analyst to be right but not that he is right, and between proving that an interpretation is plausible and proving its unique adequacy as the explanation of a specific phenomenon lies the difference between proving that typhoid bacilli can cause typhoid fever and proving that a particular patient has typhoid.[1]

Indeed there was a time when the same problem confronted the bacteriologist. He had proved that bacteria *could* cause disease, but he had not solved the more difficult task of proving that a particular patient was suffering from a particular disease, and that that particular disease had been caused by a particular organism and not by any other. The bacteriologist met that challenge by satisfying certain laws of evidence—Koch's Laws of the Specificity of Bacteria. This meant proving that a particular organism was present in every instance of the disease, that it did not occur in individuals who did not suffer from the disease either in clinical or in subclinical forms, that it was capable of cultivation in pure culture, and that when the pure culture was inoculated it would produce the disease in susceptible animals and could thereafter be recovered from the diseased animal and again grown in pure culture. These are stringent requirements. In analysis we cannot amass evidence as precise as this, but we need equivalent kinds and laws of evidence.

Every analytic session confronts us with hypotheses of extraordinary and exciting interest, hypotheses concerning the relationships of unconscious forces to human personality and behavior, hypotheses which have been proved to be possible and not impossible conjectures, but the applicability of which to the specific situation remains extremely difficult to demonstrate. In different instances we can demonstrate varying degrees of probability. Sometimes it is possible to show that presenting the patient with the hypothesis which is called technically an "interpretation" may produce profound psychological changes, from which in turn we can deduce fresh hypotheses. None of this, however, has that directness as evidence which science requires.

Let us keep in mind then what the scientist strives for (Kubie, 35, page 151[2]):

Science attempts to find approximations of truth about ourselves and the world in which we live. It depends upon (*a*) methods of gathering empirical data; (*b*) methods of testing the degree to which these data conform to external realities,

---

[1] Throughout this section I will speak of the unique adequacy of "an interpretation." This should be read as meaning a group of related interpretations, because, in translating any conscious psychological act into its unconscious determinants, we are always dealing with a group of concurrent relationships at different levels. To every conscious act, dream, or fantasy, there is not one but several meanings, and it is this constellation of meanings which I have in mind as I speak of "an interpretation."

[2] Cf. 4, 22, 71.

thus establishing approximate "facts"; (*c*) methods of interpreting causal relationships between such approximate facts; and finally (*d*) methods of testing the accuracy of these interpretations by predictions of future events. Ultimately science can accept nothing as valid until it is supported by evidence of this general nature.

It would seem to be a logically inescapable deduction from these scientific axioms that psychoanalysis will not become an exact science until some less subjective method than interpretations will be found for making articulate the relationship between conscious and unconscious processes. I shall return to this later; but whether or not interpretations someday become superfluous, certainly at the present time the most difficult challenge which confronts us in the everyday practice of analysis arises out of the process of interpretation. In our daily work each interpretation is an approximate working hypothesis. It is an operating assumption that some constellation of specific unconscious forces may have produced a certain conscious idea or action and its accompanying feelings, with the implication that these conscious psychological processes constitute a symbolic language for the masked expression of the underlying unconscious processes. Evidence for the accuracy of the interpretations is sought in the patient's further free associations and in the unlocking of doors to his lost memories. These associations and recollections may correct the interpretation, or lend it additional probability, or wholly disprove it. Only in rare instances can it be claimed that they provide positive and absolute proofs.

To what extent, then, can the introduction of other methods assist the procedures of psychoanalysis to approximate the stringent criteria of bacteriology?

Let me give a few examples of interpretations picked almost at random from daily analytic work. I will deliberately choose difficult and complex examples, because to oversimplify this critical problem in an effort to make it more acceptable to you would be a betrayal of the confidence you have showed in me by asking me to discuss these matters. I cannot mislead you by minimizing the complexity and intricacy of the phenomena for which you are seeking methods of evidence and validation.

1. As a brilliant woman artist was getting launched in analysis, she went through a series of violent and hysterical outbursts of temper against her husband. These were triggered off when in the course of a few days she read in the papers of the death of one friend, the suicide of another, and various crimes and accidents. As her thoughts gradually became free enough to roam, they finally circled around her lifelong terror of mental illness and of "losing control." To ease her tension and to sound out the rigidity of her feelings, a few casual words were said about the strange and special fear of insanity

which runs through our culture; and she was reminded how little children throw epithets at each other, saying, for instance, "You're crazy"; and how the connotations of such words alter as we develop.

Something in what was said struck home, and she suddenly swung around to face me, saying, "My God, I had forgotten all about this." Then she went on to tell a story of a village youth who silently trailed little girls home from school, hiding behind trees to watch them; he was rumored to have attacked his sister with a knife. She told of her consequent terror of going out into the yard to play, and of her strange feeling that if this "crazy" boy picked her out to follow it must be because there was something wrong with her too. Perhaps she was "crazy" too. . . . This led her to recall her feeling that her father's desertion had set her apart from other children, and yet in some strange and unfair way this again had seemed to her to be her fault. From there she went on to other matters: how unreasoningly she had blamed her mother for her father's desertion of the family, of the wild rages which this would evoke in her, of the fresh terror born of these rages, and of the fusion in her mind of her murderous rage with the concepts of insanity and of losing control. Thus the image of little children saying "G'wan, you're crazy" released a flood of painful "forgotten" memories, laden with fear and guilt. In this instance the interpretation consisted of nothing more than an underscoring of her freely expressed recurrent fear of insanity, which led her thoughts back to childhood. Automatically she herself then made the personal applications, and the other associations followed of themselves. How this happened is, if anything, less mysterious than are the resisting forces which had kept the original experience isolated and segregated in her mind.

2. Another patient had been living an impulse-ridden and wildly irresponsible life, but had finally come to realize the necessity of living with self-denial and restraint until his blind impulses could be rooted. After hearing without flinching my description of his way of life, during which perhaps for the first time he looked at himself clearly, he dreamed that he was sitting up on the couch instead of lying down, that he was looking at me and crying, that this somehow made him feel good. The dream seemed to occur high up in an office building, surrounded by transparent glass windows on all sides (whereas my office is in a basement and has no windows but for a single opaque glass-brick wall). His associations were first that the high transparent windows would let in lots of light and then of "people in glass houses." As a preliminary interpretative hypothesis I suggested that in the dream there must be a latent thought: that I am no better than he. It then developed that later in the same dream we were accusing each other of trying to seduce each other.

Thereupon, for the first time, he brought into the open the erotic component in his attachment to an older male cousin whom he had always thought he hated. In turn this made it possible for him to sense at last how feelings of hatred could mask a homoerotic impulse whose exposure he had always feared unconsciously.

Let us again challenge ourselves with the question of how we would set out to prove this interpretation. How do we prove that ghostlike figures out of his life are condensed in me, so that in his analysis I am not merely a new and unknown person with whom he has a professional relationship but also a cluster of images out of his own highly charged emotional past? From moment to moment how do I detect with certainty which of these shifting and kaleido-scopic roles I play? Often in analysis I think of my function as not unlike that of one of those old-time vaudeville performers who would hop behind a screen and out again, each time emerging with a new costume, a new mask and beard, a new gesture, a new impersonation.

A few examples follow of more complex interpretations:

3. A man had won high honors during the war by exposing himself far beyond the line of duty. Indeed, outside of the prescribed limits of his scien-tific responsibilities, he had armed himself and at great risk had taken part in the killing of many enemy soldiers. One day he arrived late for his analytic hour because of a fire which made it necessary for him to take a long detour. For some time he described this in broad generalizations of "excitement," "disaster," "war," "destruction." After a while I pointed out that such words are mere abstractions about occurrences which in real life are made up of vivid and immediate and direct and concrete impulses and experiences. I then asked on whom he might want to visit such disasters. My words evoked a long silence and then a characteristic hacking but wholly needless cough.

When asked what he had felt during the silence which had preceded his cough, he said, "Restless. I had to move. I just had to do something. So I coughed. It was as though something was stuck in my throat." These words unlocked memories, and he started to recount early recollections of building villages, castles, towers and walls in a sand lot, and then of arming himself and a young friend with stones to destroy the work of their hands. Then came the memory of a fire in a livery stable in the little town where he had been brought up, of "dozens of burned horses" lying with their bellies burst open and their guts strewn around and singed, of having felt drawn to return to the scene again and again in fascination, horror, and disgust, of having been obsessed by this long after the fire, and finally of a feeling even then as of "something stuck in my throat." Then he realized that all the smells and horrors of war had had for him a vivid sensory familiarity, a fleeting *déjà vu* quality. Thereupon a phrase occurred to him, as though written on a wall: "Killing is my business." Indeed, twice in childhood he had tried to kill his little brother; and we had long since recognized the destructive hatred which he had carried with him since the birth of this brother in his earliest years. We had recognized this as the major source of a chronic rage which made him glory in killing; yet his easy generalizations about such matters had left him untroubled; and it was only my challenge to become concrete which had produced first his silence, then the cough, and the ancient feeling of something stuck in his throat, and finally the eruption of early memories of destructive play, and of the roasted entrails of horses, fusing with the later memories of dead men in war. What does this imply in terms of unconscious primitive oral impulses toward the bodies of his father, mother, brother? How can we prove that in his childhood the ultimate destructive need had been to kill and eat his little brother, and that for this even the sanctioned murder of war had been a quite inadequate substitute?

4. A man in his middle forties said, "I feel as though I were a child beating with my fists on my father's chest. It is like beating on a locked door."

Let us consider this from various angles. The words might equally well have described a dream, or a momentary waking fantasy, or an obscure memory of an actual tantrum of childhood, or else a memory of a dream or of an old fantasy, or of a combination of all these. As a matter of fact, no matter from which type of psychological experience the feeling had derived, as we explored its meaning we would have dealt with it in essentially the same way. Accordingly, in our effort to discover why this feeling had come to mind and why it had been expressed so freely at that particular moment, we used each element in the statement as the representative of a cluster of associated ideas and feelings, each in turn with its own history, each a country of related ideas and impulses. This was true for the concepts "child," "beating," "fists," "the father's chest," "locked doors," etc. Clearly in the analysis of even so simple an image as this, the number of potential combinations is almost infinite, each combination carrying its own potential meaningfulness. Our practical therapeutic effort is to use interpretations as hypotheses which pick out for emphasis those combinations which at any moment seem meaningful in terms of a patient's current psychological difficulties. Our scientific problem, however, is to put this process of choosing combinations on a basis sounder than feeling and intuition and fragments of partial evidence. This underscores the importance of amassing the data of free associations for meticulous statistical analysis, in a search for objective laws and guiding principles. Here is where we need help from the more exact sciences, to prove that such combinations *can* be meaningful.

Let us return to the episode from which we have digressed. The patient's mother had died when he was barely two, shortly after the birth and subsequent death of a little sister. The saddened father, well meaning but ill advised, told the little boy, "Your mother went away to take care of your little sister." This statement the child had forgotten; but we were able to first reconstruct it approximately, and then to confirm it through his old nurse. Over the years his life had been an endless unconscious search to find his lost mother, and at the same time an equally unconscious effort actually to *become* and then to replace the little sister who in his unconscious fantasies was living happily with the mother who had "gone away to take care of her." At night, like an automaton, he would sometimes follow the receding figures of unknown women for hours, never approaching or molesting anybody, never knowing why he was doing this. Toward his father he had an unhappy, resentful, dependent, and hostile relationship, which had blocked this patient's career almost completely. Although he was a man of great ability, he had been unable either to pursue his father's career or to break away sufficiently to follow any other. Periodically during the analysis there would be spells of violent and for a long time inexplicable retching, almost to the point of vomiting.

The image which I have just described came at the end of a period in which fragments of dream material and of fantasy had made it clear that in a confused and childlike way he had early had to deal with a vague, secret feeling that his father was keeping his mother hidden away from him. To a child, *hidden away* means *hidden in something. In something* can mean in a house, or in a closet, or in a chest. To the literal mind of a child, *chest* has two meanings, the chest of drawers or the chest of the body, and these can be used interchangeably. Indeed, any closed space becomes a chest, and therefore suspect. Any closed space might be a place where a mother might be hidden, including equally his father's body or his own.

(I will interject here an enchanting if irrelevant story of a little boy of four, the son of artists. Because his mother had become pregnant, the youngster had been told the facts of life. They had wanted to begin early in the pregnancy to prepare him for a young rival. One day they found him sitting on the barn floor solemnly taking apart an automobile jack. When they said, "Don't do that," he answered frantically, "I have to! I have to! There may be a baby inside!" You will note that to the child of those early years "inside" means inside of anything; and an automobile jack, a closet, a chest of drawers, or the body of a parent can be quite equivalent.)

To my patient then, the feeling of beating on his father's chest was beating on a closed door, which in his infancy had hidden his mother from him. It was part of his blind and angry search for his mother. Let me add that just before this episode his wife had been called away by illness in her family, and that I had just told him that in a few weeks I was leaving for Pasadena. Why then the retching? Fantastic though it may seem, he was *at the same time not sure that his mother was not inside of himself.* For years his major sense of security had come through compulsive eating. In effigy he had had to devour everyone he loved, so that no separations could occur ever again. Thus he ate out of love, and he also ate out of hate, out of his need to possess his mother and to destroy the father who was hiding his mother from him. He ate compulsively, he could not work, he beat on closed doors and chests, he hunted for his mother, and he retched. This was his life! This was the language of unconscious pain and yearning and hate and need and loneliness in the condensed cryptograms of his unconscious. . . .

These statements are interpretations. They are working hypotheses. They are our challenge to you. How can you help us to prove and measure them?

5. The next example raises the question: to what extent are we justified in thinking of a patient's behavior as a pantomime language which can use all of the tricks of ordinary speech? We have no difficulty in accepting a patient's spoken puns. If a patient says, "You scratch my back and I'll scratch yours," we accept this as having a number of parallel connotations. But what if he dreams of scratches on his back? Or what can it mean when a woman in her mid-forties has frenzied bouts in which she scars her shoulders and neck with her own nails? Because of a severe neurosis she has never been able to establish a relationship to a man. Under treatment she begins to get well, and it is precisely at this point that the scratching starts. Certainly this is a moment when she must view her life with fresh pain. The larger part of it has been spent in a neurotic prison from which she is emerging too late to recapture the years that have been lost, too late to establish the kind of relationship with a man that she wants, too late to have the children she longs for. Therefore, the relationships between men and women among her friends serve only to increase pain and envy and resentment. She wants every man that she sees. She wants to take the husbands of all of her friends, but she also hates herself for this. A man's indifference provokes her rage, but if a man is merely friendly he creates an unfulfillable expectancy. If the doctor gives her advice over the telephone or sends her a prescription by mail, she is grateful for his attention, yet resentful at the same time, because help from a distance is a rejection when compared to seeing him face to face. Hers is no easy path, and she can do little

about it. She can never express the pent-up pain and resentment which she feels, particularly because initially it was not against the people who are now around her, many of whom are devoted to her and to many of whom she is in turn devoted. The targets of her pent-up feelings are dead figures out of her past: her psychopathic mother and her alcoholic father who had destroyed her childhood and youth. In her periods of loneliness, therefore, when the problem becomes too difficult, in obsessional-compulsive furors she attacks herself by scratching the skin of her back as far as she can reach it. She feels intense revulsion against these orgies, but at such times cannot control them. Are we justified in saying that this body language is a sorry pun, a mute appeal in which the desires for mutual love and assistance and for bodily erotic play merge with her raging impulses to attack other people from the rear—the only safe attack for a child? Hence, "You scratch my back and I'll scratch yours." Is all of this converted into the attack on herself, with all the pain and suffering self-punishment which this implies? Is this just the child who wants to go out into the garden to eat worms? Or who wants to go out into the rain and cold to catch pneumonia and die? Who wants indeed to injure herself in any way which will express her sorry vengeance against the world?

6. Take another example: an extremely attractive young woman, one of four children. For a variety of reasons she had spent her life eating her heart out in envy of her sister and brothers. She was exceptionally faithful in treatment, traveling a long distance to her analytic hour in the bleak hours of the early dawn before going to work. This was a tribute of love.

As the date of her birthday approached she carefully refrained from mentioning it, but her unconscious played an interesting trick on her. On the day *before* her birthday and again on the day *after* her birthday she overslept so late that she missed both of these sessions. In many months of analysis this had not happened before. Furthermore, during the analytic hour on her birthday she was so full of apologies for having missed the previous session by oversleeping that the fact that it was her birthday escaped even her free associations. The first missed session was on a Wednesday. Thursday was her birthday. The second missed hour was on Friday. On Saturday and Sunday, when no sessions were scheduled, she awakened at five o'clock in the morning, at least an hour earlier than she would ordinarily have to awaken to reach her sessions on time. One could hardly imagine a more adroit unconscious manipulation of the sense of time, nor a quantitatively more precise gesture of compensatory expiation. This patient achieved all of this in her sleep.

But how and why did this happen? Did her unconscious processes play these tricks on her sleeping mechanisms so as to make her oversleep on Wednesday and on Friday, and rob her of legitimate sleep on Saturday and Sunday? Did she avoid her Wednesday session because she could not bear to say to the analyst all that was in her heart: "I want to be your only child and best-loved daughter, and also your mistress and wife. I want you to make my birthday tomorrow a great and festive occasion. I want you to take me away with you for the whole day, for a lifetime, and to shut out everyone else. It must be a day in which I realize with you the longings for my father to which I dedicated my whole childhood." And did she unconsciously oversleep on Friday to avoid having to voice her reproaches and her hurt to me? Were her unconscious processes so precise in their workings that they could control her sleeping and her waking mechanisms in this way?

This is at least one possible interpretive hypothesis, which raises again the question: how would our fellow scientists set out to prove or disprove, to test and shape such a theory?

Another illustration involves a series of subtle psychosomatic problems.

7. A man came for treatment in a severe depression. This depression was punctuated by periodic explosions of "nervous tension," in which he was flooded by a variety of painful sensations in the chest, head, joints, calves, stomach, and throat. At times the throat sensations would make it difficult for him even to speak. This was a source of special embarrassment and distress to him because his professional work required much public lecturing. There were other occasions when pain would radiate from the groin into the perineum and the scrotal sac. The loss of an eye early in childhood had focused on his eyes the self-consciousness and shyness of puberty, just at the time when a small boy's sexual curiosity and sexual needs come to the fore.

In the recent past his wife had caused him severe distress in many ways. She had become an extreme alcoholic, and on many occasions had taunted him and rejected him sexually. Adversely, in the midst of a drunken orgy, when he was full of despair, resentment, and disgust, she would sometimes attempt to seduce him into perverse sexual practices, with special emphasis on *cunnilingus*. He had been deeply attached to her and in some measure sexually dependent on and even enslaved by her. This enslavement had its roots in the fact that for his own neurotic reasons he was terrified that he might be unable to cope with any other woman sexually. Therefore, his wife had been his only reassurance as to his physical adequacy as a male. Under the pressure of her alternately taunting and seductive behavior, his uncertain confidence in his potency had broken down. It was in this setting that a series of episodes occurred which present us with a characteristic problem in the validation of interpretations.

The patient visited the hospital in which his wife was under treatment for her alcoholism. He was not supposed to see her, nor she him; but as he was leaving, by chance he caught a glimpse of her in the distance walking through the gardens with a man. He learned later that the man was a rather under-sized young intern, but in that fleeting glimpse the distant stranger impressed the patient as larger and older than himself. This detail proved to be signifi-cant, because throughout his childhood and early maturity the patient had had a tendency always to become attached to some older couple, and particu-larly to the wife of some older man. Indeed his own wife had been tentatively engaged to one of his older friends when he first became interested in her. His distant glimpse of his wife in the hospital grounds gave him a brief feeling of genital and sexual arousal, followed by an immediate pain in the right groin which radiated into the testicles. This bothered him for some hours.

My silent unexpressed interpretation ran approximately as follows: He was deeply hostile to a wife to whom he was also sexually enslaved. Moreover, he had been sexually humiliated and threatened by her. The only way in which he could prove his adequacy was to conquer her sexually once again. This meant that he must take her from the unknown man with whom he saw her walking across the gardens and whose distant image was inflated by his own unconscious fantasies; hence the initial stirring of erotic feeling. At the same time this aroused feelings of guilt and fear because at that time any sexual relationship with his wife would have been tantamount to a rape murder. Con-sequently, there was at the same time a protective *hope* that he fail, which he experienced as fear of failure. By some psychophysiological alchemy this con-flict, which took place on an unconscious level in the flashing instant when he saw his wife in the distance, was translated into a waking body-dream of pain in the groin radiating into the scrotal sac. In its mechanism this is not unlike the visualized lion of a child's nightmare, or the phantom limb of an amputee.

But there was more to the story. The patient came directly to my office from the visit to his wife's hospital. He came eagerly, but to his surprise as he stood at my door he felt a sudden wave of resentment at having to discuss his problems with me. And he especially did not want to see my secretary, nor to be seen by her. At this moment, as he stood on my doorstep experiencing a surge of angry humiliation at the thought of having to face first my secretary and then me, he had an acute recurrence of the pain in his groin and testicles. In other words just as his sexual humiliation at the hands of his wife was trans-lated into the bodily experience of sexual arousal, rage, guilt, and terror, con-densed into the experience of pain localized in his genitals, so the fact that he had to pass the secretary and that his feelings of genital inadequacy were to be talked about in my presence meant to him that again he was to be exposed, mocked, and humiliated.

The patient said quite frankly that he was not sure my secretary did not share with me my knowledge of the details of his sexual life, and that this humiliated him. When a man feels genitally and sexually humiliated, there is only one way in which he can reverse that humiliation, namely, by a public exhibition of his genital prowess. In other words, his angry unconscious protest against genital humiliation took the form of an angry exhibitionistic impulse which was equally unconscious. At the same time, because of this anger, he wanted to use his genitals not as an instrument of love-making, but of hate-making. In other words, on an entirely unconscious level he wanted to attack my secretary genitally. Yet because he was at the same time a man of the highest degree of sensitivity and courtesy and consideration, he could not permit himself even unconsciously an impulse to commit a rape murder without guilt and anxiety. Was it this total constellation which was translated into the sensations of local pain?

On top of this, when he entered my presence in the inner office his throat constricted and he could not speak. Here again he experienced a conflict-laden burden of mixed feelings. On the one hand was love and yearning and gratitude, a need to cuddle in my lap as though he were a little boy, a need to suckle from my breast-penis as though I were both a father and a mother in one, and as though he were my little child. At the same time rage and envy were also active because of his need to compare himself with me genitally. Out of this arose a violent, destructive, castrative impulse toward me. We can condense all of this into the oversimplified statement that unconsciously he wanted to suckle from my penis and at the same time to bite it off, incorporating it into himself, adding it to his own genital equipment, but castrating me and through me all the men in the world, until he remained alone as the sole dominant cock-of-the-walk. This constellation of impulses brought an attendant cometlike train of guilt and anxiety. Of this, all that reached his conscious awareness was the "thickening" in his throat, the constriction, pain, burning, hoarseness, and the groin-genital pain. It was evident, furthermore, that what he wanted from me was not mere words alone but something which would give him a feeling that the imagined damage to his genitals had been undone, that I had renewed them, restored them, replaced them, or in some way equipped him anew to face women without the genital inadequacy with which his own unconscious fantasies had afflicted him, at least from the time of his eye injury. In his unconscious expectations, my function was to be a healing father who would undo the fantasied genital injuries of the past, and the actual eye injury as well. If I failed in this, then I would be the hoarding father who kept all strength and power to myself. Therefore, he must love me, envy me, feel shame before me, implore me, burn incense to me, fear me, placate me, appease me, bribe me, kill me, castrate me. Of all of this, however, he knew nothing. All that he felt consciously was the acute pain in his groin and testicles and the discomfort in his throat. These sensations constituted a symbolic body language by which he could represent the unconscious conflicts which burdened him.

I must ask this audience: how should we set out to establish and test the truth of these statements in this precise situation?

But let me pursue the story further. That night our patient went to call on an older couple for whom he felt great love and veneration. He and his wife had often visited them and been visited by them. In fact they had had an opportunity to observe his wife's embarrassing behavior; and on one occasion the older man had said to him, "I think I see the situation, and I just want you to know I am sorry." This single allusion to his wife's illness had moved my patient so deeply that he could not refer to it without choking up with tears of gratitude. The patient was a fine and gifted man who at the same time was still a small boy, deeply in need of parental approval, forgiveness, and absolution, overwhelmed by feelings of guilt toward his wife, the more remote sources of which at that time I still understood better than he did. Ultimately we both came to understand that these had had their origins in the unfair advantages which he had taken of his younger sister in childhood. With this always in the back of his mind, and with the acutely painful experience at his wife's hospital fresh in his thoughts, he called on this older couple, who were warm parental surrogates to him. He went there in great need, but when the door was opened and he stood on their doorstep he suddenly had an acute sense of constriction in his throat and found that he could not utter even his name or that of the people he had come to visit. Then came a sudden nasal "catarrh," pain in the throat, and a sense of tension and tingling in his arms that was almost unbearable. The interpretation which ran silently through my own mind was as follows: Here is a little boy who wants to hold his arms up to his parents, who wants to sit in their laps, to snuggle in their arms, to put his arms around them, to be held by them, actually to suckle from them both—from the mother-figure's breast and genitals, from the father-figure's lips and phallus. The conflict over these unconscious impulses is translated into these dreamlike bodily sensations, while appropriate accompanying glandular and secretory changes occur in the mucous membranes of the nose and throat (

correlation which on the conscious level has recently been demonstrated by Wolff and his co-workers—81; cf. also 31, 62).

When these interpretations were presented to the patient he thought about them with care, and then with some amazement replied, "That's curious. I have told you of an incident in which a big bully was fighting me and got me down and then when I was down tried to force his penis into my mouth until other boys came and pulled him off. I don't recall just when that was, but it was very early. But now I suddenly remember something that I have not thought of in years. In fact, I don't know whether I've ever remembered it before. This was the effort which I used to make to get my own penis into my own mouth."

The scientific problem with which this confronts us is specifically this: To what extent does the recovery of an appropriate memory of this kind confirm the interpretation which I gave? What other kinds of confirmation can be secured, or *alternatively, how can insight be given other than by such interpretations* (12, 13, 15, 37)?

8. As another example of the problems presented by the technique of interpretation, let me give one more clinical excerpt, superficially simple, but in its implications highly complex.

As a highly gifted and successful newspaper man talked along quite freely, this sequence suddenly occurred: something about saliva (a break), something about vaginal secretions (another break), a quick dry cough, and then a break to other topics.

The importance of this sequence to this particular man will be evident when I indicate that his life pattern had consisted of a total rejection of all bodily functions. Thus he barely ate, because food makes dirt. He barely slept because of an old feeling that bodies in bed exhale dirt. He could barely force himself to go to bed with his wife. In fact, he was unable to tolerate the idea of anybody else's body functions, and, therefore, found it difficult to maintain close relationships with any other human beings, and so had to live a solitary existence. This, however, made him feel rejected, so that he rushed blindly from the home of one acquaintance to that of another—to the dining rooms, cars, or parties of anyone and everyone he knew. He would maneuver three or four invitations for the same evening, accepting them all and popping in and out at each, and even then if he heard of one to which he had not been invited, he would be literally in despair. He needed people to make him feel free of his intolerable sense of being a pariah, and this need was as insatiable as a hand-washing compulsion. The result was that he hated and envied everyone. The homes and dining rooms and cars of others were to him symbolic also of their bodies. He would pursue girls with success, only to dash from them in a frantic panic when there seemed any danger of their accepting his advances.

Behind this façade he betrayed his secret passion for the very body dirt that he rejected. He bathed as rarely as possible. He secretly picked at every hole and aperture of his own body. His tic-like picking and his obsessional difficulty about bathing were linked to his infantile love for his "dirty" father, mother, and sister, from whom he could not emancipate himself, although on a conscious level he longed to come from a "clean" family so that he too would be clean and free of his sense of ostracism. As it was, during the New York water shortage, the only day on which he felt wholly comfortable was "dirty Thursday," when nobody else was expected to bathe either.

The sequence mentioned (saliva, vaginal secretion, and cough) could therefore be interpreted partially in several ways. It was in a sense an epitome of his entire existence. There was a great deal of collateral evidence that this patient had strong necrophagic and coprophagic impulses. These linked him to his father, who was an inveterate user of saline cathartics, and to his mother, who had an organic disease of the nervous system which ultimately destroyed all control of her sphincters. She died when the patient was quite young, leaving the patient with deep conflicts over everything that had to do with the body. In all positive feelings toward other human beings there was a violent impulse to bore in *head first* or *mouth first*, which brought him up against equally violent repugnance and revulsion. In fact, the entire pattern of his life was a reaction formation against such oral impulses as these.

These are what we call interpretations. Some are indeed fantastic, or at the least implausible. The moment I finish an analytic hour and put such an interpretation down in words, I began to doubt it myself. True, the fact remains that it sometimes works; but to this you will answer, and rightly, that although therapeutic results are interesting they prove nothing. The history of medicine is full of stories of right medicines used for wrong reasons, and of the right reasons being advanced for using wrong medicine. Cod-liver oil was used for hundreds of years before anybody knew anything about vitamin D or its influence on calcium metabolism and the prevention of rickets. At this stage of our knowledge too many variables are at work for us to be able to say that an apparent therapeutic result proves the validity of an interpretation, or that a therapeutic failure proves that the interpretation was either incomplete or incorrect. Therefore, as I have already indicated, an interpretation is always presented as a working hypothesis, and our only tests of its validity are derived: (1) from the patient's associations to it, which may confirm, correct, or reject it; (2) from alterations in symptoms; and (3) finally, but only rarely, through our ability to predict future behavior. We need better tests than these.

We are justified in affirming that every moment of life represents the influence of conscious, unconscious, and preconscious processes. Our task becomes how to estimate the relative roles of each. Free association to each component element is our basic exploratory device. It gathers the data, but it cannot prove the validity of our interpretations of the data. Among the patterns of free associations we select some for emphasis, on the basis of hunch, feeling, intuition, and logic. Apparently we are right often enough to feel justified in respecting these as crude approximations to truth. I recently had the good fortune to hear Anna Freud describe a series of interpretations which had led to the complete cure of four manifest male homosexuals. This cannot fail to be both impressive and challenging. Clinically, it is gratifying. Scientifically, it is not precise enough. I repeat: Here is where we need your help.

Furthermore, when we try to put such an interpretation into adult language, words themselves mislead us. Adult speech can describe only the conscious symbols into which the unconscious residues of the confused preverbal thoughts and feelings of childhood are translated. A language which can communicate these preverbal experiences without adultomorphic distortions is still lacking and is urgently needed so that we will be able to communicate better with the child who is within the man, so that we can understand him and so that his unconscious can understand us.

The primary emphasis of any interpretation can be on the genesis of a conflict, i.e., on its history, or alternatively on its manifestations at any current moment. In either case the issue is: how can its implications be proved both to science in general and to the patient in particular? Or is there a better way of bringing unconscious material to the surface of consciousness without interpretation? Is there any way by which unconscious levels can be enabled to reach direct expression without masking distortions, which would eliminate the necessity to interpose interpretations of unconscious, conflict-laden impulses into their symbolic meanings?

To explore this possibility, we need techniques for direct moment-to-moment alterations of levels of consciousness, whether by hypnotic, electrical potentials, magnetic field, pharmacological, biochemical, or physical maneuvers. Often as I sit listening to a patient I have thought to myself, "At this moment I would like to be able to press a button which would throw this patient into some form of communicative 'sleep,' in which I could ask his unconscious to translate directly the idiosyncratic meaning to him of the words his conscious self has just uttered. If I could do this, we would understand his illness almost at once." It is not inconceivable that some such fundamental technical innovations may, like prosperity, be just around the corner.

Let me illustrate my meaning by indulging in a few more fantasies. Let us suppose that conscious, preconscious, and unconscious processes give off electrical discharges with different characteristics (as to amplitudes or periodicities), or that they have refractory phases of different characteristics. Conceivably, we could then have concurrent records of different concomitant levels of psychological processes and of their interrelated physiochemical processes. The patterns of electroencephalographic changes might vary with fluctuations in the patterns of free associations in response to interpretations, or to transference forces, and also in response to variations in physiological and pharmacological influence. Such studies might even provide biophysical and biochemical indices of the relative dominance of conscious and unconscious processes. Related to such studies there would also be the possibility of exploring the role of reverberating circuits in various levels of the central nervous system in establishing deviant patterns of psychological behavior. Or let us suppose that, concurrent with the fluctuating dominance of conscious or unconscious processes, variations could be demonstrated in those enzyme systems in the brain which influence oxidation and reduction potentials, or its metabolic balance, or its carbohydrate consumption, or the rate and loci of manufacture, utilization, and destruction of the substances which transmit the nervous impulse. Here again we can look to the exact sciences to provide us with more precise quantitative and qualitative correlates.

I repeat that we do not need pallid laboratory facsimiles of facts that have long since been clinically evident to anyone who would look through the clinical microscope of analysis with open ears and eyes and an open mind. Such experimental demonstrations have value chiefly as teaching devices for elementary classes, or to persuade the reluctant skeptic who has not wanted to look through the microscope himself, but they are not pathways to new knowledge. We have more important tasks for our friends in experimental and clinical psychology and in the exact sciences, and to these I will turn next.

II

FUNDAMENTAL PROPOSITIONS OF PSYCHOANALYSIS

Psychoanalysis is a qualitative exploratory technique out of which quantitative hypotheses evolve so insistently and so persistently that it would almost seem as though psychoanalysis cannot get along without them. These quantitative and qualitative hypotheses often are compellingly plausible, in the sense that they seem to be adequate either as explanations or at least as descriptions, but as I have already tried to indicate they are nonetheless difficult to subject to rigorous proof (3, 7, 18, 33).

The techniques of proof must encompass all major areas of psychoanalytic theory. These can be variously classified as dynamic, economic, genetic, structural (or metapsychological), clinical, and psychosocial. As conceptual and terminological constructs, these are far from systematic; among them there is much overlapping; and although I shall attempt to indicate some of the conceptual redundancies in this brief survey, I shall not myself be able to avoid them altogether.

The Dynamic Premise

The first challenge is in connection with the concept which is basic to psychoanalysis, namely, that there are unconscious processes which we cannot perceive by simple self-examination alone, but which nonetheless in conjunction with our conscious processes are continuously shaping and influencing our behavior and indeed every psychological experience as every moment of life. In essence this was qualitatively demonstrated and accepted long ago, but we still lack instruments for measuring the relative roles of conscious and unconscious forces in any psychological act. Unhappily this limitation does not hinder some analysts from making quantitative assumptions with unquestioning confidence.

Let us make sure that we still are clear about a distinction already made above, namely, the distinction, on the one hand, between the *dynamic unconscious,* which influences human life but which is not accessible to conscious self-inspection, and, on the other hand, those borderline processes of which we are unconscious but which can be made conscious relatively easily merely by taking thought. These last are psychological processes which were shunted out of the center of the stream of conscious awareness during the process of learning. All learning is by repetition; and through repetition, many intermediate steps, which at first have to be taken one by one, are woven into synergistic patterns. As these patterns form, conscious attention is withdrawn from the individual intermediate steps and is directed only to the whole pattern. Freud called this type of unawareness variously the "descriptive subconscious" or the "preconscious." William James called it the "fringe of consciousness." There are no dynamic barriers against the emergence of psychological data from this fringe of consciousness into full consciousness. They remain on the fringe only because they usually function as elements in integrated patterns of thought and action and not alone. It is through the economy which they make possible that we are able to walk without pondering each step, to talk without thinking through every movement with which we enunciate, or to do complex mathematical processes in our sleep. It makes possible the intuitive leaps of creative thought, whether in science or in art. There is much to be learned from an experimental investigation of the boundaries between these major areas of psychological function, i.e., conscious (CS), dynamic unconscious (UCS), and preconscious (PCS), and of the laws which govern their interactions in varying states of consciousness, such as walking, dozing, daydreaming, hypnagogic reveries, sleeping, dreaming, hypnosis, deliria, narcosis, etc. The mere fact that they exist apart from the dynamic unconscious, however, can be accepted as demonstrated.

By implication this basic dynamic proposition brings with it four interrelated concepts, namely, "repression," "dissociation," "resistance," and "displacement." The usual analytic assumption is that each of these is a separate process or "mechanism," each of which can vary independently of the other. Thus in analytic literature one reads about "weak" or "strong" resistances or repressions, etc.

The observed clinical facts are (a) that conscious process can be rendered unconscious (repressed), and (b) that as an inherent part of repression, resistances form which make it impossible for the repressed processes either to become conscious spontaneously or to be unveiled by direct self-inspection, with the result (c) that energetic forces which originally were part of the previously conscious processes become detached from them when they are repressed ("primary dissociation"), and then (d) become manifest in the various disguised forms (of which displacements are one example), which we encounter in the psychopathology of everyday life (Freud, 21), in personality structure, and in neurotic symptoms. Each step of this has been reproduced in experimental hypnosis to the satisfaction of the most exacting skeptic (Erickson, 9). This still leaves unclear, however, the question of whether these are four separate processes or four aspects of one process; and whether, if more than one process is operative, each functions as an independent variable apart from the others, or always as part of a synergistic unitary pattern. In other words, do they always change together, or under appropriate circumstances and pressures can each move with varying "strengths," or in separate directions? For example, does "strong" repression always mean "strong" resistance and "strong" dissociation, or may repression be "strong" and one of the others "weak," whether these be processes, forces, or effects? Here is where we are in need of clever conceptual definitions and then of experimental help.

Indeed for clearer definition we need more precise qualitative and quantitative devices. I often wish that through the coming years our colleagues in clinical psychology would make it their major concern to search for such quantitative devices. If it is true that in every moment of human life our every act and thought and feeling has multiple determinants, and if it is true that of these determinants some are conscious and some are unconscious (in the dynamic sense), then in order to understand the dynamics of any moment of human experience the most essential requirement would seem to be that we develop instruments for ascertaining with precision the relative roles played by conscious and unconscious determinants. We can recognize important qualitative differences between behavior in which conscious processes play the preponderant role and behavior in which unconscious processes predominate, but we have no means at present of measuring directly the relative concurrent influence of the two groups (Fig. 2).

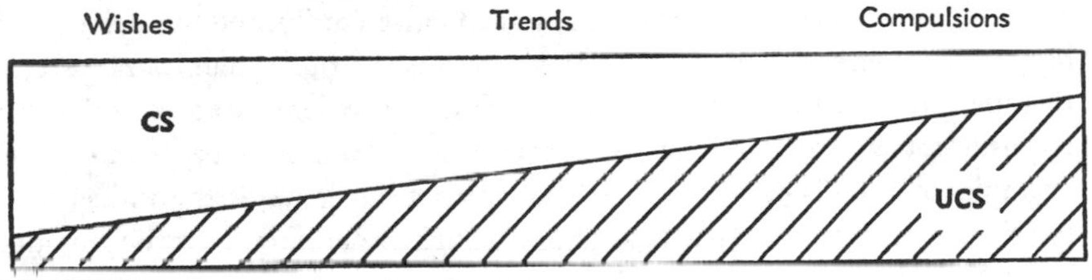

Fig. 2.—Every human thought or feeling or act or pattern of living falls somewhere along such a diagram as this. The technical and quantitative problem is to determine where. It will be noted that the diagram indicates that there are no acts in which UCS processes play no role, and none which are devoid of CS determinants. If this is true, then in all probability the ends of the scale are theoretical abstractions.

There are many conceivable approaches to this problem. For instance, as already suggested, there might be differences in the electrical activity that accompanies conscious, preconscious, and unconscious psychological processes, or differences in enzyme action or distribution, and perhaps in the consequent rate of manufacture, storage, or destruction of those chemical substances which mediate the transmission of the nervous impulse. It would be a contribution of enormous significance to have some way of making a continuous registration of the interplay of these various aspects of physiological function to correlate with conscious and unconscious psychological experiences.

Thus a basic area for experimental investigation has to do with the demonstration and measurement of forces which govern the dynamic interaction between unconscious and conscious processes. Actually, we know more about the influence of unconscious forces on conscious behavior than about the reverse. In other words, we know a little more about the processes of falling sick than of falling well. This may seem strange, yet the reason will be quite obvious. It is due to the special technical difficulties in studying the influence of conscious on unconscious processes. When unconscious forces break through into consciousness in the form of symptoms we become aware at once that something unexplained has erupted into the conscious stream of life experience. Thus conscious awareness provides its own direct registering apparatus. But when conscious processes influence unconscious processes, their influence is hidden behind the very screen which separates us from our own unconscious levels. Therefore the influence of the system CS on the system UCS can be determined only through secondary boomerang effects, i.e., through the resulting alterations in the influences which these same unconscious processes have previously exercised. This requires precise quantitative experiments which have never been designed satisfactorily, and the lack of such basic experiments circumscribes our knowledge of the dynamics of psychotherapy. Indeed the solution of this technical problem is an essential prerequisite for any fundamental clarification of the processes of therapy. For example, our understanding of so fundamental an issue as the influence of insight hinges on this. It is a strange oversight, therefore, that the question has never even been posed.

The "Mechanisms of Defense"

For this reason everything that can be said about the laws which govern the relationships of unconscious and conscious processes must deal chiefly with the direction in which they have been studied, i.e., how unconscious processes can produce conscious processes which can both represent and at the same time mask the nature of their unconscious origins. In analytic terminology this relationship between a psychological act and its UCS roots is given a variety of descriptive names: condensation, displacement, substitution, abstraction, *pars pro toto*, reversal, denial, projection, isolation, undoing, etc. These have all been grouped together as "defensive" devices of the ego (Anna Freud, 19). This involves aspects of psychoanalytic theory which have not yet been considered here, but we may point out that these terms describe some of the many forms which the disguising process can assume. It is wholly unjustifiable to treat each of them as the outcome of a specific "mechanism." This is an example of the recurrent fallacy in psychoanalytic theorizing which I have already discussed at some length, and to which I shall have occasion to refer again when I discuss the tendency to confuse descriptive and explanatory concepts (33). For the present it suffices to remind ourselves that pulse, blood pressure, cardiac output, oxygen need, and oxygen consumption are all measurable adjustment processes which can be said to serve defensive functions, but which are the products not of independent physiological processes but of closely interdependent mechanisms with common roots and special variables. The same is true of psychological processes, yet we tend consistently to forget this in our theoretical formulations.

The influence of UCS on CS processes has been studied in the full waking state, in the spontaneous dreams which occur during sleep (20), in artificially induced dreams under hypnosis (16), in hypnagogic reveries (79), in delirious states, and in all major and minor psychopathological manifestations. This work has been invaluable. It has confirmed the fact that such relationships exist, but there have been no adequate facilities for a round-the-clock study of these relationships as they occur in nature. Nor have the possibilities been exploited for studying them under the influence of variations in such potent physiological and pharmacological processes as body temperature, oxidation and reduction potentials, carbohydrate metabolism, hypoglycemic states, acid-base balance, water and salt disturbances, toxic states, drugs, and other active agents. As a base line for other studies it is essential to know how such variables influence UCS CS relationships, and how patterns of personality structure, age, and culture interact with such biophysical and biochemical influences.

Consider sleep, for instance, as the most "normal" (statistically, at least) of the dissociative processes. It is clear that the polarity between "asleep" and "awake" is relative and not absolute. Sleep is a psychologically active state, and we are never completely asleep, nor completely awake (78). Nevertheless, except for studies of dreams and of the hypnagogic reverie (79) and some rudimentary investigations of the processes of inducing hypnotic states, this vast reservoir of information about the most spontaneous of all dissociative processes has scarcely been tapped (78).

Many a tired soldier has fallen asleep seemingly "well," to awaken in the torments of severe combat neurosis. Cases are recorded in which men have gone to sleep in balance, only to awaken in a full-blown psychosis, in certain instances even in malignant, irreversible psychoses. This phenomenon must be studied, beginning with the banal but subtle daily experience of falling asleep—that evanescent transitional twilight in which our sensory anchorage in reality weakens—with the result that every night our frail psychic vessels drag their anchors perceptibly or imperceptibly toward dangerous shoals and rocky shores.

Nor have there been systematic studies of those more ordered psychological processes which can also occur in sleep, and which enabled Kekule, for instance, to solve in his sleep the structure of the benzene ring, and O. Loewi to discover the chemical transmission of the nervous impulse in a dream, and Poincaré to solve mathematical problems in sleep, and a gynecologist to dream how to tie a surgical knot deep in the pelvis with his left hand. These are the experiences which justify our saying that there is nothing we can do consciously that we cannot also do unconsciously, in the dissociated state. In some earlier work, Margolin and I (53) pointed to the fact that as conscious controls relax, during the process of falling asleep (as under the influence of hypnosis or of anesthesia or other drugs), the mental apparatus automatically returns to its more highly charged storm centers, in such a way that these areas stand out like islands, much as minimal organic lesions in the central nervous system which ordinarily produce only subclinical manifestations may unleash full-blown clinical symptoms under the influence of relative hypoglycemia or anoxia.

All such work requires clinical physiological and psychological laboratories organized in ways which have not yet been approximated. Certain phases of these organizational problems will be discussed below, and we shall then see that cultural anthropological and socioeconomic variables will have to be included in the broad scope of the investigations.

The Symbolic Process

This brings us directly to another problem which is fundamental for the understanding of both normal and pathological psychology.

In earlier sections we indicated that our key is the *symbolic process*. If we were incapable of the symbolic representation of psychological experience we could make no abstractions from experience, and our psychological functions would be limited to central sensory afterimages of past experiences. As Adolf Meyer pointed out long ago, without the processes of symbolic thought the full range of our mental functions could not go far beyond the level of the "phantom limb." To this I would add that *there could then be neither language nor the neurosis*. It is no accident, therefore, that in every child these two should develop in such close relationship, but precisely how and when they diverge in each life story has not yet been studied carefully enough. Nor have the influences of cultural variants been evaluated in terms of their impact on the dichotomy between CS and UCS symbolic processes. The cultural anthropologists who have written so much and so loosely about the influence of culture on the shaping of secondary manifestations of the neurotic process have neither considered nor discussed the influence of culture on this fundamental dichotomy, which is the point of origin of the neurotic process itself.

If it is true that our understanding of the psychological process in man depends upon our understanding of the symbolic function and its development, then it must be equally true that our understanding of psychopathology depends upon the precision of our knowledge of the distortions of the symbolic process which result from the dichotomy between symbolic representations of CS and UCS inner processes. The major emphasis of this distortion can occur at either of two points in symbolic function, and the essential difference between the neurosis and the psychosis depends upon which emphasis is predominant. Where both types of distortion exist, which is usual, the neurotic process and the psychotic must coexist in varying admixtures.

Let me develop this point further. Pavlov proved that conditioning and learning depend upon a state of craving. As indicated elsewhere (30, 37, 40, 42), cravings arise in body tensions, with the consequence that the symbolic thought world of the child starts with his own percepts of parts of his own body, of his own body products, of his apertures, and of the sensations associated with his body needs. No new percept can be perceived apart from the residue of previous percepts and the resultant pre-existing concepts. As experiences multiply, therefore, there can be no new percepts apart from older concepts, and vice versa, although in different experiences the two can be intermixed in different proportions. Consequently, the growth of the symbolic process starts with what the infant needs, the parts of the body which become involved in these needs, how these needs become wants, and how they are represented in feeling, in thought, in speech, and in act. All of this is focusd internally at first, every new external stimulus making its initial impact on our psychic life only by relating itself to that which was already present. Thus in the initial stages of development every external percept must be apperceived in relation to some prior internal experience. *Hence, it is mathematically predictable that every unitary symbol must have both an internal and an external point of reference.*

This is manifested clearly in the speech of childhood, of which examples are given from the reference just cited (30) : A little boy squats beside a dog defecating in the street and watches with interest. Then the boy walks further and squats beside a coal wagon which is emptying coal out of its rear chute, and says, "Look at the coal wagon doing uh-uh." Or after defecating in the woods himself, he looks at the fecal mass which happens to stand erect and says, "Look at the Empire State Building." In the first instance he treats the coal wagon as though it were a human body. In the second he treats a body product as though it were a building. The two-way reference of the symbol is obvious, and throughout life the sample principle governs all normal symbolic functions as well as their distortions. For example, the difference between the role of the symbol "cat" in an individual with a cat phobia, and the role of the symbol "cat" in an individual with delusions about cats is definable in these terms. In the neurosis the primary distortion is in the link between cat as cat, and cat as a representative of unconscious inner psychological conflicts. In the psychosis the primary distortion is in the linkage between the cat as cat, and cat as an unconscious symbol of hated, loved, and threatening objects in the external world. Inevitably, as we have said, the two are always intermixed, but in varying proportions.

That is why in the neurosis we are self-deceived predominantly about ourselves, and in the psychosis predominantly about the world outside of us. Again, however, it will be clear that these polarities are areas of relative and not absolute difference, which can be represented best in our familiar diagram (Fig. 3).

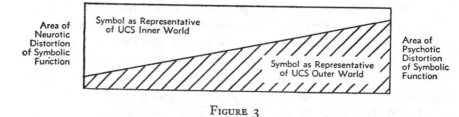

FIGURE 3

This defines for us another area of validating research. How does it come about that certain psychological processes of which we are conscious will be expressed symbolically in language, while other psychological processes of which we are unconscious can also be expressed through a symbolic act, but in this case one whose link to the internal process is severed, as occurs in the neurosis? This can be studied developmentally in the parallel evolution of normal speech and of the universal neurotic episodes of childhood, and their subsequent evolution into the neurotic problems of the so-called normal adult. These come to us for clinical study, when unsolved unconscious problems are reactivated in those periods of decompensation which we call the neurosis (or psychosis).

The neurotic process takes many forms, and the resulting distortions of symbolic function are variously classified, but I am not convinced that these clinical classifications are sufficiently basic to be of value. Therefore, until we can define our own clinical entities which represent separate developmental distortions, I would not feel justified in asking help from nonclinical disciplines in studying them.

I realize that throughout this section I have been more concerned with areas of research than with techniques. That is because psychoanalytic research is passing through a phase in its development through which all scientific disciplines must work their way, a phase in which a good technique which has no questions to answer is even more futile than a good question without the means of answering it. To apply this to the case in hand, at this moment in the history of psychoanalytic research the experimental scientist does not know enough about the subject to know what questions are appropriate and significant. Too often he undertakes to investigate theoretical concepts which are already in the discard, or bases his work on naïve clinical groupings which the analyst has come to regard as mere superficial masks of the neurotic process, comparable to the manifest content of dreams. All that we can hope to do at this time is to clear some of this confusing underbrush out of the path of the experimental scientist, so that future investigations in this field will be more mature and sophisticated than they usually have been up to the present time.

Genetic Theories

We have indicated that psychoanalysis is the art and science of interpreting human psychological experience in terms of the confluent interplay of conscious and unconscious processes. It is not always recognized that psychoanalysis also constitutes a biological approach to psychology, since it derives both conscious and unconscious processes from biological roots. Actually this is the fundamental significance of the analytic concept of instincts: that all behavior derives its fundamental *vis a tergo* from a body need, and that one or more such body needs (or instincts) infuse in varying degrees all psychological functions. Psychologists and biologists regularly disagree with one another about the meaning of the term "instinct," and find common grounds for rejecting the idiosyncrasies with which the concept is used in psychoanalytic literature. Part of these difficulties are semantic in origin and can be eliminated by greater precision in the use of words. Part of them are more basic and conceptual, however; but an essential core remains which the analyst cannot yield without abandoning his fundamental working hypotheses. This is the concept that the roots of all behavior lie in certain biochemical and biophysical necessities of the body, and that in the human being every biological need is subject to distortions of greater or lesser complexity under the influence of psychological processes (3, 7, 23, 24, 29).

Thus, even so primitive a body need as breathing can be overdriven by compulsive psychological superstructures or inhibited by phobic mechanisms. *In man, therefore, the amount of instinctual activity in which he indulges never measures directly or alone the underlying biochemical requirements which it may seem to serve. Indeed in human life the biochemical function of any biogenetic act is almost incidental to its psychological function.* To what extent this is true for the lower animals we do not know. It may be a peculiarity of the human being alone. Certainly it is a major source of many of our neurotic troubles. One of the more familiar examples of this is the compulsive overeating of many adolescents, and the reverse of the same medal—the child who develops what is called "anorexia nervosa" and refuses food even to the point of death. Quite frequently the same child passes through the compulsive phase into the anorexic stage, but the caloric requirements of the body are no greater in one phase than in the other. The same phenomenon is observed in anyone who passes through a period of compulsive sexual hyperactivity (so-called "nymphomania" or "satyriasis") into psychic impotence or psychic frigidity. The study of such patients indicates that in the first phase an obsessional-compulsive overdrive has taken hold of a pattern of activity which originally served a biochemical or instinctual body requirement, and that in the second a phobic inhibitory mechanism has taken hold of this same biogenetic activity. The fact that this can happen to man is one of the numerous special disadvantages of being a member of the human race, because it seems to be more or less peculiar to us that our biological requirements are so highly sensitive to the influence of the conscious and especially unconscious components of our psychological apparatus.

This subjugation of the simple body need by complex superimposed psychological necessities occurs because in the human being the act of gratifying a biological necessity becomes in itself a form of unconscious symbolic behavior, a language which is used for manifold unconscious purposes. This is why the biochemical kernel of any act that, superficially regarded, seems to serve biological needs may actually play only a small part in determining the act. To the extent to which such behavior pursues symbolic gratifications, it can never reach its goals, and consequently becomes insatiable. Therefore, we must constantly ask ourselves how much of any pattern of behavior is organically determined and how much of it is the result of the interaction of these complex superimposed psychological forces.

This issue was first raised some years ago by Bertram D. Lewin and me in our published discussion of a paper by Hoskins (50), and later in a paper on "Instincts and Homoeostasis" (34). I cannot here go into all aspects of this basic and intricate issue, but I hope that the discussion has made it clear that this is another area where we need instruments which we now lack, instruments which would enable us to make quantitative estimates of two interacting and concurrent components in the determination of behavior, i.e., the biochemical and the unconscious psychological ingredient in instinctual acts. Let me emphasize the analytic position that in human beings there is no action which can be called "pure instinct" in the sense of being solely an expression of a biochemical necessity alone, and also no action which can be said to be solely psychological, in the sense of being devoid of the influence of biochemical necessities. Furthermore, psychoanalysis indicates that on different occasions even in the same man, any act (breathing, eating, drinking, or sex) can be determined by quite different instruments; we could place any particular act at the proper point on a scale, at one end of which would be the theoretical pure instinct and at the other end the theoretical pure psychological motivation (neither of which occurs in pure culture in nature), with every admixture of the two falling between. Once again this is best illustrated by our familiar diagram (Fig. 4).

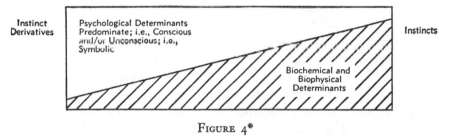

FIGURE 4*

* As already indicated under different circumstances, any act can fall at different points on this scale. Respiratory functions tend in general to operate at one end and sex at the other, with the other body needs distributed approximately in the following order: respiratory, water intake, food intake, water output, food output, sleep, general activity, sex. The reasons for this were discussed in the study to which I have already referred (Kubie, 34).

You will see at once that this diagram is identical with others which I have already used to illustrate the relationships between conscious and unconscious determinants in behavior in general (Fig. 1), the role of reality and symbol in psychic functions (Fig. 2), and the relative roles of symbols of internal and of external experience (Fig. 3). This does not mean that "instinctual" is identical with "unconscious," or that "psychological" is identical with "conscious," but rather that this type of distribution of relative roles seems to be characteristic of every basic attribute of human psychological behavior. It is doubtful, or at least uncertain, whether the same is true among lower animals, where we cannot assay the role of *conscious* symbolic, much less of *unconscious* symbolic functions. This is why the major part of any experimental work in this field must be done on man himself, which makes even more urgent our need for instruments which would enable us to ascertain with greater precision the position of any particular act on all such spectra.

You will notice that I have not even mentioned the different classifications of instincts which have been advanced at various times during the evolution of psychoanalytic theory, such as erotic and destructive instincts, or libidinal and ego instincts, or life and death instincts. This is because these again are descriptive only in terms of the resultants of behavior and not in terms of the genesis or dynamics of behavior. Consequently, they lie outside the scope of these considerations, which have to do with the areas in which the experimental approach can validate and deepen our knowledge.

On the other hand, I cannot be as cavalier about that aspect of the analytical theory of the instincts which has to do with various transitional and overlapping stages in the development of body needs. Fortunately, however, these are not so complicated as is generally believed. Inevitably the first stage has to do with the child's respiratory processes, a phase in instinctual development which psychoanalytic literature has largely overlooked. Therefore, the first phase described in psychoanalytic literature deals with the child's ingestive processes, the second with his excretory processes, and the third with his genital and reproductive processes. Each of these has been variously subdivided, however, usually into two subphases, the earlier of which is relatively passive, inturned, peaceful, and accepting; the second more outgoing and aggressive, demanding, and at times destructive. These are quite obvious and commonsense descriptions of phases through which every child passes; and, as Professor Hilgard has indicated, it has been possible to confirm them in considerable measure in laboratory observations of the human child and in some instances in the lower animals.

What is both more difficult and more important than the confirmation of these overlapping and approximate stages or phases of instinctual development is our need for methods by which we can accurately determine those fixation points which leave charges of *fixed* needs, which remain in the personality as it passes on to subsequent phases. Fixation points are phases in which a child's psychological development becomes focused, with the result that this particular phase subsequently exercises an exaggerated influence on the child's further development and behavior. To differentiate such "fixations" from regressions and to follow their ultimate fate in the adult personality require methods more precise than those which are now available. The analogy that comes to mind is something that seemed an equally fantastic and unrealistic and chimerical hope only a few short years ago, namely, the hope of being able to follow the course of specific molecules through the body economy. This has become possible through tagging molecules with special radioactive or other properties.

Such investigations will clarify many basic problems about *fixation*, e.g., how it occurs, whether fixation is something that occurs only in infancy and childhood and therefore is without precise later analogues, or whether the process of fixation is identical with the obsessional-compulsive phenomena of clinical experience except that it occurs in infancy and earliest childhood and is focused directly on some early phase of instinctual development. The result of such an obsessional accentuation of a particular phase of development would be that its characteristic patterns of thought and feeling and behavior would become a magnetic pole to which behavior will return automatically in periods of stress throughout the rest of life. In other words, are *fixation* and *regression* two separate mechanisms, or are they just two words for inseparable aspects of one process, a conjoint consequence of an early obsessional-compulsive state, focused on one of the instinctual functions?

A consideration of the fate of early instinctual needs involves us in certain other theoretical issues. In a previous section we pointed out that early needs apparently require gratifications that will be both "appropriate" (implying qualitative differences in gratification) and "adequate" (implying quantitative specifications). These statements, for which Hilgard presented what experimental evidence exists, imply that even at an early age a child can be subjected to both qualitative and quantitative frustrations (73). Consequently, a study of the influences of early frustrations on the evolution of human behavior requires both quantitative and qualitative evaluations of needs and gratification, of possible indigenous variations in basic bodily requirements, and of variations in both internal and external reactions to frustration. More specifically, we have to learn how frustration can lead to fixation, and in turn what determines when such fixations are expressed through compulsive exaggerations and when through phobic inhibitions. In turn this will lead to a study of the incidence of primitive rage which may infuse the original need when it is frustrated. And finally will come the study of what determines the fate of this primitive rage, whether it will become diffuse, defiant, and destructive, with secondary manifestations of guilt and fear, or alternatively whether it produces the intimidated child, who generates guilt and fear merely at want-ing that which has been forbidden, with consequent limitation of and damage to his own further development (18, 55, 56, 58, 73, 74).

Nor can the instinctual ontogeny be studied apart from the evolution both of the child's intellectual development and of his capacity to relate himself to other human beings. Of all instinctual needs it is only the respiratory body need that the infant can serve fully for himself and without assistance from adults. Consequently, every other step in his instinctual odyssey involves him in a human relationship and is accompanied by highly charged affective re-actions to those who serve or frustrate him. Much of the complexity of human development, and consequently many intricacies of our analytic concepts, de-rive from this fact. Our unconscious identifications with others, both loving and hostile, and the incorporation of their images into our own psychic or-ganization, the loving and the hating of those images, both when these are projected outward and when they are internalized, and the unconscious in-fluence of such processes on later attitudes both to others and to ourselves—all of this is integral to the complex story of instinctual development. Here again we need instruments which shall be appropriate for every age and capable of precise qualitative definition and quantitative appraisal.

Theories of Personality Structure (Metapsychology)

This brings us to theories and concepts concerning the organization of the personality as a whole.

You have all heard such terms as "id," "ego," and "superego." You know that the id is a name for the reservoir of conscious and unconscious instinctual needs of which we have just been talking, and that it is always pressing for both direct and indirect, open and disguised gratifications. You know that the ego is our technical name for those aspects of the personality by which the *individual* perceives the outside world, reacts to it, seeks the gratification of his instinctual needs, and defends the security and integrity of his own body. You know that the superego is that aspect of the personality by which both consciously and even more unconsciously the individual criticizes and eval-uates himself, by which he also limits and controls and shapes the expression of his needs, and under whose influence he unconsciously punishes and de-prives himself. These superego processes are represented consciously by his developing system of ethical controls and standards. It is commonly assumed that id functions are in large part unconscious, and that the same thing is true of superego functions, whereas a larger part of ego functions operate in the light of consciousness. (Cf. the recent restatement of these concepts by Hartmann, Kris, and Loewenstein, 23, 24, 30.)

Perhaps you may have observed that I have chosen my words carefully. I speak of the individual as seeking *his* gratifications under the pressure of forces which arise in the *id* section of his make-up, but which are shaped by compulsive overdrives and phobic inhibitions, which are the products of the activities we call "superego" functions. I take care deliberately not to speak of the *id's* gratification. *Gratification,* like *frustration,* is an experience that comes only to a whole man, not to his parts. Similarly I speak of the ego as an instrument of the whole individual by which *he* shapes his efforts at gratification and mastery and control and defense. I am similarly cautious in my use of the superego concept. In each case my fear is of allowing a subtle, anthropomorphizing tendency to inflate these abstractions from the whole personality, endowing each with a spurious independent existence, which then would allow us to indulge ourselves in allegorical imagery and figures of speech about strife *between* them. Whole books have been written in this vein. (Cf. Anna Freud, *The Ego and Its Mechanisms of Defense,* 19.) There are fashions in analytic theorizing. Currently one hears much of *ego* analysis; as though one could analyze *ego* functions apart from the rest, and as though defense were a military campaign waged by one facet of the person against the others. These are conceptual and terminological naïvetés and confusions which must be simplified and clarified by analysts themselves before we have a right to appeal to the experimental scientist for help with them.

About this tripartite view of the human personality, however, there are some basic problems that can be approached experimentally. We need experimental techniques to clarify more fully the stages of personality growth with respect to id, ego, and superego development, i.e., the genetic problem. We also need techniques by which to determine to what extent these divisions of the personality are mere abstractions, aspects of an indivisible unit, as I have claimed; or alternatively to what extent they become entities which can function independently of one another, sometimes even in mutual opposition; and finally whether it is possible to measure separately the influence of each of these three facets or components of the personality so as to determine whether they vary quantitatively. Unless such quantitative variations can be demonstrated, it is hard to justify the use of such terms as "weak" and "strong" in speaking of them. (Cf. Kubie, 33.) Therefore, their isolation in the laboratory for independent qualitative and quantitative appraisal is as essential as is the isolation of a bacterial organism or of a chemical compound.

The validity of many current psychoanalytic efforts to explain behavior depends on the answer to these questions.

CONCEPTS OF CAUSAL RELATIONSHIPS IN PSYCHOANALYTIC PSYCHOLOGY

This brings us to a theoretical issue which is of fundamental importance in all psychological research. In no science is the boundary line between description and explanation as clear as one might like it to be, but this obscurity is especially troublesome in psychology, and particularly in psychoanalysis. A few fundamental considerations may be useful as a guide in the designing of experimental approaches to this problem.

The Problems of Chronology

Psychoanalysis is a system of hypothesis based on sequences. A sequence of events may never prove a causal relationship, but it makes causal relationship possible. This highlights two facts about analysis: (1) There are so many variables in human life that it is hard to be sure that any apparent repetition of sequences constitutes sequences of similar events. (2) This ambiguity is further increased by the difficulty of distinguishing clearly between factual events of a patient's life and the patient's fantasies. The historical data which any patient offers include both gaps and embellishments, embellishments which may be slight or extensive, or which may mistake old dreams and fantasies for actual happenings. "Memories" consist, therefore, of composite recollections: events told the patient, family legends, events actually recalled in whole or in part, fragments of old waking fantasies, the residues of old dreams, the partial bodily reliving of one's own emotional participation in all of these, plus the screening of earlier events by superimposed memories of analogous later events. Sometimes the statement is made that events and fantasies about events are of equal value in the explanation of human behavior. This, of course, is not accurate. It is true that both are meaningful, but they cannot be identically meaningful. Hence, methods are needed which would make it possible to distinguish the role of actual events from the role of fantasies in any life history.

The validation of chronological sequences is rarely easy. Sometimes this can be done by canvassing other members of a family, either directly or through social service agencies. Sometimes, however, this merely multiplies the sources of error, since through repetition an entire family may have given credence to a legend. Consequently, there is no guaranty that fantasies shared by different members of a family will always correct one another. Sometimes they merely lend an added semblance of validity to something which is nontheless untrue. On the other hand, the difficult and time-consuming piecing together which occurs in analysis may also leave many sequences uncertain. Occasionally it is possible to test and correct memories under hypnosis by regressing the patient to an early age and having him relive the supposed memories as though he were actually experiencing the events as they occurred (80). For obvious reasons, however, this can have only a limited applicability even in experimental work. Consequently, other confirmatory devices must be found.

Trigger Mechanisms vs. Causal Mechanisms

The ancient confusion between description and explanation in psychological theory takes several forms. One of these is the failure to differentiate between two types of causative relationships. The finger that pulls a trigger releases a bullet, but it does not impart to the bullet its energy. There are many such trigger mechanisms in psychological affairs. The phobia is the most familiar example of this, merely because it is easy to recognize. Laughter, however, is another trigger response, although its species similarity to a phobia has been overlooked. Tears, sudden waves of depression, acute elations, obsessional and compulsive furors, sudden regressions, sudden rages, equally sudden states of apathy, lethargy, or even sleep, acute dissociated states, and sometimes states of partial or complete multiple personality—any one of these may be set off by subtle and inconspicuous moments which because of their symbolic meanings exercise a trigger action. In all such episodes the trigger is not the cause. Nor is it in any realistic sense analogous to a catalyst. Triggers are effective stimuli solely because of their unconscious symbolic implications. Clearly, therefore, there is a vital difference between a cause and a trigger, but their clear definition and their experimental isolation has not been achieved.

Epithets as "Explanations"

Again, characterizations which merely describe human traits are often misused as explanations, not only in popular parlance but in more pretentious pseudotechnical jargon as well. Thus a man beats a woman *because* he is "sadistic." She allows herself to be beaten *because* she is "masochistic." A frightened soldier runs away *because* he is afraid. Something happens *because* it is a habit. A woman behaves in a certain way *because* she "identifies" herself with her mother. Which of these formulations are explanatory? Which are descriptive figures of speech? Popular psychologizing constantly deludes itself into thinking that it has explained something when it has merely redescribed its conscious manifestations. Psychoanalysis recognized this fallacy early but unhappily walked into the identical trap when it made the tacit assumption that descriptions of unconscious relationships were always and necessarily more explanatory than conscious relationships. No one has yet succeeded in defining clearly either a boundary line or a transitional zone between descriptive and explanatory concepts and their respective terms. Until we can made this differentiation it is premature to attribute more explanatory significance to descriptions of unconscious than of conscious processes.

Content or Cause?

Closely related to this is another persistent problem, which has to do with the relation of the content of a psychological state to its cause. This problem is not disposed of by Whitehorn's suggestion that we substitute the word "meaning" for the word "cause." This is mere verbal juggling. The real problem is deeper and tougher than that. We know that when a child has a nightmare about a lion, it is not a lion that he fears, and that the dreamed image of the lion is merely a projected symbol of some internal sources of his terror. The same is true of the object of a waking phobia or of the terrifying visual hallucinations of an alcoholic delirium. The same principle applies to the content of an elation, rage, or depression. Thus a patient may claim to be depressed "about" something, which actually has only a masking and symbolic relation to the true causes (or meanings) of the depression. When the conscious content as "cause" or "meaning" fails adequately to explain some psychological moment, we seek its explanation in its unconscious content. As in the analysis of dreams we move from the manifest to the latent content in our efforts to explain any psychological experience. Yet our methods of determining the actual function of both the conscious and unconscious contents in any psychological constellation are equally lacking in precision; and although we take as our model the relation of the manifest to the latent content of a dream, we fail to carry this through consistently. We are no more justified in taking it for granted that the unconscious content is the "cause" of a mental state than the naïve layman is justified in making the same assumption about its conscious content. Therefore, it is equally important to determine when unconscious fantasies are products of a mental state, when they are mere clues to their explanation, or when they constitute their uniquely adequate and complete explanations.

Assumptions Concerning Quantitative Changes

Similar caution applies to all efforts to explain behavior by assumptions concerning quantitative changes. In any system in which a large number of forceful processes are in unstable equilibrium, any qualitative or quantitative change in any of them, or even in change in the direction of one, may so upset the equilibrium of all as to produce quantitative changes in the resultant activity. Indeed, if the balance is sufficiently sensitive, the equilibrium of the whole group of forces can be moved into action or silenced into inaction by a relatively minor change in one component. In this way quantitative changes of major magnitude can result from the mere rearrangement of quantitatively unchanged units of force. Under these circumstances it is never justified to assume quantitative changes in any one of the component forces, until and unless each one of them can be measured. This fact is obvious, but in psychoanalytic theories it is consistently overlooked (Kubie, 33; Benjamin, 3).

Furthermore it is difficult to decide what indices of quantity changes can be used. Does an increase in the *frequency* of an act mean that it is more strongly driven or more weakly opposed? Or that a more powerful force is at work to overcome greater obstacles? Or merely that the act occurs frequently because it happens to be an easy avenue of discharge? It has taken the physiologist long years to discover all the possible meanings of a change in rate (frequency) of the heartbeat. It may take an equally long time before we will be entitled to draw any deductions from the mere fact that some pattern of behavior has persisted for a long time.

All such ruminations concerning quantitative changes and relationships will remain vague and general until we know more precisely how quantity changes are mediated in the central nervous system. At present we do not know whether the discharges which subserve conscious and/or unconscious processes can vary in quantity, or whether they operate on an all-or-none basis, as in simpler components of the nervous system. So also we do not know whether quantitative changes in conscious or unconscious processes depend upon variations in the intensity or frequency of discharge of the same neurones or on variations in the number of central neurones which subserve the activity. Such possibilities as this can be subjected to experimental investigation. This is not too difficult in lower animals, where, however, any correlations with either conscious or unconscious processes present major problems. But such studies are far from easy when carried out in human beings, where correlations with both conscious and unconscious processes could be made. This fact exemplifies one of the major dilemmas of research in this field.

Perhaps I have said enough to indicate some of the pitfalls which are involved in the use of such quantitative metaphors as force, energy, and the so-called economic principle in attempts to explain human behavior. They are useful, descriptive metaphors, in so far as they help to visualize changes; but when they are used to *explain* changes, then no matter how technical and specialized our terminology, and whether we are speaking of conscious or unconscious processes or of mixtures of the two, we are nonetheless liable to every fallacy of popular speech. It is all too easy to use descriptions as though they were explanatory, and to illuminate them with *ad hoc* quantitative metaphors, and then to use these metaphors as pseudo explanations in order to expand their apparent explanatory significance. Analytic theory provides many examples of these sources of error; until they are weeded out, a closer liaison with the more exact sister discipline will continue to be difficult.

Other Theoretical Issues

Without overburdening this discussion with a complete catalogue of work to be done, I will list a few other basic questions which urgently need to be answered by appropriate experiments.

1. Are there innate traces of universal human experiences which have not been experienced by the individual during his own life? For instance, is there a drive specifically toward a mother's breasts in children who have never been nursed? What is the meaning of fantasies or dreams about parental intercourse, which occur in orphans who have been brought up in asylums throughout their lives? How does one measure the force invested in certain types of archaic, primitive, or infantile fantasies and impulses? And if these are inherited traces of past experience, why, in spite of the fact that the human race has been divided into male and female for quite a number of years, do we remain wholly unreconciled to the anatomical differences between the two sexes? How does the language of the dream in the congenitally blind differ from the visual imagery which constitutes the predominant dream language of the sighted? In such dreams what sensory modalities are used?

2. These questions are linked to the problem of the influence of emotions on memory (Rapaport, 69), to questions of organic preverbal memory of the earliest phases of life, and finally to problems of racial memory.

3. Again, what about the claims of parapsychology? And how would the data and technique of psychoanalysis be influenced if telepathic communication of some kind is found to be possible? Or extrasensory perception? Or even precognition?

4. Finally, I will merely mention the problem of the specificity of the genetic propositions which have been advanced to explain the various constellations of neurotic symptoms.

These problems lead too far for full discussion here.

RESEARCH IN THE SOCIAL AND CULTURAL
APPLICATIONS OF PSYCHOANALYSIS

The recognition of the universality of the neurotic process is becoming more general. Consequently, we hear more and more about social, economic, and cultural factors in the neurosis. This makes it all the more striking that there have been no systematic comparative inquiries into the relative incidence of the various manifestations of the neurotic process in any components of our own culture, much less in other cultures. Such studies are essential for a rounded study of the neurotic process in human affairs.

Similarly we hear a great deal about mental hygiene, with the implication that we know how to keep people well, how in short to prevent or arrest the neurotic process. This again has never been put to a critical test. There has been no systematic effort to find out whether an all-out application of existing knowledge will affect the incidence and the evolution of neurotic disturbances, which would seem to be important if only to indicate whether or not we are on the right track.

Finally we hear a great deal about the importance of providing adequate services. Yet we hear little about how to solve the fundamental difficulty of training when there are not enough teachers, or about the development of training aids such as films, or about cultural indoctrination to overcome the great cultural resistance to psychiatric knowledge, or about the need to develop a new professional group to meet that part of the shortage in personnel which is due to the long time it takes to train psychiatrists. It will become evident that these issues, which would seem to be purely practical, are actually of great importance in any effort to solve the basic scientific issues which we are considering.

Research in the Cultural Anthropology of Psychoanalysis

Psychoanalysts as scientists and psychoanalysis as a body of knowledge about human personality need the co-ordinated help of their fellow scientists —social psychologists, clinical psychologists, psychiatric social workers, men trained in the techniques of opinion-polling and random sampling, and cultural anthropologists. Their help is needed to fill a serious gap in our knowledge of the vital statistics of the neurotic process. Kinsey's studies of the incidence of sexual anomalies (36) are by far the greatest contribution to such knowledge that has yet been made, but for lack of full technical competence the work was done so uncritically that most of it will have to be done over again. It is to our shame that there were no adequate basic studies to guide Kinsey; i.e., no studies of the incidence in various segments of the population of even the simplest neurotic symptom, and no correlations of these with even such external facts of life as economic status, occupation, population density, national, racial, and religious origins, differences in culture and customs, family structure, family size, ordinal position in the family, age gaps between siblings, family clusterings of neurotic symptoms or trends, intellectual capacity, education, and the like. Even less has there been any effort to correlate these cultural and socioeconomic factors with the onset of the neurotic process in infancy or early childhood or with its later fate in puberty and adolescence. None of this is easy, but such data are essential for any understanding of the interaction between endogenous developmental factors and exogenous cultural factors in the evolution of the neurotic process. Furthermore, such knowledge is essential for any precise testing of the preventive value of early psychotherapy, analytic or otherwise.

The Preventive Applications of Research in Psychoanalytic Knowledge

Any study of the value of psychoanalytic knowledge for the prevention of neurotic disturbances would require similar interdisciplinary teamwork. Such a study would consist in essence of an evaluation of the effects of early psychiatric education, consultation, advice, and guidance for young parents, and in the early treatment of both the young parents and of infants and young children in a statistically adequate sample of the young couples in some relatively stable community.

One would start by assembling a large group of young couples who either had not yet had their first children or who were "expecting," or whose children were in the first weeks of life. Such couples would then be organized into a prepayment group for periodic psychiatric examination of their children, for early and continuing psychiatric treatment as indicated, and for consultations and educational programs for the young parents, both individually and in groups, all of this to be continued over a period of ten to fifteen years. A control group of young couples from the same community would have to be assembled. The appraisal of results would be in terms of comparative morbidity and mortality records, comparative growth records, comparative costs of medical care, comparative school progress (as indicated by general scholastic standing and by special tests and examinations performed by the staff of the project), adjustments to homes and siblings, athletic adjustments, social adjustments, social service and police records, and psychosexual development. Comparison of children from the test and control groups would require the co-ordinated efforts of both medical and nonmedical personnel, including psychiatrists, clinical psychologists, specially trained educators, psychiatric social workers, etc.

In addition to prepayments from those members of the community who either elected to become subjects of the test or who were selected for that privilege, the investigation would have to be supported by grants from foundations. It would be preferable if the staff held university positions so that the work would be carried out in affiliation with or under the auspices of a university. Without such affiliation it would probably prove difficult to recruit a staff of high caliber, and even more difficult to hold the staff together for the long period of observation which would be necessary.

For instance, the study might well be carried on under the auspices of such an organization as the Institute of Human Relations at Yale, or the Department of Social Relations at Harvard, with the Department of Psychiatry of the Medical School. Or it could be under the auspices of a special Institute for Research in Psychoanalytic Psychology. As the site for such a study, a compact community of moderate size, with a relatively stable population, which afforded an adequate cross-sectional representation of the economic, educational, racial, national, and industrial make-up of the country as a whole would have special advantages. The schools should be good and fairly uniform in quality; and the community should be interested in establishing certain group health services, of which such a study as this might well be a part. (Cf. Kubie, 38.)

A RESEARCH INSTITUTE IN PSYCHOANALYTIC PSYCHOLOGY

I will close this survey of areas of future research by discussing what kind of organization would constitute the minimal essential prerequisites for mature research of the kind which we have been considering. The question leads our thoughts back to the fact that psychoanalysis had to start and indeed persists largely as a form of private practice. This is an unusual way to introduce into medicine a new therapeutic technique, and this historical fact has in itself been a source of much skepticism about analytic integrity. It is possible to demonstrate that its status as a form of private practice has been a basic source of strength in the past, but it is equally certain that it will ultimately destroy psychoanalysis if private practice should continue to be the exclusive or predominant field of psychoanalytic activity in the future.

Yet it was no accident that psychoanalysis has been largely a private practice. At the start nothing else was possible because of the nature of the material, the high degree of intelligent co-operation required of patients, the long and uncertain duration of treatment, and the immediate hostility of organized medicine. These past fifty-odd years of analytic history constitute one of those occasional episodes in medicine in which the affluent have been the guinea pigs instead of the poor. If we consider the difficulties and limitations on strict controls which are imposed by the conditions of private psychoanalytic practice, it is astonishing that psychoanalysis has been able to make even the modest progress which it can rightfully claim.

The practical and psychological limitations of scientific work in private practice are obvious, yet it is worth while to review them to guide us in planning more favorable conditions for future research. I should place first the fact that each analyst works for so many months or years with only a few patients. As a direct consequence, even in the course of a lifetime of exclusive devotion to the psychoanalytic treatment of patients, no analyst will have been able to analyze deeply more than a few representatives of any one psychopathological constellation. When an internist reports on what happens in pneumonia, his report is based on his experience with hundreds of patients. When an analyst discusses some condition, such as height phobias, for instance, he will base his report on, at most, a mere handful of such patients. Furthermore, even when over many years an analyst has accepted patients as they came along, he can never claim that he has had an opportunity to survey a statistically adequate random sample of the field. As an example, I have been in practice for more than twenty years, yet there are many conditions which have never come my way. Informal inquiries indicate that the same is true for my colleagues. It is inevitable, therefore, that an analyst's judgment will be influenced unduly by the statistically inadequate, if random, sample which chance has brought to him. With the length of time that each analysis requires in the present state of knowledge, there would seem to be no way of eliminating this source of error completely.

While this problem is not peculiar to private practice, its distorting influence is greatest under these circumstances. With group or institutional practice, two partial solutions to the problem are at least conceivable. One analyst might decide to specialize in height phobias, for example, analyzing nothing else; another might specialize in a certain type of male homosexuality and nothing else, etc. The scientific disadvantages of this are precisely those that would arise if a physician concentrated on only one kind of illness or on one constellation of symptoms within an illness. His judgment would then be influenced by the fact that he was not continually exposed to contrasting experiences, so that he would not have an opportunity to observe how often the data on his special group of patients might be duplicated in patients suffering from quite different conditions. Therefore, such superspecialization as this would not be a satisfactory way of solving the problem, unless perhaps it were done in an appropriate research institute which was manned by analysts who had already had several years of broad analytic experience with a random assortment of patients. This is one of many reasons why the organization of an institute of this kind, including on its staff several full-time analysts of broad previous experience, is essential for future progress.

Another conceivable solution might be to pool the experience of many analysts in a central registry with central records. This procedure would present many new difficulties, such as the problem of assembling, recording, and reproducing data and then of analyzing them, while preserving at the same time each patient's privacy, etc.

Moreover, under conditions of private practice it is difficult to exercise control over the many variable factors which operate in a patient's life outside of the analysis itself. Frequently the analyst works under conditions comparable to that of a cardiologist treating outpatients with myocardial insufficiency. Two patients might have essentially identical cardiac defects, but one might be doing a desk job and the other that of a day laborer. One might have an apartment with an elevator and the other a walk-up flat. One might be living in an atmosphere of domestic harmony and the other in an atmosphere of constant emotional assault. No cardiologist would evaluate the results of a therapeutic regime without taking into account these variable external conditions, and if he wanted to improve his therapeutic results he would have to control the outside stresses as well. The analyst faces comparable problems. The attitude of the referring physician, the emotional support given by the family, and many other external situational strains play a role which can rarely be controlled in private practice. In fact, the outside world's behavior toward an analytic patient is largely an obligatory and automatic expression of the neurotic problems of those who make up that world, and, therefore, is not an attitude which will yield easily to direct or indirect advice. Consequently, there is no way of stabilizing or controlling the influence of outside forces except by lifting a patient out of his ordinary life and placing him in a special treatment center, where the constancy and uniformity of the total situation can be controlled at least in some measure, and where the influence of those external variables which cannot be eliminated could be observed closely enough to make it possible to evaluate them. From this point of view the military services, especially in times of peace, might provide an ideal setting for such investigations.

Such neurosis treatment centers would have the additional advantage of providing an opportunity to remedy another defect of private practice for research purposes, namely, the difficulty of making follow-up studies of the subsequent histories of patients after the completion of treatment. Two generalizations may be made: (*a*) that in private analytic practice our therapeutic failures tend to avoid subsequent contacts with their analysts, and (*b*) that for a considerable time after the termination of successful treatments conscientious analysts tend to avoid postanalytic contacts with their therapeutic successes. This is because one of the important goals in analysis is to help patients toward greater independence as they resolve the neurotic problems which have fostered dependency. Even the most discreet inquiries by the analyst can in some measure jeopardize this postanalytic independence, whereas follow-up inquiries and interviews by some relatively impersonal organization (such as a research institute or a neurosis treatment center) would not entail this risk for the patient to the same degree.

A number of subtler but equally potent forces minimize further the research value of private practice. Some of these are peculiar to analysis, some are shared with all medical practice. Thus no therapist can be a wholly detached and objective person. In analysis we strive to achieve an attitude which Ernest Jones characterized as one of "benevolent curiosity"; but I doubt that any analyst can spend months and years with his few patients without investing in each of these therapeutic odysseys an enormous amount of hope and eagerness as well as deeper feelings. If he claims that the outcome is a matter of indifference to him, he either has fooled himself or else he should not be an analyst, because such indifference would indicate a pathological withdrawal of feeling from the fate of his patients and from his own years of effort. Therefore, in spite of efforts to be objective, the good therapist will always be in some measure an ax grinder. This is true of all medical therapists but particularly true of psychoanalysts. Add to this the natural enthusiasm of a group of devoted and extremely hard-working people who stake their entire scientific and professional lives on the evolution and fate of a single technique, plus the enthusiasm that is engendered by having to battle against a considerable amount of persistent popular and professional bias, misunderstanding, and hostility, and it will be clear that it is unrealistic to expect perfect scientific detachment.

Finally, private practice is not the best place for making or keeping records. In the past we have been dependent largely on one of the most frail and vulnerable of all human instruments, namely, memory. As has been pointed out elsewhere (46, 47, 54), so long as we depend upon recorded impressions and memories, the subtle differences with which we are concerned over long drawn-out periods of observations become sources of error. Over a period of many months, daily observation of a process which waxes and wanes continually by just perceptible increments and decrements gradually dulls the perception of even the keenest observer, paralyzes the memory through the monotony of repetition, and renders the written word literally useless as an instrument of record. After a time, the observer can no longer differentiate clearly and surely what the patient has said from what he himself has said, or which came first. To this I would add that since the process of analysis makes use of the free associations of the analyst as well as those of the patient, the memories of both must be subject to selective influences in an identical way, if not to the same degree.

Hence, it is impossible for the analyst to make adequate records of what transpires between himself and his patient merely by writing notes either during or after each session. He can capture certain fragments, but what he captures will be guided by his own emotional involvement. The patient storms the analyst's emotional citadel with complex challenges. Both as therapist and as observer the analyst attempts to deal with these in such a way as to keep himself from becoming emotionally stirred up by them, so that he can clarify them to the patient. To do this requires great freedom and agility, and tying himself down to his pencil would inevitably limit the flexibility of the analyst's associative responses.

Moreover, what transpires between the patient and the observer employs a language which uses many means of communication. Gesture and expression and posture all enter into it, and although in practice relatively less use is made of these components of language than of words, they sometimes are an essential ingredient in the total response. So they should not be omitted from an inclusive scientific investigation.

These various considerations lead to a conclusion which may have been obvious from the start, namely, that in psychoanalytic research the analyst cannot be both therapist and observer. In addition to someone to observe the patient, we need an observer to observe both the analyst and the interaction between the patient and the analyst. We need, in short, methods by which the entire process can be observed and recorded. Bales and others (1) in the Department of Social Relations at Harvard have recently begun a systematic study of this technical problem.

Furthermore, if it is essential that the raw material of the analytic interview must itself be subject to scrutiny by more than one observer, it is equally important that this be done on more than one occasion. From moment to moment so much happens that it is impossible for any psychiatrist or analyst, no matter how astute he may be and no matter how phonographic and photographic his mental processes, to retain by unaided memory an adequate record of the course of treatment. Consequently, it is impossible for him to review it to himself without retrospective alterations and even more impossible to report it to his colleagues without unconscious distortions. This is not only because of the essential limitations of memory but also because of the emotional involvements of the analyst. Every hour includes things that he wishes he had said or left unsaid. He becomes aware of mistakes. Doubts assail him. No matter how secure he may be, what he recalls and records must be influenced in some measure by a deep need to put his best foot forward. (Cf. Kubie, 46, p. 32.) It is impossible, therefore, ever to reproduce in words a moment of life which can never recur. One needs not only the observer who observes the observer but also methods of mechanical reproduction of language, gesture, expression, posture, and even color. This means a not inconsiderable laboratory, which will introduce its own artificial distortions and deviations from the therapeutic situation to which we are accustomed.

There is a long period in the development of any science during which research consists of the amassing of crude observations and the gradual ordering of these tentative data into tentative theories. During this stage there is uncertainty and disagreement about the empirical data themselves, about the methods by which these data can be observed with precision and discrimination, and about how they can be recorded and reproduced for later study. A science begins to emerge from this phase of approximation only as it develops techniques by which observations of the essential empirical data can be reproduced undistorted, so that many workers can repeat the same observations and interpret them in joint or parallel investigations.

In several recent symposia on the special problems of research in psychiatry and psychotherapy (46) it has been emphasized that a fundamental defect of research in analysis, and indeed in all psychotherapies, has been the fact that only one person could observe the empirical data of the therapeutic process, and that only once. Past attempts to evaluate a therapist's report of what he and his patient did and said have had to depend upon the faulty observations, the faulty recall, and the faulty records of one observer who was himself emotionally involved in the events he was trying to report. In other words, four sources of error were interposed between the objective data of any psychotherapeutic procedure and those who would evaluate them: inaccuracies of primary observation, flaws of memory, the emotional involvement of the therapist in the situation which he was also trying to observe dispassionately, and the inadequacy of the written word as the record of a moment that had passed and could never return. Such data give rise to controversies, but they are hardly the stuff out of which fundamental scientific advances can be fashioned.

It seems clear, therefore, that if we are ever to understand psychoanalysis deeply, we must begin by solving the problem of how to make adequate recordings of the therapeutic process *without at the same time distorting the process*. These considerations are additional reasons why the work should be done by men who have had broad and varied experience with the therapeutic situation under all kinds of circumstances.

The first objective of any investigation must be the development of methods for recording the psychotherapeutic process with minimal distortion, so that it can be reproduced accurately for subsequent re-examination and restudy. For this purpose interviews would be carried on under standardized conditions in which all significant variables, both psychological and physiological, could be controlled with greater precision than is possible in the ordinary interview situation. This means a standardization not only of the many subtle psychological variables already discussed but also of all relevant physical variables. This implies extremely complex and costly equipment, including such items as sound-proofed, air-conditioned, and temperature-controlled chambers, with one-way mirrors for direct observation. The chambers themselves might be equipped with mirrors so arranged as to make possible the simultaneous viewing and photographing of an individual from several angles, both for full observation and for laterality comparisons. There might be provisions for observing and recording sleep and other intimate body functions, provisions for infrared still photography and for infrared motion pictures with sound tracks, and for concurrent (or alternative) continuous wire or tape recordings. Infrared illumination would make possible direct observations during nocturnal sleep, as well as in the daytime. The special reasons for including such provisions have already been indicated. Connections would also be provided for EEG, EKG, and other special electrophysiological recordings, comparable to the electrophysiological studies made during the war on men in tropical and arctic chambers.

The second goal of such a research program would be the qualitative and quantitative analysis of the material gathered under these conditions. Its purpose would be to begin the study of the data with an analysis of the subject's *free associations*: those produced (*a*) spontaneously when alone, (*b*) in the presence of one or more observers or therapists, (*c*) in response to selected stimuli, (*d*) in response to interpretations, (*e*) in varied physiological states, and (*f*) more specifically in relation to states of consciousness which would be varied purposefully by means of physiological, pharmacological, and psychological agents. This material could be subjected to precise quantitative and qualitative scrutiny (much as radio broadcasts from enemy countries are analyzed quantitatively and qualitatively by official monitors, for the purpose of

sonality must be studied from one individual to the next in their total settings. Therefore, in studies such as these, the use of matched pairs is of little value, and the technique of control is correspondingly complex. It requires rather the use of statistically adequate random samples, each unit of which must be studied in sufficient detail to make it possible to compare the individual units with respect to many traits instead of one. Hence, controls can be achieved only by contrasting details within the individuals who make up the random samples which constitute the groups to be studied.

3. *Personnel.*—In addition, all studies of the psychoanalytic process depend not only on the adequacy of the techniques to be used but also on the maturity and sophistication of the personnel in their use of the specific techniques which are to be studied. This implies that the personnel must be experienced technically and also sufficiently secure and objective and mature to be willing to subject themselves to critical observations while in action, without undue sensitivity, and to observe others in action without unduly destructive aggressiveness. In this connection the comments of Drs. H. W. Brosin and David Shakow are highly relevant (48).

Such an investigation of the analytic process would ultimately attempt to find answers to a number of interrelated questions concerning that hallmark of Homo sapiens, the symbolic process. Such answers will illuminate both the genesis of the neurosis and its resolution: (1) How often do transitory diffuse dissociative states occur as the initiating repressions produce those dichotomies between CS and UCS which launch the neurotic process? How often are these transient dissociative states overlooked? (2) To what extent does the therapeutic impact of eliminating these repressions depend upon a procedure by which such transient episodes of pathogenic dissociation can be reproduced or relived? (Cf. Kubie and Margolin, 53.) (3) How are the various dissociative phenomena interrelated (e.g., pathogenic dissociations arising out of the process of repression, spontaneous dissociations under the influence of explosive affective states, hypnotically induced dissociations, the dissociation of hypnagogic states, of hypnosis and of sleep, etc.)? (4) What is the difference between, on the one hand, the process of sleep which plays a healing and reintegrative role so that we awaken restored and, on the other hand, the process of sleep which facilitates a pathogenic regressive and/or dissociative process during which human beings become more disturbed? (5) What are the therapeutically most effective methods of inducing and controlling dissociative states? By hypnotic procedures? By electrical (or even magnetic) potentials? By the use of a wide variety of pharmacological agents (including not only the usual sedatives but also the analgesics, the curare-like substance, drugs, which influence or reproduce various effects of the neurohumoral substances, etc.)? (Cf. Kubie, 45.) (6) To what extent are the altered states of consciousness which can be produced by various pharmacological, physiological, and psychological maneuvers allied both to the phenomena of normal and/or pathogenic sleep and to hypnotic phenomena? (7) How can dissociative states best be used? (a) For the fuller exploration of free associations? (b) For the free and spontaneous translation of unconscious symbols? (c) For the recovery of repressed pathogenic conflicts? (d) For the reliving of past experiences with and without induced regressions to earlier age levels? All of these questions converge on a problem which has often been discussed but never investigated. (8) What is the therapeutic meaning of that form of insight which consists of the penetration of the barrier between CS and UCS levels? (a) What are the reasons for its therapeutic efficacy when it succeeds, or for its failure when it fails? (b) What are its emotional as well as its intellectual components? (c) What is the difference between insight which is therapeutic in its influence and the spontaneous symbolic insight of the schizophrenic with its characteristic therapeutic impotence?

These questions are neither a systematic nor an exhaustive list. They serve merely to exemplify certain pressing issues. They have grown out of analytic and other experiences, and they need to be explored. It remains true that all such studies must include manipulations of the state of consciousness, which in turn requires physiological as well as psychological controls. Obviously, studies of varied states of consciousness must include running records of EEG changes and of concomitant changes in blood chemistry, etc. To omit these physiological correlates would be equivalent to studying cardiac physiology without a sphygmomanometer or an EKG.

All of this can be summarized by pointing to the need for research laboratories focused on one of the most fundamental conundrums of human life— the interplay of CS and UCS forces in health, in disease, and in our culture in general. Ultimately, what would this mean? It would mean a many-sided organization to co-ordinate the several disciplines. Its work would include genetic research on the evolving distortions of the symbolic process in many cultures, on the early dichotomy between the symbolic representation of conscious and unconscious processes which occur in infancy and childhood, on the two-way interactions between the various levels of organized psychic function. This would require active participation by the neurophysiologist, the biophysicist, the biochemist, the pharmacologist, the clinical psychologist, the cultural anthropologist, and the biostatistician, as well as the psychoanalyst. Their work would range from these areas to the most concrete applications of psychoanalytic psychology, to the vital statistics both of the overt neuroses and of the universal neurotic component in so-called normal human life, with comparisons of the influence of cultural forces on the fundamental neurotic process. Thus our institute would include subsections on psychoanalytic psychology, psychotherapy, clinical psychology, social psychiatry, cultural anthropology, specialist training, and educational techniques.

This is a dream for the future: an institute, in our field the very first of its kind, in which "unfettered scientists could pursue unchartered courses to unanticipated goals." As with the Rockefeller Institute at the turn of the century, the value of such an institute would not necessarily be in its world-shaking discoveries. It would be rather in the extent to which it would raise the general level of research in this field throughout the world.

SUMMARY

1. A brief reference is made to Professor Hilgard's two lectures in March 1950.

2. The major contribution of experimental science will not be limited to confirming psychoanalytic observations in the laboratory but rather to providing psychoanalysis with instruments of greater qualitative and quantitative precision. Areas of theory and technique are discussed in which such instruments are urgently needed, as well as the importance of making it possible to prove the validity of psychoanalytic principles, not merely in general, but when they are applied in specific instances.

3. This leads to the discussion of basic features of analysis as an operational process, to wit: (*a*) free associations, (*b*) transference phenomena, (*c*) interpretations. These must be reproduced and/or controlled in any experiments whose purpose it is to illuminate the analytic process.

4. In such experimental work, the relationship of the human subject to the experimenter must parallel as closely as possible the relationship of an analytic patient to an analyst so as to (*a*) make experimental situations comparable to the clinic, (*b*) illuminate CS and UCS elements in the relationship, and (*c*) reduce the number of exogenous variables in the experimental as in the therapeutic situation. Thus the stereotyped monotony of psychoanalytic technique and the so-called "analytic incognito" must be duplicated as far as possible in experimental procedures, because both of these basic components of psychoanalytic technique are essential in order to limit the total number of external variables and to restrict their points of origin to the unconscious processes of the patient (or subject).

5. Details are described of examples of self-translating psychoanalytic data

occurring spontaneously in the state of nature, i.e., in the psychopathology of everyday life, in the untutored speech of infants and children, in the transparent dreams of naïve young people, under experimental hypnosis, and, finally, during the course of analytic treatments.

6. This brought up the critical scientific challenge, namely, how to prove that any particular constellation of interpretations of CS–UCS relationships is *adequate* and *uniquely necessary* as the explanation of any psychological phenomena. The validity of interpretations is the critical test of the validity of psychoanalytic theory. The effectiveness of interpretation as a method is the critical issue in psychoanalysis both as an investigative and as a therapeutic procedure. At the same time interpretation is the most vulnerable element in psychoanalysis. The search for a substitute for the process of interpretation has barely started; it will require help from allied psychological disciplines and from the more exact sciences.

7. The clarity of a group of psychoanalytic concepts and assumptions is considered in terms of their readiness for experimental investigation.

8. The social, cultural, and preventive aspects of psychoanalytic practice are reviewed as areas for basic investigation.

9. The concept of an Institute for Research in Psychoanalytic Psychology is considered.

ADDENDUM

Since these lectures were given, an important new field has opened up for investigation through the implications of the work which is being done in the Montreal Neurological Institute under Dr. Wilder Penfield. This involves the electrical stimulation of various areas of the cortex, and more particularly of the external convexity of the temporal lobe as well as some of its deeper structures, while the patient is being explored operatively under local anesthesia. The patients have been cases of psychomotor epilepsy. The work is summarized in the book by Drs. Wilder Penfield and Theodore Rasmussen, *The Cerebral Cortex of Man*, the Macmillan Company, New York, 1950 (248 pages); and more recently in Dr. Penfield's Presidential Address, "Memory Mechanisms," before the American Neurological Association, June 1951 (the *Archives of Neurology and Psychiatry*, February 1952, Vol. 67, No. 2, pp. 178–98). A detailed discussion (Kubie) of the psychiatric and psychoanalytic implications of Dr. Penfield's work appears in the same journal on pp. 191–94; and this discussion has been elaborated into an article entitled, "Some Implications for Psychoanalysis of Modern Concepts of the Organization of the Brain," which was read before the annual midwinter meeting of the American Psychoanalytic Association in New York, December 1951. This is now in press.

The Position of Psychoanalysis in Relation to the Biological and Social Sciences

THE SETTING AND PREHISTORY OF PSYCHOANALYSIS

I SHALL NOT ATTEMPT to recapitulate the points made by Dr. Hilgard and Dr. Kubie in their lectures, but rather to review the development of psychoanalysis at its present stage of evolution from a methodological point of view. In this way I hope that some perspective may be gained regarding the field of psychoanalysis.

Psychoanalysis did not spring full born from the head of its Zeus, Freud, but went through a long history of evolution and change. For anyone who may be interested in the genesis of psychoanalysis, the recent book of Freud's early notes and his correspondence with Wilhelm Fliess (10) from 1887 to 1902 is particularly illuminating.[1] In one way the history of psychoanalysis is relatively uncomplicated, since its originator (who died only a little more than a decade ago) remained its principal contributor and guiding spirit until the very end. Thus one can approach psychoanalysis both from the historical and methodological points of view through a study of his works. At the same time, however, the task is rendered complicated by this very fact. The figure of Freud has dominated the field of psychoanalysis so completely that perhaps undue weight has been attached to his every sentence and word.

However, every science is in the process of constant growth and change, as is all life itself. There is nothing which science can accept without question, without doubt. The true scientific spirit is the antithesis of dogma, of faith. Scientific method is more basic than scientific "fact" or theory. We are constantly faced with the necessity of assimilating "new facts" which have been revealed to us by the application of the scientific method to "old facts." Laws, theories, hypotheses represent generalizations concerning a certain accumulation of data. They never represent an end point, a final codification. Even as a new theory or law is promulgated it opens to us new vistas, new areas of which we were hitherto unaware, which ultimately may lead to its reformulation or even its replacement by a different law. Psychoanalysis, then, if viewed

---

[1] Up to the present time a translation of this book from the German has not yet appeared. However, commentaries on certain parts of this correspondence are available in English (26, 30).

from this general point of view, must be looked upon as an attempt to codify certain observations regarding human thought and behavior, resulting from the application of a certain methodology. It has not the final definitive answers. Rather, it is a pathway into aspects of human nature which had not come under scientific scrutiny at the time Freud began his work.

I should like to state that I have deliberately attempted to exclude my own personal views and theories from the following lecture. Rather, I have attempted to present the generally accepted principles of psychoanalysis as they appear at the present time. Of course it is impossible to be completely objective in so fluid and controversial a field as psychoanalysis, so that I am sure anyone who wishes may easily find statements with which he can take issue. This is inevitable and unavoidable. However, I am not avoiding the expression of my own views for fear of criticism or attack. On the contrary, it is my feeling that I would be subverting the purpose of this series of lectures by presenting my own side of controversial questions without being able to present in detail the substantiating clinical and scientific evidence therefor. The purpose of these lectures is to acquaint an audience of scientists from other fields with the basic principles underlying, and the basic evidence for, psychoanalytic concepts. I shall attempt to adhere as closely as possible to this purpose.

In order to understand the position of psychoanalysis in relation to the biological and social sciences, we must briefly examine its history and development. It is only in this context that we can look upon it objectively and view its accomplishments and limitations. Historically it must not be forgotten that psychoanalysis derives from medicine. Its founder was a physician and remained within the medical sphere all his life. The starting point for the development of psychoanalysis lay in the fact that neurotic symptoms were unamenable to cure by any method then known. Even more important was the fact that they seemed meaningless, unpredictable, and inexplicable. No type of approach seemed to yield a satisfactory explanation of their existence. Freud entered the scientific scene at a time when the impact of the Darwinian evolutionary theory was tremendous. The bewildering chaos of animal life had suddenly become ordered, logical, coherent, rational. The principle of evolution had revolutionized the approach to life. Man had taken his place in the evolutionary scale as a highly developed animal. He was no longer a divine creation, static and unchanging, but a phenomenon of nature, who could be studied and examined as a product of natural forces. If biologically man was a natural phenomenon, then perhaps psychologically he was also. In this intensely biological and rational atmosphere Freud approached the problem of the neuroses of man.

The basic problem which first confronted Freud as a physician and as a scientist was the elucidation of the neurotic symptoms which he observed in his patients. While on the surface they appeared to present a bewildering array of disconnected data, perhaps beneath the surface there lay some unifying or ordering principle, some common denominator, which would make them also coherent, rational, logical. They, too, in spite of their diversity, must be amenable to systematic study, just as were the biological phenomena of nature, as had been demonstrated by Darwin. Yet none of the objective methods of investigation had yielded any rational explanation for the diversity of neurotic symptoms. A new technique, a new method of observation was necessary. With the development of a new specialized technique of observation, theoretical formulations of significance emerged.

The prehistory of psychoanalysis begins with Freud's contact with Charcot and Bernheim (17). With these men he observed the use of hypnosis to remove hysterical symptoms, at least temporarily. He was particularly impressed and puzzled by the fact that through posthypnotic suggestion individuals could be made to do things for reasons of which they were completely unaware. Yet later they could become aware of the suggestions given them which had caused them to behave as they had. In other words, the ideas motivating their actions were still present in them, although they did not know it. Herein lies the germ of the concept of unconscious forces, which forms a basic cornerstone in the development of psychoanalysis. Freud reasoned that if individuals could be made to do things for reasons unknown to themselves, perhaps unknown forces also lay behind neurotic symptoms which cause them to develop and yet remain beyond the conscious control of the patients. Even more important, perhaps if the patients became aware of the reasons for their symptoms they could then control and overcome them.

Freud then began to investigate the neurotic symptoms of his patients by means of hypnosis. In conjunction with Breuer (4) he was able to demonstrate that psychological traumata in the past life of his patients, of which they were completely unaware, played a dynamic role in the genesis of their symptoms. Further, he could demonstrate that if the individual could become aware of these events the symptoms could be resolved, at least temporarily.

Four important deductions resulted from these observations:

1. The source of neurotic symptoms was not to be found in the pathophysiological sphere, but in the psychological.
2. Neurotic symptoms were not random, meaningless, purposeless phenomena, but were *determined* by factors within the individual, and could be understood if these factors were discovered.

3. The forces which created the conflict and which resulted in the appearance of the symptoms were unknown to the patients themselves.
4. Sexual traumata in the childhood of the individual appeared as dominant factors among the forces which lead to the appearance of neurotic symptoms.

THE TURNING POINT OF PSYCHOANALYSIS

In his early studies Freud was convinced of the objective reality of the traumatic experiences of his patients. He was able in numerous instances to confirm the actual occurrences through outside sources. For instance, in a paper on the "Defense Neuro-psychoses" in 1894 (12) he clearly states that the sexual traumata of his patients were objectively confirmed. In fact he goes to great pains to assure his readers of the existence of objective evidence for his findings.

However, shortly thereafter he found that he could no longer maintain this point of view. He states (18):

When this aetiology broke down under its own improbability and under contradiction in definitely ascertainable circumstances, the result at first was helpless bewilderment. . . . Perhaps I persevered only because I had no choice and could not then begin again at anything else. At last came the reflection that, after all, one has no right to despair because one has been deceived in one's expectations; one must revise them. If hysterics trace back their symptoms to fictitious traumas, this new fact signifies that they create such scenes in fantasy, and psychical reality requires to be taken into account alongside actual reality. This was soon followed by the recognition that these fantasies were intended to cover up the auto-erotic activity of early childhood, to gloss it over and raise it to a higher level, and then from behind the fantasies, the whole range of the child's sexual life came to light.

In another article he states (15):

These [hysterical symptoms] now no longer appeared as direct derivations of repressed memories of sexual experiences in childhood; but, on the contrary, it appeared that between the symptoms and the infantile impressions were interpolated the patient's fantasies (memory-romances), created mostly during the years of adolescence and relating on the one side to the symptoms into which they were directly transformed. Only after the factor of the hysterical fantasies had been introduced did the structure of the neurosis and its relation to the patient's life become perspicuous. . . .

I quote these paragraphs at length because they represent a turning point in the history of psychoanalysis. Up to this point Freud had concerned himself with the elucidation of symptoms in neurotic individuals. However, if the events which resulted in neurotic symptoms were apparently products of the patient's fantasy, then subjective psychological factors had to be granted a reality which they had never been given before. (It should be understood, of course, that fantasies derive from and have their ultimate basis in real experiences.)

Freud drew certain important conclusions from these observations:

1. Neurotic symptoms are determined by the past experiences of the individual, whether these experiences were real or fantasy.

2. Neurotic symptoms cannot be understood by the study of their objective manifestations. They can only be understood in terms of their symbolic meaning, i.e., as a compromise between conflicting forces.

3. The fantasies, the imagined occurrences, have as much if not more force than the real events by which they are ultimately determined.

4. These fantasies differ in their characteristics from logical thought processes.

Freud therefore concluded that only by increasing the dimensions of observation to include subjective experiences could he arrive at an understanding of the observable clinical phenomena of the neuroses. Fantasy, however, is not confined to pathological states alone. It is a universal phenomenon in all human beings. Thus, having observed the importance of fantasy in pathological states, Freud speculated that it might also play a significant role in nonpathological states as well. This is not at all unusual in the history of medicine. We have frequently been led to the study of the physiological function of an organ by first having our attention focused upon it through its dysfunction. The dysfunction alters the normal function so that we can examine it more clearly. I shall return to this point of the transition from pathological to normal states later.

However, I should like to make one thing clear before proceeding with my main line of thought. In so far as psychoanalysis is a method of treating sick individuals, it retains many of the features common to all other specialties in medicine. There is no field of medical practice which is not part "art" and part "science." The actual treatment of the individual patient cannot be reduced to completely scientific experimental terms. That is, in actual practice we do not have optimal control of all the variables in each case. There always remains an uncontrollable element. Research in clinical medicine, because of the nature of the material with which it deals, can never control the variables in its experiments as well as can be done in the laboratory. I would like to differentiate carefully what I am going to discuss from the actual use of psychoanalysis as a method of treatment. What I wish to deal with here are the data, the techniques, the observations, and the theories which have been derived from clinical observation.

THE SUBJECT MATTER OF PSYCHOANALYSIS

Before we can proceed further I think it is important that we clarify for ourselves the problem of the subject matter of psychoanalysis. What aspect of natural phenomena did psychoanalysis take upon itself to examine? This may seem a superfluous question, because in most fields of science it requires no elucidation. However, psychoanalysis occupies a unique position in this regard. It is my feeling that much of the controversy about psychoanalysis and much of the confusion which exists with regard to it is based upon the lack of clarity about this basic point. If the scope of the natural phenomena which psychoanalysis has chosen to observe is clearly understood, much of the obscurity surrounding it will be dissipated. Up to the time of Freud it was generally accepted that methods of observing objective factors, if sufficiently refined and controlled, would lead ultimately to the solution of the mysteries of nature. This was also assumed to be valid for human thought and action. Freud introduced the concept that human reactions could not be understood by the observation of objective factors alone but only through the observation of additional subjective factors, the motivations underlying overt action. Whereas all other branches of science attempt to exclude, to minimize subjective intrusions, feeling that they invalidate their results, psychoanalysis, in contradistinction, attempts to exaggerate, to stimulate these very factors, in order to observe and examine them, taking them as its proper subject of observation.

With the full realization of the significance of fantasy (that is, imagined occurrences) in the life of the individual, Freud broadened the scope of psychoanalysis far beyond the realm of the neuroses to which it had until then been confined. For fantasy is not confined to the realm of pathology. It is part of the common experience of all men. With the recognition of the reality of the subjective, psychoanalysis burst through its bonds in the pathological and extended itself into a whole realm of psychic activity. From this point on, all types of subjective experience became the focal point of psychoanalytic investigation, and have remained so until the present time.

Psychoanalysis, then, becomes a field which deals primarily with the nature and characteristics of the *"nonrational"* elements in the human being. I have deliberately chosen this term (nonrational) rather than other more generally accepted terms in order to delineate this important problem of the proper subject matter of psychoanalysis on a descriptive level. I hope that the significance of this choice will become evident in what follows. By the term "nonrational" I mean to include the broad realm of psychological phenomena which are not, or at least are only in part, subject to the direct control of the logical thought processes of the conscious mind. These include fantasy, daydream, night dream, nightmare, irrational feelings, impulses, and emotions, and convictions, prejudices, slips, etc. I do not mean to imply that feelings and impulses are always nonrational. The more they are correlated to and commensurate with the stimuli from the external world, the less nonrational is their character. Psychoanalysis attempts to observe and describe those factors which precede purposive overt action and logical thought. Putting it in other terms, we might state that logical thought and overt behavior represent a final common pathway upon which innumerable stimuli impinge. If I may be permitted an analogy from the field of neurology: Conscious thought and action may be compared to the lower motor neuron of the nervous system, the final common pathway for all motor and secretory discharge. However, the stimuli which impinge upon this pathway may arise from diverse sources and traverse many paths within the central nervous system before reaching this final common pathway. It is these stimuli which are comparable to the processes which psychoanalysis attempts to investigate.

Psychoanalysis is related to biology by the fact that man has much in common with other animals. However, man is a particular kind of animal with certain characteristics which differentiate him from other animals.[2] Man is organized on a different order of complexity and so functions on a different level of integration because of his very biological characteristics. Most important from the psychoanalytic point of view is his ability to symbolize both the external and the internal world, particularly through his language ability, that is, his ability to use one object to represent something else. Perhaps we might even characterize psychoanalysis as the study of certain aspects of the processes of symbolization in the human being. The realization of the significance of symbolization, in the processes which precede the coming-into-consciousness and the carrying-into-overt-action in the neurotic individual, forms another one of the bridges to the investigation of the role of these processes in the normal individual.

Psychoanalysis is also related to and part of the broad field of psychology, which classically takes as its province the study of the special senses of the human being and the conscious aspects of human behavior. In this way these

2 If we appreciate the nature of the subject matter chosen by psychoanalysis, we can understand better the theoretical objections raised by Dr. Kubie to the attempt to validate psychoanalytic observation and theory by means of animal experimentation. We do not know if animals experience subjective phenomena similar to those experienced by human beings. There are certain observations which would lead us to suspect that they possibly do. However, even if this were definitively established, we have no method by which they can communicate to us the content of these subjective experiences. And it is just this content which is the subject matter of psychoanalysis.

two fields supplement and complement each other. Psychoanalysis is further related to those fields dealing with the social aspects of human beings, in so far as the symbolic process enters their sphere of observation. Since nonrational processes also occur in the social and cultural fields, psychoanalytic investigation and theory have bearing in the fields of anthropology, ethnology, sociology, history, etc. These fields must formulate their principles and theories at their own integrative levels, and cannot be subsumed under psychoanalytic concepts alone. But their principles, in so far as they deal with the nonrational elements in their observations, must be correlated with the findings of psychoanalysis. In addition, psychoanalysis finds application in the aesthetic fields (art, literature, etc.) but only in so far as the objects produced reflect nonrational elements. Psychoanalysis cannot "explain" a work of art, but it can cast some light on the subsurface forces manifested therein.

If we now return to our outline of the course of development of psychoanalysis and examine the major works of Freud, following his realization of the significance of psychic reality, we can easily trace the application of this finding in his scientific investigations. Parallel to his numerous clinical papers on the neuroses, we find in the heroic first decade of psychoanalysis (1895-1905) his major observational works. The very titles of his books in this period illustrate the scope of his investigations and the transition which I have stressed. We have the *Interpretation of Dreams* (1900), the *Psychopathology of Everyday Life* (1904), the *Three Contributions to the Theory of Sex* (1905), and *Wit and Its Relation to the Unconscious* (1905).

What do we find in these books if we reduce them to their simplest common denominator? The subject matter of psychoanalysis had extended beyond its original domain, the neuroses and their symptoms, into all aspects of human thought and action in which nonrational factors enter. Freud applied the findings which he had made in relation to hysterical symptoms, namely, that impulses, forces, fantasies, ideas of which the individual was unaware expressed themselves in symbolic ways, that unconscious forces played a definite role in determining the manner of overt expression.

The subject matter of psychoanalysis, then, is the nonrational, the nonlogical, the emotional elements in the human being. Rational action, purposive behavior, logical thought processes are not directly within the province of psychoanalysis. These processes are considered derivative, secondary to what lies behind them. I cannot emphasize too strongly that psychoanalysis does not directly concern itself with rational manifestations as such, but rather with what leads up to, what motivates, what brings about conscious reactions. Psychoanalysis investigates the nature of the processes behind conscious thought and purposive action but not the character and quality of rational processes in themselves. It attempts to answer the question of what nonrational factors enter into the conscious behavior of the individual, and it stops there. It does not attempt to explain the nature of external reality but rather deals with those factors which cause different individuals to apprehend this reality differently, e.g., it does not attempt to explain the laws of logic as such but rather why one individual uses them in one way and another in a different way. Its field lies in the exploration of the effect of inner reality on the ways in which individuals relate to external reality. In any given situation there is a mixture of internal and external reality factors, as was pointed out by Dr. Kubie in his lecture, both in his text and graphically through his diagram. One of the great problems in psychoanalysis, to which some of its practitioners have unfortunately fallen prey, is the failure to realize this constant admixture. They have sought a unitary and exclusive "cause." They have fallen prey to the mechanistic will-o'-the-wisp of simple cause and effect. As will be discussed later, such thinking cannot be applied in the psychological and social spheres. It is "pretty" because of its simplicity, but basically fallacious. We must be careful of the "either—or" and look for the "both—and." For practical purposes we must recognize that in some situations the external environmental factors dominate so completely as to minimize the role of internal factors, and vice versa. Theoretically, however, neither the one nor the other can be completely excluded.

It should be pointed out that Freud never presumed that he had fully explained rational thought and action by the elucidation of the unconscious forces which lie behind them. What he did attempt to demonstrate was that the surface appearance was not the complete story.

It is my feeling that much of the misunderstanding surrounding psychoanalysis stems from the fact that it is expected to furnish a total answer to human behavior, which it does not presume to do. Psychoanalysis may, for example, be able to demonstrate the emotional basis for the interest of a particular scientist in his particular field, but it does not presume to explain his actual scientific activity in this field. The significance of the influence of external reality upon the rational activities of the individual lies in other disciplines than psychoanalysis. Parenthetically it might be added that unfortunately some psychoanalysts themselves do not always fully appreciate the nature of the subject matter in their chosen field, so that they at times wander into strange pastures and express opinions in areas beyond the province of their specialized competence and knowledge. Because psychoanalysis has emphasized the importance of unconscious forces, it does not follow that they are the *only* factors or, in a given situation, the predominant factors involved. This is particularly true with regard to the application of psychoanalysis to related fields.

It may seem that I have labored the question of the sphere of operation of psychoanalysis, but I feel that it is necessary in order to continue with the rest of my discussion. I hope that I have succeeded in defining the area of observation of psychoanalysis, its scope and limitations.

THE METHODOLOGY OF PSYCHOANALYSIS

In my opening paragraphs I stated that psychoanalysis developed a specialized technique of observation in order to investigate those natural phenomena which came within its province. Each science develops a specific methodology in order to investigate its chosen objectives. The technique developed permits particular observation of its data, but by limiting its scope it of necessity eliminates other aspects of the problem. This is part of the method of science. Science isolates its material in order to better examine it. It pays a price for this isolation in that it divorces its object from its natural relations with the rest of the world. Only at a later stage can it reintegrate its object in its natural setting.

The basic purpose of a methodology is the control of the variables which encroach upon the object under investigation. A science must establish its techniques and experimental situation in such a manner as to control and limit the variables which tend to obscure its data. As I have previously stated, the methodology of scientific observation and investigation of natural phenomena is more basic than the theoretical conclusions derived from the data observed. Theories may change, may stand or fall with further observation, but as long as the method meets the criteria of scientific accuracy the data thereby gathered remain valid observations of nature, provide the "facts"—the raw material with which science works.

Theories are attempts to synthesize, to generalize, to find order and regularity in the raw data. But they are not irreplaceable. They grow and change with the increase of observational data. However, unless the methods permit accurate observation of the phenomena of nature, they will sooner or later fall and be replaced by others. The whole history of science consists of constant changes in the hypotheses, the theories, the laws which have been derived from the data.

Because of the nature of the observational data required in psychoanalysis, the problem of technique and experimental situation is crucial. After the recognition of the significance of unconscious factors in the genesis of neurotic symptoms, the basic methodological problem became to devise some method whereby the manifestations of these unconscious forces could be more thoroughly observed and investigated. This involved the exclusion of the disturbing element of rational logical thought, which interfered with the production of the subjective material which Freud wished to investigate. He at first attempted to continue his investigations by means of the technique of hypnosis. However, he quickly found that this technique was too uncertain, too erratic for consistent use.

Freud then sought other means to achieve his end. This means he found in the technique of "free association." Freud states: "The history of psychoanalysis proper . . . begins with the new technique that dispenses with hypnosis" (19). But in order to achieve free association, or an approximation thereof, a certain setting was required. If we look upon free association as the technical instrument of Freud's methodology, we may look upon the setting in which it occurs as the experimental situation. This experimental situation consists of two parts: (1) the complete privacy of the patient and the analyst (subject and observer), and (2) interviews of a specified length at fixed frequent regular intervals over a considerable period of time. With these two factors of isolation and of time, Freud achieved in some measure the necessary conditions under which variables could be controlled sufficiently to yield observational (clinical) data from which generalizations could be made.

Let us examine further the instrument and the experimental situation. The technique of free association attempts to fulfill the need to eliminate conscious control over thought. It does so by requiring the patient to eliminate the discriminatory faculty of consciousness and to say anything which comes to his mind without regard for relevancy, coherency, logic, social amenity, etc.; in short, any type of control which he ordinarily uses. This may sound simple, but it is extraordinarily difficult to achieve, as anyone who may have tried it can testify. It is difficult to do when one is completely alone, and more so in the presence of another. Because of this latter factor, the experimental situation necessary to achieve this follows logically, i.e., privacy, frequency, and regularity. It is only in privacy that one can approximate free association. It is only if one sees another individual frequently and regularly for a considerable period that one can overcome the barriers of the logical processes sufficiently to produce actual free association.[3]

---

[3] In part, the "analytic incognito" represents a corollary to this aspect of the experimental situation. The anonymity of the analyst encourages free association. Knowledge of the personal and social life of the analyst tends to create barriers, due to the awareness of him as a distinct individual. Parenthetically, the analytic incognito also is a factor with regard to the problem of the reduction of the number of variables complicating the analytic situation. The factor of control of variables will be discussed later.

However, there is an underlying assumption inherent in the technique of free association which requires discussion at this point. The paradox of free association lies in the assumption that it is not "free," but rather determined. In other words, the assumption is that apparently random thoughts, superficially disconnected, are determined beneath the surface by some connections of which the subject is unaware. The lack of relation between the utterances is only an apparent one. If we look beneath this surface we will be able to find their real significance.

This assumption is actually an extension to the psychological realm of what has long been recognized and accepted in the physical realm—the principle of determinism, the principle that there is a relationship between two events or occurrences which follow one another in time. Freud extended the concept of determinism to psychological phenomena with far-reaching effect. Causality, however, is a relative matter. It depends upon the ability of the observer to control the number of variables involved in the experimental situation. If most or all of the variables can be controlled, we may speak of the relation between stimulus and response as specific and exclusive. If, however, as in the experimental situation in psychoanalysis, there remain many uncontrollable variables, we can merely speak of a sufficient or apparent relation, without being able to attribute exact specificity or exclusiveness to it.

The technique of free association permitted the exploration of hitherto inaccessible data in the realm of psychology. By at least partially diminishing the effect of rational processes, Freud was able to investigate these interrelationships and observe an entire realm of natural phenomena which had been hitherto unexplored.

I have attempted to elaborate here the methodology of psychoanalysis in order to demonstrate that, granting the choice of subject matter, the methodology devised is one which permits adequate observation. However, it must be recognized that the technical instrument of free association represented a marked departure from the type of technique which had hitherto been used in the observation of natural phenomena. It is an instrument which is difficult to control and, above all, useless in the presence of other observers. It is, therefore, understandable that scientists in other fields should question the nature of the data in psychoanalysis because of the nature of the technique. Both the data and the technique depart radically from our general concept of scientific observation. It is for this reason that I have spent so much time in elaborating the type of observational data sought in psychoanalysis. Because of the unique character of the material, a unique approach is required. Herein lies the paradox of psychoanalysis: the very things which other fields of science seek to exclude from their experiments, which they consider nullify and distort their results (the "gremlins" of the experimental situation, so to speak) are the phenomena which psychoanalysis seeks to explore. The very thing which other fields use as a means for observation psychoanalysis chose to exclude from its observation. Rational thought and action obscure and disturb the observational data of psychoanalysis as much as nonrational phenomena obscure and disturb the observational data of the natural and physical sciences.

THE CLINICAL PHENOMENA OF PSYCHOANALYSIS

Let us turn our attention to the clinical phenomena which emerged as a result of the application of this method. The first observation which was made, when free association was used under the prescribed conditions, was that associations brought into consciousness a whole series of events and occurrences, feelings, fantasies, attitudes, and impulses from the past life of the patient, reaching far back into childhood. Much of this material had not been hitherto consciously remembered. Nor could it be elicited by direct questioning. The nature of the recalled material dealt with those aspects of the life of the individual which were consciously alien to his personality or unacceptable in the eyes of society. In other words, the apparently random talk which resulted from the use of "free association" led to the exposure of things which distressed and disturbed the individual but of which he was not previously aware or about which he felt guilt and shame. The patient re-experienced traumatic situations in his past life, particularly as they related to emotionally significant people.

What was the nature of the things about which disturbance was felt? Much of it dealt with sexual content: feelings, desires, impulses, fantasies, acts which the individual felt were wrong, bad, immoral, perverse, forbidden. Other things which entered dealt with hostile and violent feelings toward people, particularly those toward whom the individual consciously felt tender and affectionate, and conversely with tender feelings toward those to whom the patient felt consciously hostile and antagonistic.

Up to this point I have not mentioned dreams, which play an important technical role in psychoanalysis. Actually, the use of dreams is secondary to the technique of free association. Without the latter we would still be in the stage of soothsaying and superstition with regard to this practically universal phenomenon. Dreams actually could be included under the more general heading of fantasy. They serve as an endless source of observational data. In the history of psychoanalysis they play a vital role. Freud called them the "via regia to the unconscious." But without the leaven of free association they have little significance in themselves. They furnish us with invaluable keys to the unconscious processes in the individual, but only when they are used as a starting point for free association.

The dream served as the focal point for the investigation of the nature and characteristics of the unconscious processes. With the application of the technique of free association to the dream material the hidden aspects of the dream could be elucidated. This perhaps requires further elaboration. The "manifest content" of the dream is the dream as it is initially recalled and presented by the dreamer. When the dream is used as the starting point for free association, i.e., when the dreamer takes the dream content as the stimulus and says whatever occurs to him about any of its elements, the "latent content" gradually emerges. The manifest and latent contents revealed themselves to be quite different. In unraveling the disguises of the dream it was found that certain processes were used to prevent clear expression of the significance of the dream. These processes were called by Freud the "dream-work." They distorted the dream so as to mask its underlying meaning to the dreamer. These processes include condensation, displacement, symbolization, and plastic representation. Again, perhaps brief elaboration is necessary at this point. Free association revealed that the manifest dream was a much condensed version of the latent dream content. Separate events, people, objects could be easily telescoped into one. A person in a dream could be found to have the attributes of several different people in real life. Similarly, significant things could find representation in trivial aspects of the dream, or vice versa, i.e., they could be displaced and thereby distorted. In a similar manner many things in the dream could be revealed by free association to represent other things, i.e., to become symbols. And last, dreams were predominantly visual in character, representing the translation of thoughts and wishes into images, which in turn have to be retranslated into words. It could also be observed that events in the dream were lumped together without regard to sequence in time or space, that contradictions existed side by side, and that things could be turned into their opposites. These processes and qualities are all associated with the state of unconsciousness. It will be obvious that these characteristics are in many respects the opposites of those associated with conscious processes, namely, logic, order, consistency, and sequentiality in time and space.

Further observation revealed that free association could not be easily carried through by many patients. When they attempted to use free association, resistances arose. The patients could not proceed freely and easily. They had no thoughts, they blocked, they discarded certain words or ideas, they were ashamed of certain ideas—in short, they resisted carrying out the conditions of the experiment as prescribed for them. These resistances were felt by the patients within themselves as blocks. They defended themselves against the thoughts, ideas, words which came to their minds. Either those thoughts were irrelevant or inconsequential, or they were too shameful, or too frightening, etc. Freud described many of these resistances in detail. Others have elaborated on various ways in which patients have been unable to co-operate. Thus, a long list of resistances was elaborated. Basically they all are related to the process of repression, the first resistance described by Freud. Repression (the active banishing from consciousness of ideas or impulses which are unacceptable to it) is a dynamic concept, i.e., the concept of a force which ejects, excludes. It appears to me that such mechanisms as intellectualization, rationalization, projection, denial, conversion, introjection, reaction formation, etc., are descriptions of the vicissitudes to which the repressed ideas and impulses are subject, the modes of handling the repressed material. They are not necessarily in themselves dynamic. The manifestations of certain of these different mechanisms and the experimental evidence for their existence were discussed by Dr. Hilgard in his lectures.

A further peculiar clinical phenomenon also became apparent under the stimulus of the use of the technique of free association. This is subsumed under the concept of transference. Freud observed that the resistances to free association which patients manifested develop in relation to the analyst (observer). To quote Freud (14):

They [the transferences] are new editions or facsimiles of the tendencies and fantasies which are aroused and made conscious during the progress of the analysis; but they have this peculiarity, which is characteristic for their species, that they replace some earlier person by the person of the physician. To put it another way: a whole series of psychological experiences are revived, not as belonging to the past, but as applying to the person of the physician at the present moment.

The phenomenon of transference, which is one of the clinical cornerstones of psychoanalysis, is definitely demonstrable within the experimental setting of psychoanalysis. Because of the intensity and duration of the contact and the resultant relationship between the patient and physician, the transference takes on a particularly intense character.

Up to this point I have dealt with the clinical phenomena which appeared when the methodology of psychoanalysis was applied to the analysis of neurotic individuals. Let us turn to the application of the methodology to the so-called normal. I mentioned earlier that the recognition by Freud of the importance of fantasy in the genesis of neurotic disturbances represented also the first step in the transition to the normal. For since all individuals have fantasies, perhaps psychoanalysis could be applied to similar phenomena as they occurred in nonneurotic individuals as well, and to phenomena which appeared to be related to symptoms in the neuroses. This material broadened the scope of investigation of psychoanalysis considerably and serves as the basis for the widespread interest in it. Had it remained purely a technical medical method of handling neurotic disturbances, the interest in and controversy over psychoanalysis would never have reached the proportions which it has. However, Freud, by applying his technique of free association to himself and to the many nonrational aspects of human thought and action, made psychoanalysis into a study of all human beings.

Similar resistances to those which made free association difficult for patients in the analytic setting could also be observed in the nonanalytic situation. The patient's characteristic mode of resistance in analysis was also manifested in the manner in which he handled situations out of the interview. From the concept of resistances, then, there could be generalized the concept of characteristic modes of defense. It is because they are not peculiar to the analytic situation as such that they were the first aspects of psychoanalysis to be "domesticated" by clinical psychology, as so aptly put by Dr. Hilgard. It is also because they exist outside of the analytic situation as such that they can be examined experimentally and verified.

We have now reached the point at which we can raise a basic question: Are the phenomena observed by means of psychoanalytic technique demonstrable by this technique alone? Can we expect validation from extra-analytic observation?

It is, of course, entirely possible to dismiss the findings of psychoanalysis by saying that, because of the technique and experimental setting, the observations obtained are artifacts and not natural phenomena. However, there are few serious scientists who would today adopt this attitude. They may question some aspects of the material and the theoretical conclusions derived therefrom, but they cannot discard the structure *in toto*.

Let us first examine the question of the scientific basis for the use of free association, the technical instrument of psychoanalysis. It was stated that the assumption underlying the use of free association was that it was not free, but rather determined by unconscious conflictual forces. If we knew the nature of the disturbing conflict in an individual and could induce him to use free association, would the unconscious conflict emerge into consciousness? Luria (33), in an ingenious experiment, was able to confirm the validity of this technique. He first administered word association tests to a number of normal subjects. These tests contained certain words relating to the conflict situation to be suggested to them later. The subjects were then placed in deep hypnosis. A situation was suggested to them in which they had done something about which they felt conflict and guilt. Posthypnotic amnesia was suggested and they were awakened. The word association test was readministered. The results differed markedly from the original prehypnotic test. They showed marked blocking on the key words connected with the episode suggested under hypnosis. However, a further test was done which was most significant. They were given an indifferent stimulus word, and requested to say whatever words came into their minds. From this indifferent stimulus, the word chain wandered through many associations until gradually more and more words dealing with the hypnotically suggested episode appeared. This finally led, through the production of many of the significant words, to a conscious recall of the whole episode. This experiment has been repeated by others and confirmed.

Actually, while it furnished experimental evidence for the validity of the technique of free association, it leaves open the question which psychoanalysis would pose for itself. What is the meaning of the conflictual situation to the subject? Where does it fit into the unconscious fantasies of the individual concerned? This can only be elucidated by further exploration in the analytic setting.

In general we may look for extra-analytic confirmation of analytic concepts in those aspects of observation and theory which are not directly related to the use of the technique of free association. The more "biological" the behavior the more likely is the validation through the use of experimental animals.

Dr. Hilgard referred to Masserman's (34) interesting article on animal experimentation. In this Masserman demonstrated that he can produce the same behavioral patterns by frustration in animals as appear in human neuroses. There is no question of the fact that there are numerous and striking analogies. But one must not compare these experiments with psychoanalytic research. Masserman mentions in his article that each cat reacted differently to the frustration experiments. Psychoanalytic investigation proper begins at the point at which these experiments end. Its problem, in its own frame of reference, is this: What in the previous life experiences of one cat makes it develop a ritual, in another a phobia, in a third anxietylike symptoms, etc.? This is the crucial question of psychoanalysis, not that frustration produces neurotic patterns of behavior. What is the history, the background which led to this pattern? It is here that we need means of communication with each cat. To examine the problem of neuroses in cats we would have to talk cat language, if there is such, or teach a cat to speak our language in order to tell us its fantasies, previous experiences, and feelings. Without this we do not advance in the strict psychoanalytic sense.

I do not mean to minimize thereby the significance of Masserman's work but to show its relation to the specific problems of psychoanalysis. In these experiments, for example, he had investigated the problem of the nature and genesis of aggression. His findings in this regard are of significance and importance, but unfortunately are aside from the main thread of our discussion at this time.

We might state that the affectual responses of human beings (primitive automatic responses) are subject to animal experimentation, but not those in which the subjective processes play a significant role. That the human being should respond in some measure in the same manner as other animals is not surprising. That the same general type of stimulus should produce the same general type of response in both animals and humans is also to be anticipated. *However, the events which occur between the stimulus and the response are the things with which psychoanalysis is concerned.* These events can only be examined in human beings, not in animals, because we have no way of communicating with the animal. Psychoanalysis has demonstrated, if nothing else, that conclusions regarding the processes leading to a specific type of response cannot be reached by evaluation of the objective behavior alone.

THE THEORETICAL STRUCTURE OF PSYCHOANALYSIS

It was stated earlier that the development of psychoanalysis began under the impact of the Darwinian theory of biological evolution. The fruitfulness of the application of this theory to psychology should not blind us to the fact that it also placed certain limitations on the development of psychoanalysis by binding it so strongly to biology.

It would indeed be very interesting to examine the various theoretical constructs which were developed by Freud to explain the variety of phenomena which were revealed by the methodology which he developed. It would be even more fascinating to study the history of his theoretical structures and see how they evolved in a constant struggle to explain the clinical data. However, I am afraid this would take us too far afield. I shall, therefore, confine myself to a discussion of the libido theory. I chose this aspect of psychoanalytic theory to discuss, in part, because it is the most widely known and, in part, because it represents an attempt to synthesize a coherent picture of the development of the human being, which closely parallels in form, if not in content, the biological theory of evolution.

The existence of sexual aberrations of all types is not a psychoanalytic finding. The deviations from normal genital union had been described and catalogued extensively before Freud began his work (5, 29). The recent Kinsey (28) report certainly furnishes sufficient evidence regarding the wide variety of sexual experiences in the human being. However, no explanation bringing these phenomena under a unified head had been forthcoming. Freud, by broadening the concept of sexuality beyond that of genital union of the opposite sexes, was able to bring a series of enormously diverse phenomena under one unified concept. By so doing he also brought under the heading of sexuality many phenomena which had not hitherto been considered sexual.

What led Freud to the assumption of his basic concept of infantile sexuality (23), about which so much question exists?

Inherent in his whole approach to the problem of sexuality is the concept of psychological evolution, of the genetic (historical) development of the human mind. Clinically this concept forced itself to his attention in two ways: first, in the historical material produced by patients through the use of free association; second, in the clinical phenomenon of the transference, in which the patient transferred inappropriate attitudes from individuals in his past life to the analyst. If we accept the concept of biological evolution, both phylogenetic and ontogenetic, we must accept the concept of psychogenetic evolution if we are to regard the psychic manifestations in human beings as having a biological, i.e., a material, origin. Herein we see also the impact of the Darwinian evolutionary theory upon Freud. In the scientific atmosphere in which Freud emerged it was inevitable that human psychic phenomena be examined from this point of view.

With the use of free association, Freud found in his neurotic patients evidences of fantasies and experiences which included all the manifestations of the so-called perversions of adult life. Moreover, these experiences or fantasies related to the early childhood of the patients. Since no one questioned the fact that the perversions of adults were of a sexual nature, Freud reasoned that the phenomena in childhood were of a sexual nature also. The relation of fantasies in neurotic patients to the activities of adult sexual deviates was very striking. The nature of the material produced by the patients dealt with feelings and impulses which centered around the mouth, the anus, and the phallus. These he called the erogenous (or erotogenic) zones. In other words, Freud found that there was a genetic relationship between adult perversions and the infantile fantasies of his patients. This led to observations regarding the activities in children. There is no doubt of the fact that there is, among children, a great deal of activity which must be considered sexual in the broader Freudian use of the term. There are many extra-analytic observations confirming the existence of the behavior in children which psychoanalysis considers to be in the sexual sphere (37).

In the psychoanalytic investigation of the neuroses and the perversions it was found that the psychogenesis of these illnesses could be traced back to a series of childhood fantasies and traumata which the individual had not been able to master and which had caused him to remain "fixated" at that level of psychosexual development, or, having advanced beyond it, to have "regressed" to it as a result of later traumata. Freud at one time illustrated his concept of fixation and regression by means of a military analogy which may be useful here. If an army meets with strong resistance, its advance halts, i.e., it is blocked at this point. If it overcomes the resistance and continues to advance into hostile territory, it must leave relatively large forces behind to protect and safeguard its lines of communication, thereby relatively decreasing the number of forces at its disposal for further advance. In terms of the libido theory, each stage of development represents an advance into new territory. Depending upon the amount of conflict and difficulty which the individual has had at the particular stage of development, he will have more or less energy (force) at his disposal to tackle new problems. Freud also noted that if an adult met with frustration in his sexual expression, he returned to some form of infantile sexual activity. There is no question of the fact that regressive behavior results from sexual frustration, but this does not confirm the psychoanalytic concepts regarding their psychogenesis. It is my feeling that in this field, up to the present time, there is no technical approach other than free association. If we accept free association as a scientific instrument, we must perforce accept its conclusions with regard to the interrelationships of the phenomena of sexuality.

To explain the observed phenomena, Freud postulated an energy, libido, in the form of a drive or instinct, with certain properties which differentiated it from more physiological drives. In these latter, a somatic change gives rise to a sensory experience, which precipitates a specific action leading to the elimination of the somatic change which caused the urge to appear. In other words, somatic tension leads to a specific mode of discharge of this tension. Examples of such drives are breathing, thirst, hunger, urination, etc. These drives are characterized by their urgency and the need, from the point of view of the organism, of relatively immediate gratification. Postponement endangers the integrity of the organism (32).

On the other hand, the sexual drive does not show the characteristic of the need for immediate gratification. It can be postponed, delayed in discharge without endangering the integrity of the organism. It can change its aim and object if frustrated in its original goal. And it can be repressed, i.e., the individual can become completely unaware of sexual tension. It is interesting to note that in the presence of prolonged life-endangering situations, e.g., in concentration camps, the sexual drive disappears almost completely (25). There is sufficient extra-analytic evidence to confirm these characteristics of the sexual drive (9). And there is little controversy in the analytic field about the phenomenology of the sexual drive.

On the basis of his observations, Freud constructed his libido theory. Reduced to a bare outline, this theory states that the libido or sexual energy is concentrated around the various erogenous zones at different periods of the individual's development. During the first year of life it is predominantly around the oral zone, during the second and third years around the anal, and during the fourth and fifth years of life around the phallic zone (41). It then undergoes repression (the basis for the universal phenomenon of infantile amnesia) during the latency period, following the resolution of the Oedipal phase,[4] and reappears during puberty and adolescence under the stimulus of the development of the gonads, reaching its final form normally in genital sexuality. Only if the various stages, the various shifts of the libido energy, are successfully worked through by the individual will he be able to achieve genital maturity. The vicissitudes to which the individual is subjected in relation to his external relations with the world will condition whether he successfully masters each developmental level and goes on to the next. For the child the external world consists primarily of his mother and father or their surrogates, who can modify, form, shape, direct, influence the manifestations of the libido. But basically the energy is biologically predetermined in its course. On the basis of the various shifts of libidinal energy, the individual develops various reactions to, and relations with the external world (object relationships). Briefly the individual proceeds from a state without object relations in which the external world does not yet exist (the "primary narcissistic state"), through total then partial "incorporation" (identification), to "ambivalent" aims in which the object is an instrument for one's own pleasure, to real love ("object love") in which the object is accorded a right to exist outside of one's self (7). In this somewhat unwieldly sentence I have skeletonized an extremely complicated and intricate structure dealing with the

[4] The "Oedipus complex" is probably the most widely known and often misunderstood psychoanalytic concept. Therefore, it deserves special comment for this reason. However, it also occupies a key position in the libido theory, and in the controversy about this theory. In psychoanalytic literature the term "Oedipus complex" has been largely abandoned because of the narrowness of the concept of the complex. The Oedipal phase or conflict is considered to represent the climax of infantile sexual development. Around it the prototypes of future object relations crystallize, in the working through of the child's relations with its parents of both sexes.

whole problem of the psychoanalytic concept of the interrelationship between the individual and the world around him. In nontechnical language it represents an attempt to explain theoretically the observable ways in which children and adults relate to the external world in terms of the forces impinging upon them from within and without. It is not my purpose here to give a detailed account of this structure but rather to point out that such a theoretic structure has been developed.

In relation to this theory of the instinctual energy of the libido and its characteristics, psychoanalysis has elaborated a corresponding theory of the structure of the personality (id, ego, superego) and the various mental qualities (conscious, preconscious, unconscious). Dynamically the personality is viewed as deriving all its psychic energy from the "id," the reservoir of all instinctual urges. The individual at birth is all id; i.e., impulses seek direct discharge and immediate gratification. As the restrictions of the external world are imposed upon the infant, the ego forms. One might conceive of the ego as a bud which develops out of the id (as it appears in one of the rare diagrams used by Freud to illustrate his concepts [13]) or as a crust surrounding the id through which contact with the external world is established and maintained and the internal processes are channelized. The superego develops relatively late in the child's life, in relation to the phallic phase, under the impact of the Oedipal conflict. It derives from the ego (hence its name) and represents the internalization of external, primarily parental, dictates and demands upon the child. It is equivalent to, but not identical with, what is commonly called the conscience. These three aspects of the personality constantly interact to produce overt thought and behavior.

The theory of the mental qualities describes phenomenologically the states to which mental phenomena are related. Conscious material is that of which we are aware at the moment. Preconscious material is that of which we may not be fully aware but which can be easily recalled. Unconscious material, however, consists of all that which not only cannot be recalled "at will" but also cannot be recovered except through special means, e.g., free association, whether in the analytic situation itself or spontaneously under unusual circumstances, "in a flash" so to speak (24).

I should like to point out the areas of agreement and the areas of controversy in psychoanalysis around these theoretical constructs. There is little controversy among analysts regarding the phenomena which psychoanalysis has described. The great controversy lies in the question of the theory to explain the facts. This has been the cause of the numerous splits which have occurred in psychoanalysis both before and since the death of Freud, and which continue to the present day. This is, of course, not unique to psychoanalysis. In fact, it might be said that it is a healthy sign which signifies growth and development. The tremendous advances in physics, chemistry, biology, etc., have all resulted in controversies and splits on theoretical levels.

Perhaps if we were to accept Freud's own evaluation of psychoanalysis, much of this controversy, which unfortunately often becomes personalized and bitter, could be avoided, or at least could be maintained at the level of dispassionate scientific differences. Freud states (20):

Any line of investigation, no matter what its direction, which recognizes these two facts (transference and resistance) and takes them as the starting point of its work may call itself psychoanalysis, though it arrive at results other than my own. But anyone who takes up other sides of the problem while avoiding these two premises will hardly escape the charge of misappropriating by attempted impersonation, if he persists in calling himself a psychoanalyst.

Freud himself then places primary emphasis on the observable phenomena which result from the application of his technique rather than on the theoretical constructs developed to explain them. What underlies these controversies within the field of psychoanalysis which can lead to a situation such as that described in a recent report of the American Psychoanalytic Association Committee on the Evaluation of Psychoanalytic Therapy? This report states (36): "In order to evaluate a subject, one must first know of what that subject consists and since apparently there were no two individuals, not only of the Committee but of the society as a whole, who would agree to a definition of psychoanalysis, the Committee was at a loss as to how they were to know just what they were evaluating." I believe that the differences lie mainly in the theoretical approach rather than in questions of basic technique and data.

One broad group emphasizes the immutable basic biological nature of man and uses the libido theory as its theoretical structure. It reduces the observational data to their origin in the biological substratum of man. It is primarily interested in the forms of expression of these biological drives in the id which "contains everything that is inherited, that is present at birth, that is fixed in the constitution—above all, therefore, the instincts, which originate in the somatic organization and which find their first mental expression in the id in forms unknown to us. . . . This oldest portion of the mental apparatus remains the most important throughout life . . ." (21).

Another broad group (which I shall call, for the sake of brevity, the biosocial) accepts the existence of this biological substratum but does not necessarily regard it as immutable. It concerns itself more with the relation of man to the external world. It focuses its attention primarily on the problems of object relationships. It approaches the problem of the genetic development of the individual not in terms of what biological factors are thereby demonstrated but rather in terms of what effect object relationships have on the individual. The biological forces are not considered specific predetermined dynamic forces with specifically delimited goals, but a plastic energic substratum which can be molded and formed in different directions by the social and cultural milieu in which the individual exists.[5]

Perhaps it is best to illustrate the difference in approach through an example. The first group regards the Oedipal phase as a biological phenomenon, universal in all human beings, "not only in the life of the individual, but also in the history of the human species as a whole" (22). The other group regards this phase as a cultural phenomenon, dependent upon historical conditions, and not as a universal and invariable biological phenomenon.

Perhaps we might state the difference as one of approach. For one group man is approached as a biological animal with his psychological superstructure to be explained in biological terms. For the other, man's psychological development is on a different integrative level, which cannot be explained in biological terms alone. Psychological manifestations are inextricably interrelated to social, cultural, and economic factors which mold the underlying biological substratum.

Analogies are dangerous, but I should like to venture one which may serve as a partial illustration of the difference. In the development of language we know that the human being is born with the capacity to produce vocal sounds. There are definite inherited anatomical and physiological limitations to the types of sounds which may be produced. However, whatever the biological limitations upon the range of sounds which the human being can produce, the development of the specific language ability is dependent upon the social, cultural, and economic environment in which the individual is brought up.

In psychoanalytic terminology we might say that the first group poses its problems primarily from the point of view of an id psychology, while the other primarily concerns itself with the elaboration of an ego psychology, without primary interest in the derivation of the forces from specific biological

---

[5] I should like to emphasize the fact that the two broad groups which I have differentiated here on the basis of theoretical considerations should under no circumstances be confused with the existing organizational groups within the psychoanalytic societies. What I am discussing here deals with certain underlying assumptions which form the basis for further work or elaboration, and which are often taken for granted. In examining the work of individual psychoanalysts or the tenets of different schools, one often finds a nominal acceptance or espousal of one or the other group of assumptions outlined above, or an attempted union of the two divergent attitudes. However, critical examination may reveal the predominance of one or the other direction. In any case, the acceptance of either set of premises does not by any means coincide with organizational affiliation and should not be confused with it.

drives. The first group looks upon the biological substratum as defining and, so to speak, predetermining the modes of psychological expression. The second looks upon it as delimiting, in a physical sense, the modes of psychological expression, but not defining, directing, and predetermining them.

The ramifications of these basic theoretical problems extend throughout the field of psychoanalysis. Such concepts as the nature and meaning of aggression, the problem of sublimation, ego strength, feminine psychology, homosexuality, etc. are all inextricably tied to the basic theoretical assumptions which I attempted to delineate briefly above. Whether aggression (with its assumed destructive quality) is a basic biological phenomenon, as, e.g., Freud postulated in his last theoretical formulation of the life and death principles (11), or whether its destructive aspect is a result of the frustration of constructive strivings in the individual by reality factors depends ultimately upon whether theoretically one wishes to reduce to a strictly biological basis or to a basis which we might call "biosocial."

The assumption of the biological superiority of the male genital over the female, as epitomized in Freud's quotation "anatomy is fate" (16), is also obviously based upon biological primacy. It has been pointed out (43) that this is one of the very few places in which a value judgment has been accepted in psychoanalysis. Obviously, the biosocial group tends to reject this purely physical difference as a sole determinant (42). Similarly, the theoretical concept of inherent bisexuality has created differences of interpretation (35). One could continue illustrating the differences in theoretical formulations resulting from the basic theoretical differences of approach which I have only briefly sketched, but they would be only variations on an underlying theme.

It is important that we recognize that there is much which is unknown, and that much psychoanalytic discussion is on a theoretical and not on an observational level. It is not the data so much which are in question as it is the theoretical interpretation thereof. In such a complex and abstruse field, in which the methodological struggle to control the variables in the experimental situation is tremendous, one can easily fall victim to the very forces which one is attempting to understand—the nonrational elements in the human being.

THE VALIDATION OF PSYCHOANALYTIC CONCEPTS

We may now turn our attention to the question of the validation of psychoanalytic observations, concepts, and theories. This is unquestionably the most difficult aspect of our problem from the scientific point of view. I have endeavored throughout my presentation to demonstrate the distinctive character of the phenomena dealt with in psychoanalysis. Because of this, the methodology used to approach and examine them must differ radically from the usual methods of observation in scientific fields. Free association as a technical instrument may seem questionable to an audience of scientists.

Fliess (8) states the problem in the following way:

Those disinclined to recognize psychoanalysis as a science because it fails to comply with certain accepted standards of method (experiment) or result (expressibility in mathematical symbols) might be reminded that in the last analysis, standards derive from science, not science from standards. The latter reflect exigencies of scientific investigation and are therefore conditioned by the nature of the object of this investigation. As far as the object proper of psychoanalysis is concerned, it must be recognized as fundamentally different from any other. It is an object conceived as composed of elements whose perceptory sources are those of internal perception. To be sure, the verbalizations of an analysand, the text of a myth, an historical document, or the content of a work of art are subject to external perception; and as such, are no different from the point of a needle over a scale, a change in color, or an ultra-microscopic alteration in shape. But their observation is analytic only in so far as the data elicited by it are indicative of certain products of internal perception, in the patient, the author (individual or collective), the historical personage, or the artist. These perceptory products are elements of the "inner" world; and their observation is scientific inasmuch as it allows for the establishment of ordering principles whose adaptation to the observable data is comparable to that of hypothesis to experience in the sciences studying the "external" world. The obvious differences in method of observation as well as description employed by analysis as compared with the rest of the natural sciences reflect merely the dissimilarities of their objects.

The predicament of the theoretician in psychoanalysis—and it is here that he will ask forebearance—stems from the potency, not the deficiency, of his method. While the latter enables him to make new observations he has, in abstracting from these, to rely upon old metaphor, handed down to him from the sciences that have outgrown it. He must posit nonspatial "loci," describe processes as "dynamic," ignorant of the forms of energy sustaining them, and even postulate "economic" relations between quantities which he is altogether unable to measure. Yet, at present at least, he can do no better than work for a closer adaptation of these concepts to his particular subject; in other words, for the improvement, made possible by the collection of further empirical data, of their definition.

In other words, we must use language which is not particularly adapted to our subject matter, discuss forces, the physiological nature of which has not yet been elucidated by biology, and speak in terms of quantity for which we have no instruments of measurement.

This seems to present a rather hopeless situation. But if such phenomena as are observed by psychoanalysis actually exist in nature, we must not throw up our hands in despair. Psychoanalysis has attempted to cope with the problem of descriptive symbols for its unusual subject matter by developing new words to describe new phenomena. Although psychoanalysis is often re-proached for its strange jargon, we must face the fact that every field of science develops its own set of symbols to describe its phenomena. I do not mean here to condone the deficiencies of psychoanalytic terminology, on which most ana-lysts themselves agree. Our terms are regrettably ambiguous in many respects. However, efforts are being made to clarify and simplify the confused semantic problems in psychoanalytic terminology.

While it is also true that we do not know the nature of the biological forces which create the drives in human beings, beyond the fact that they are probably physiochemical in nature and therefore not problems of psychoanalysis but of biology, we can still work with them. The science of physics has worked with electricity and achieved brilliant results, although we know little about the exact nature of electrical forces.

My feeling regarding quantitative factors in psychoanalysis is that we are not yet at a point at which we can even approach this problem. The develop-ment of quantitative measurement in many sciences has had to wait until technological advances permitted an exact approach. Perhaps we must wait for some technological devices before we can speak of the quantification of any of our data. It is possible that here closer relationships may be established between neurophysiology and psychoanalysis through chemical and electro-encephalographic investigations. It is also just as possible that entirely new methods and instruments will have to be devised. While we must strive to-ward the goal of quantifying our data we must be wary of the opposite trap, into which we sometimes tend to fall. Because we have no valid methods of quantitative measurement, it is not only dangerous to speak in such terms but also conducive to overlooking the significance of other factors if we attribute necessary significance to quantitative changes. This danger was discussed several years ago by Dr. Kubie (31).

Let us turn to another frequent reproach regarding the unscientific nature of psychoanalysis—that regarding the lack of objectivity of the data. It has been stated that because the analyst himself is part of the experimental situa-tion, the material derived therefrom must be subjective. This is in part true, and is one of the reasons for the attempt to intrude the personality of the analyst as little as possible, by means of the "analytic incognito" and the analytic setting. However, in many fields of science it has now become necessary to include the observer in a "closed system." Psychoanalysis has also attempted to do this in a crude way by standardizing the role of the observer as much as possible.

The problem of objectification and verification is an extremely complicated one in psychoanalysis, doubly complicated by the need for privacy in the experimental setting. It is my feeling that this latter factor is not an insuperable obstacle. In his lectures Dr. Kubie presented an elaborate and detailed plan for making the raw material of the psychoanalytic interview available to other investigators, including detailed methods of attempted control of many of the variables which enter into the experiment. However, I do not feel that this presents any final answer to the problem involved. I shall discuss the question of control of variables in more detail a little later. Even without such detailed controls the mechanical recording of interviews as they are at present carried out would permit ample verification of the raw observational material. This possibility, which did not exist in Freud's day, incidentally, illustrates that which I stated above regarding the problem of technological advance. It is not so much a matter of the lack of observational material but of its overwhelming mass and the amount of time and energy which would be required to analyze it which is the real problem.

However, no matter how excellent the recorded observations, unless they are oriented around some theoretical point of reference they do not yield data of much relevance. There existed a tremendous mass of biological data before Darwin, but its very mass was overwhelming until the ordering principle of evolution clarified it and placed it in some pertinent frame of reference. In many respects psychoanalysis is in the position of pre-Darwinian biology, or pre-Mendeleef chemistry. It has some general ordering principles around which to orient its data, but no one, least of all Freud himself, would pretend that they were more than tentative formulations.

If repetition of observation and agreement of observers are, in part, criteria of a science, we must grant that this exists within the sphere of psychoanalysis, granting the validity of the setting and technical instruments. In the objective sciences one does not expect repetition and agreement except under closely controlled conditions. The very nature of the analytic experiment is such that it differs markedly from that which is usually accepted as an experimental setting. In any experimental setting involving multiple variables it is not possible to perform a short term, cross-sectional experiment. If we deal with single additive variables which can be individually controlled and varied by the experimenter, with the others held constant, we can by a series of cross-sectional analyses arrive at a final composite result with a degree of specificity. However, when dealing with multiple variables, particularly when in the nature of the material many can never be controlled, the experiment must of necessity be of a longitudinal nature, i.e., extended in time, with repeated observations. Only in this way will individual variations be reduced and a statistical generalization be reached. While each portion of the experiment may yield a different result, the total result at the end may be generalized, because the differences caused by the multiplicity will average out over the long term. Thus, while each analysis will vary in its details, and while the material produced by the individual patient will vary with the individual analyst in the course of a total analysis, the material will be comparable to other analyses of the same analyst, or of different analysts. It is the whole analysis as a unit which must be regarded as the experiment.

Before we approach the question of the possibility of prediction of results from a theory as a criterion of validity, we must first examine in a general way a very important question which I mentioned above. This has to do with the question of single versus multiple variables (6). The ability to predict with a reasonable degree of accuracy differs markedly in different sciences. Prediction depends ultimately on the ability to control the variables present in an experiment. Only if we are able to control all the variables in a given experimental situation and vary one at a time may we expect a reasonably high degree of accuracy of prediction. The more exact the controls, the more exact the demands for accuracy.

In the field of psychoanalysis there is the explicit and implicit assumption of the overdetermination of neurotic symptoms and of overt behavior in general. That is, behavior is always a resultant of multiple stimuli, not of single stimuli. May I recall to you the analogy I mentioned earlier—of the lower motor neuron as the final common pathway. The conscious contraction of a muscle in response to a stimulus depends not only upon the impulse transmitted to the anterior horn cell through the pyramidal tract but also upon the synergic action of all the other impulses received by the anterior horn cell from the other pathways converging upon it. In such complex phenomena as are dealt with in psychoanalysis we always find more than one factor contributing to observed behavior. In other words, we cannot expect the elucidation of any one single factor as the single direct cause of a specific action, thought, psychiatric syndrome, or character trait. In any specific instance we may anticipate a certain dominant factor (or group of factors), but without being able to grant to it the specificity which may be necessary or attainable in other fields. Due to this factor of multiplicity we cannot anticipate prediction with the degree of accuracy which exists in the exact sciences. He who looks for such specificity is looking for a chimera.

Overdetermination, or the principle of multiple or additive factors, also explains in part the lack of specificity regarding interpretations in psychoanalysis. There are so many possibilities due to the complexity of the experiences of each individual that one can never feel with certainty that any specific interpretation is the only possible one in a given situation. It can only be stated that on the basis of what is thus far known at a particular point in an analysis we can postulate the following hypothesis or explanation (interpretation). This may be changed later by new data which become available. Actually this is a basic scientific approach: a hypothesis on the basis of the known, which opens new paths into the not yet known. This is basically the main function of psychoanalytic interpretation. Underlying this is the assumption of all scientific endeavor: the more we know (are conscious) of the factors involved in a given situation, the better we can control and work with it, and the more easily can we look for further unknowns. Each interpretation attempts to explain some of the factors elucidated, but it is always indeterminate. It can never be final, absolute, specific. All the findings of psychoanalysis point to the principle of multiplicity of determinants in the interplay of psychological forces in the individual. We must think in terms of interrelationships rather than single relationships in the explanation of psychological phenomena.

This principle also explains, in part at least, the reason for differences of interpretation of the same material by different analysts. With multiple determinants present, one analyst may stress one aspect of the data and interpret that, while another may stress another aspect and interpret that. Very often, critical examination reveals that seemingly divergent interpretations are in actuality complementary and not contradictory.

Herein lies one of the contradictions in the theoretical structure of psychoanalysis which I attempted to delineate briefly earlier, in discussing disagreements among groups of analysts. Paradoxically, while Freud stressed the factor of overdetermination rather than unitary determinants in regard to his clinical data, he searched for a unitary source of these data. We cannot in the human being isolate the biological from the psychological, the psychological from the cultural. They are all interrelated, fused, intermingled. We must look for the constellation, the pattern, the *Gestalt*, rather than a single causal pattern. No single incident, no single experience, no single trauma calls forth an inevitable specific type of response. It is a total situation, repeated and reinforced through the life of the individual which is of significance. We cannot therefore expect the specificity which we find in those sciences which exercise much greater control over their subject matter than we can ever hope for in psychoanalysis. And even in these sciences, I gather from my general reading, this procedure of isolation and control of single variables is now felt to be not entirely adequate to explain all its phenomena. This basic problem of unitary determinants versus multiple determinants raises the question of the possibility of validation of psychoanalytic data by laboratory experimentation. I believe this is what Dr. Kubie meant when he stated that we must be careful not to simplify the experimental situation to such a point that we no longer study the phenomena we set out to observe.

If we narrow our concept of a science to those fields which are able to exercise sufficient control over their material so as to elucidate the single additive factors which affect the object of their experimentation, we must exclude psychoanalysis from this realm. If, however, we are willing to accord some scientific stature to a field which can only deal with its material in terms of multiple variables, we may grant psychoanalysis a place in the group.

Psychoanalysis here reveals its close relationship to the social sciences, with which it shares in common the principle of multiple variables. Nowhere in the social fields is it possible, with the exception of rare and unusual instances, to isolate single factors in a direct cause and effect relationship. We might say that the social sciences differ fundamentally from the physical and biological sciences in this basic assumption. Due to the very nature of their subject matter, they must operate on the basis of the principle of multiple determinants.

Are, then, psychoanalytic data and theory verifiable in the laboratory? I am afraid that we must face the fact that they are not subject to direct verification in this manner at the present time. Derivative data, such as the mechanisms of defense or the presence of conflicts and of unconscious forces, may be verified, but the detailed derivation of these factors in the analytic sense at present cannot be subjected to any type of experimental validation, except by the use of the analytic method itself. I do not underestimate the type of experimentation and clinical validation offered by Dr. Hilgard in his lectures, as, for example, with Blum's Blacky test (3) or Keet's microneurosis (27), but the extension of this material beyond these limits is not yet feasible. Incidentally, I might mention that the Blacky test provides a degree of validation of psychoanalytic theory with regard to internal consistency, but, because it remains within the framework of analytic theory, does not provide "objective" validation of the underlying assumptions.

Does this mean that psychoanalytic theory and data cannot be validated at all? This I do not feel is true, although the results will not meet all the strict criteria to which one is accustomed in the physical and biological sciences. I believe it is possible to obtain objective evidence of at least certain general hypotheses of psychoanalysis. Certainly it is possible to investigate in the laboratory the nature and quality of the underlying forces present in human beings, as to a certain extent has already been done. Let me mention briefly some of the experimental clinical work in this field. Psychoanalysis has theoretically maintained and clinically demonstrated that the mother-child relationship is of primary importance for the emotional, intellectual, and physical development of the child. Spitz (39) in his clinical studies and films has demonstrated these effects. Moreover, he has been able to establish some correlations between the relation of mother to child and the emotional reactions in the child which result therefrom. He has also, through his experimental-observational method (40), demonstrated that the symbiosis between a specific mother and a specific child develops only at about the age of six months. His data ultimately may lead to certain revisions in psychoanalytic theory. Further, he has demonstrated that at least behaviorally (38) we cannot assume the presence of anxiety before this same age, thus confirming the theory that anxiety depends upon object relationships. We cannot yet relate specific occurrences or chains of events to specific constellations in the adult, but perhaps with further observations we may be able to do so. However, such studies will require observation over long periods of time. With relevant material gathered in childhood, correlations may evolve which may do much not only to prove or disprove current theories, but to open new avenues of approach and new theoretical advances. Such studies have already begun in several places, but it will be many years before definitive results will be available.[6]

If we wish to discuss the possibility of extra-analytic verification and clarification of some aspects of analytic results, we might consider the possibility of the following type of research project. Through it the predictive ability of analytic observation might be tested, as well as some significant correlations (or lack of correlations) between analytic data on the one hand and objective behavior and conscious attitudes of the patient on the other. Independently of the patient under analysis, but with his knowledge and consent, a team of competently trained workers (psychiatric social workers and psychologists, for example) could interview the relatives, friends, business associates, etc., of the patient at frequent intervals, and obtain data as to his reactions, attitudes, behavior, and the changes therein from time to time. The analyst would keep detailed records (mechanically recorded if desired) of the progress of therapy. In addition, he might attempt to formulate and predict certain reactions and attitudes of the patient at significant points in the course of the analysis. At the conclusion of the analysis the various data would be studied so that relationships between analytic material and overt behavior would be correlated. In this way much information could be obtained regarding the relation of conscious behavior and unconscious material, as well as the effect of external

[6] Studies at the University of California (Berkeley) Institute for Child Welfare under Dr. Jean McFarlane have been in progress for a number of years. The Judge Baker Foundation in Boston also has undertaken a project of this nature which may well yield interesting results in the future.

events on unconscious productions. I would be the first to admit that there are many loopholes in such an experiment, but it might yield some verification of psychoanalytic data and also lead to some new aspects of the problem. Such type of investigation has been done in a limited way in regard to the physiological sphere. T. Benedek (1), for example, has made significant observations regarding the correlations between the type of psychological material produced and changes in the menstrual cycle of women.

CONCLUSION

I have attempted to demonstrate that psychoanalysis is a field which is related to the biological sciences in that it looks upon man basically as a biological phenomenon. It is related to the social sciences in that it views man as a product of the society in which he lives. In attempting to approach the problem of the psychological development of man, psychoanalysis adopted the principle of evolution from biology and applied it to psychology, choosing as its sphere of observation the nonrational aspects of human thought and action. In order properly to observe the phenomena it wished to observe, it had to exclude or diminish the processes of rational thought and action. To accomplish this it developed a technique and methodology which permitted proper observation of its data.

It has often been said that one of the difficulties with psychoanalysis is that it has made no advances since Freud. This is not true, although it may appear so on the surface. When the sun rises over the horizon, the stars are no longer visible to the naked eye. Freud has been the towering figure in psychoanalysis, whose light shown so brilliantly that he has obscured all others, and, to a certain extent, still does. However, the stars are still in the sky, whether we perceive them or not. We are still too close to Freud to have any real perspective on him. But others have advanced slowly but surely on the way. As in every field, there are always those who are so dazzled by the brilliance of a genius that they cling desperately to his findings, frightened to advance beyond him. But there are others who question, search, and probe, with lesser brilliance perhaps, but with true scientific spirit. Although Freud chartered many paths in unknown fields, he opened many more fields to further exploration.

However, it is difficult to discuss these developments in more than general terms because they would involve a more detailed and technical discussion of aspects of psychoanalytic theory than would be desirable here. I have attempted to indicate at various points in my discussion some of the advances which have been and are being made. In general, it might be stated that there has been a marked tendency toward the further development of an ego psychology. The role of the ego was at first conceived of as primarily defensive. Increasing focus has been placed upon its synthesizing and integrative functions. The recognition that the ego has other than merely defensive functions has also led to a re-evaluation of its role in the total personality structure.

Every field of science requires some time to recover from the impact of a towering figure arising in its midst. As a colleague recently remarked: "I sometimes wonder how we will recognize another Freud when he appears." I am not worried about this. For as in every field of science, a great figure can arise only on the basis of the slow patient work of innumerable scientists who form the firm foundation upon which he plants his feet. It has been demonstrated sufficiently, I believe, that Freud was a pioneer in the dim fields of the human mind which he chose to investigate. But he arose in a definite historical period and was subject to its influences. As in all fields of science, we must constantly evaluate, examine, criticize, test, and probe. To view any scientific theory as dogma is to violate the spirit of science itself. If psychoanalysis wishes to find a place in science, it must also accept this dictum.

Whether one wishes to accord psychoanalysis the rank of a science or not depends upon one's personal point of view. I have attempted to present here a methodological approach to this problem. I have tried to demonstrate that psychoanalysis occupies a position between the biological sciences, which are objective in the character of their subject matter, and the social sciences, which must include subjective elements in their subject matter. Psychoanalysis has its roots in the physical and biological nature of man but spreads its branches into those fields dealing with social, cultural, and environmental factors. It cannot be judged by the criteria of the physical and biological sciences alone because it rests on the principle of multiple determinants, which it shares with all the fields whose subject matter is on a higher order of complexity than its own (social sciences). It cannot exercise the degree of control over its observations which is required in the exact sciences. Its subject matter is on a different integrative level than that of these sciences. Its hypotheses and principles cannot have the specificity and definiteness which is demanded in the exact sciences. Psychoanalysis must content itself at its present stage of development with establishing what appear to be significant, but not exclusive, correlations rather than specific causal relationships. But the great question is whether we can exclude from the broad field of scientific endeavor such important aspects of human activity as psychoanalysis attempts to investigate.

References

Hilgard—*Experimental Approaches to Psychoanalysis*

I. PSYCHODYNAMICS

1. ABRAHAM, K. *Selected Papers on Psychoanalysis.* London: Hogarth Press, 1927
2. ADORNO, T. W., FRENKEL-BRUNSWIK, ELSE, LEVINSON, D. J., and SANFORD, R. N. *The Authoritarian Personality.* New York: Harper & Brothers, 1950
3. BARKER, R., DEMBO, T., and LEWIN, K. "Frustration and Regression: An Experiment with Young Children," *Univ. Iowa Studies Child Welf.*, 1941, **18**, No. 1
4. BLUM, G. S. "A Study of the Psychoanalytic Theory of Psychosexual Development," *Genet. Psych. Monogr.*, 1949, **39**, 3–99
5. BRENMAN, MARGARET. "Dreams and Hypnosis." *Psychoanal. Quart.*, 1949, **18**, 455–65
6. COOPER, L. F. "Time Distortion in Hypnosis," *Bull. Georgetown Univ. Med. Cent.*, 1948, **1**, 214–21
7. DAVIS, H. V., SEARS, R. R., MILLER, H. C., and BRODBECK, A. J. "Effects of Cup, Bottle, and Breast Feeding on Oral Activities of Newborn Infants," *Pediatrics*, 1948, **2**, 549–58
8. DOLLARD, J., DOOB, L. W., MILLER, N. E., MOWRER, O. H., and SEARS, R. R. *Frustration and Aggression.* New Haven: Yale University Press, 1939
9. FARBER, L. H., and FISHER, CHARLES. "An Experimental Approach to Dream Psychology Through the Use of Hypnosis," *Psychoanal. Quart.*, 1943, **12**, 202–16
10. FENICHEL, OTTO. *The Psychoanalytic Theory of Neurosis.* New York: W. W. Norton & Company, Inc., 1945
11. FRENKEL-BRUNSWIK, ELSE, "Mechanisms of Self-Deception," *J. Soc. Psych.*, 1939, **10**, 409–20
12. FREUD, ANNA. *The Ego and the Mechanisms of Defense.* London: Hogarth Press, 1937
13. FREUD, S. *Character and Anal Erotism.* Coll. Papers, 1908, **2**, 45–50
14. ———. "The Interpretation of Dreams" (1900), in *Basic Writings of Sigmund Freud.* New York: Modern Library, 1938
15. ———. *New Introductory Lectures on Psychoanalysis.* New York: W. W. Norton & Company, Inc., 1933
16. ———. *The Psychopathology of Everyday Life* (1904), in *Basic Writings of Sigmund Freud.* New York: Modern Library, 1938
17. GOLDMAN, FRIEDA. "Breast-feeding and Character-Formation," *J. Personality*, 1948, **17**, 83–103
18. HAMILTON, G. V. *A Research in Marriage.* New York: Boni, 1929

19. HERMA, H., KRIS, E., and SHOR, J. "Freud's Theory of the Dream in American Textbooks," *J. Abnorm. Soc. Psych.*, 1943
20. HILGARD, E. R. "Human Motives and the Concept of the Self," *Am. Psychologist*, 1949, **4**, 374–82
21. HUNT, J. McV. "The Effects of Infant Feeding-Frustration upon Adult Hoarding in the Albino Rat," *J. Abnorm. Soc. Psych.*, 1941, **36**, 338–60
22. HUNT, J. McV., SCHLOSBERG, H., SOLOMON, R. L., and STELLAR, E. "Studies of the Effect of Infantile Experience on Adult Behavior in Rats. I. Effects of Infantile Feeding Frustration on Adult Hoarding," *J. Comp. Physiol. Psych.*, 1947, **40**, 291–304
23. KLEIN, D. B. "The Experimental Production of Dreams During Hypnosis," *Univ. Texas Bull.*, 1930, No. 3009
24. LANTZ, BEATRICE. "Some Dynamic Aspects of Success and Failure," *Psych. Monogr.*, 1945, **59**, No. 271
25. LEVY, D. M. "Experiments on the Sucking Reflex and Social Behavior of Dogs," *Am. J. Orthopsychiat.*, 1934, **4**, 203–24
26. ———. "Fingersucking and Accessory Movements in Early Infancy," *Am. J. Psychiat.*, 1928, **7**, 881–918
27. MILLER, N. E. "Theory and Experiment Relating Psychoanalytic Displacement to Stimulus-Response Generalization," *J. Abnorm. Soc. Psych.*, 1948, **43**, 155–78
28. MORGAN, C. T. "The Hoarding Instinct," *Psych. Rev.*, 1947, **54**, 335–41
29. ORLANSKY, H. "Infant Care and Personality," *Psych. Bull.*, 1949, **46**, 1–48
30. PATTIE, F. A., JR. "A Report of Attempts to Produce Uniocular Blindness by Hypnotic Suggestion," *Brit. J. Med. Psych.*, 1935, **15**, 230–41
31. RAPAPORT, D. *Emotions and Memory.* Baltimore: The Williams & Wilkins Company, 1942
32. SEARS, R. R. "Experimental Analysis of Psychoanalytic Phenomena," in HUNT, J. McV. (ed.), *Personality and the Behavior Disorders.* New York: The Ronald Press Company, 1944, 306–32
33. ———. "Experimental Studies of Projection: I. Attribution of Traits," *J. Soc. Psych.*, 1936, **7**, 151–63
34. ———. "Personality," in STONE, C. P. (ed.), *Ann. Rev. Psych.*, 1950, **1**, 105–18
35. ———. "Survey of Objective Studies of Psychoanalytic Concepts. A Report Prepared for the Committee on Social Adjustment," Social Science Research Council, New York, *Bulletin,* 1943, **51**
36. SEARS, R. R., and WISE, G. W. "Relation of Cup Feeding in Infancy to Thumbsucking and the Oral Drive," *Am. J. Orthopsychiat.*, 1950, **20**, 123–38
37. SHARPE, ELLA F. *Dream Analysis.* London: Hogarth Press, 1937
38. SYMONDS, P. M. *Dynamic Psychology.* New York: Appleton-Century-Crofts, Inc., 1949
39. ———. *The Dynamics of Human Adjustment.* New York: D. Appleton-Century Company, Inc., 1946
40. TRUE, R. M. "Experimental Control in Hypnotic Age Regression States," *Science,* 1949, **110**, 583–84

41. WELCH, L. "The Space and Time of Induced Hypnotic Dreams," *J. Psych.*, 1936, 1, 171–78

II. PSYCHOTHERAPY

1. ALEXANDER, F. *Fundamentals of Psychoanalysis.* New York: W. W. Norton & Company, Inc., 1948
2. ALEXANDER, F., and FRENCH, T. M. (eds.) *Psychoanalytic Therapy.* New York: The Ronald Press Company, 1946
3. ANDERSON, O. D., and PARMENTER, R. "A Long-Term Study of the Experimental Neurosis in the Sheep and the Dog," *Psychosom. Med. Monogr.*, 1941, 2, Nos. 3 and 4
4. ELLIS, A. "An Introduction to the Principles of Scientific Psychoanalysis," *Genet. Psych. Monogr.*, 1950, 41, 147–212
5. FENICHEL, OTTO. *Problems of Psychoanalytic Technique.* Albany: The Psychoanalytic Quarterly, Inc., 1941
6. ———. *The Psychoanalytic Theory of Neurosis.* New York: W. W. Norton & Company, Inc., 1945
7. FROMM-REICHMANN, FRIEDA. "Notes on the Personal and Professional Requirements of a Psychotherapist," *Psychiatry*, 1949, 12, 361–78
8. HEBB, D. O. "Spontaneous Neurosis in Chimpanzees: Theoretical Relations with Clinical and Experimental Phenomena," *Psychosom. Med.*, 1947, 9, 3–19
9. KEET, C. D. "Two Verbal Techniques in a Miniature Counselling Situation," *Psych. Monogr.*, 1948, 62, No. 294
10. KUBIE, L. S. *Practical and Theoretical Aspects of Psychoanalysis.* New York: International Universities Press, Inc., 1950
11. LANDIS, C. "Psychoanalytic Phenomena," *J. Abnorm. Soc. Psych.*, 1940, 35, 17–28
12. LA PIERE, R. T. "Review of Three Psychoanalytic Books," *Am. Sociol. Rev.*, 1948, 13, 346–48
13. MAIER, N. R. F. *Frustration: A Study of Behavior Without a Goal.* New York: McGraw-Hill Book Company, Inc., 1949
14. MASSERMAN, J. H. *Behavior and Neurosis.* Chicago: University of Chicago Press, 1943
15. ———. "Experimental Neuroses." *Scientific American*, 1950, 182, 38–43
16. MASSERMAN, J. H., and YUM, K. S. "An Analysis of the Influence of Alcohol on Experimental Neuroses in Cats," *Psychosom. Med.*, 1946, 8, 36–52
17. MILLER, N. E. "Theory and Experiment Relating Psychoanalytic Displacement to Stimulus-Response Generalization," *J. Abnorm. Soc. Psych.*, 1948, 43, 155–78
18. PAVLOV, I. P. *Conditioned Reflexes.* London: Oxford University Press, 1927
19. ———. *Conditioned Reflexes and Psychiatry.* New York: International Publishers Co., Inc., 1941
20. ROGERS, C. R. "A Coordinated Research in Psychotherapy," *J. Consulting Psych.*, 1949, 13, 149–220
21. SEARS, R. R. "Experimental Analysis of Psychoanalytic Phenomena," in HUNT,

J. McV. (ed.), *Personality and the Behavior Disorders*. New York: The Ronald Press Company, 1944, 306–32

22. ———. "Survey of Objective Studies of Psychoanalytic Concepts. A Report Prepared for the Committee on Social Adjustment," Social Science Research Council, New York, *Bulletin*, 1943, **51**

23. SEEMAN, J. "The Process of Nondirective Therapy," *J. Consulting Psych.*, 1949, **13**, 157–68

24. SPRAGG, S. D. S. "Morphine Addiction in Chimpanzees," *Comp. Psych. Monogr.*, 1940, **15**, No. 7

KUBIE—*Problems and Techniques of Psychoanalytic Validation and Progress*

1. BALES, ROBERT F. *Interaction Process Analysis: A Method for the Study of Small Groups*. Cambridge, Mass.: Addison-Wesley Press, 1950

2. BARTEMEIER, LEO, KUBIE, L. S., MENNINGER, K. A., ROMANO, J., and WHITEHORN, J. "Combat Exhaustion," *J. Nerv. Ment. Dis.*, 1946, **104**, No. 5, 358–525

3. BENJAMIN, JOHN D. "Methodological Considerations in the Validation and Elaboration of Psychoanalytical Personality Theory" (Approaches to a Dynamic Theory of Development, Round Table, 1949), *Am. J. Orthopsychiat.*, 1950, **20**, No. 1, 139–56

4. BERNARD, CLAUDE. *An Introduction to the Study of Experimental Medicine*. 1859. Translated by H. C. Greene. New York: The Macmillan Company, 1927

5. BRENMAN, MARGARET. "Dreams and Hypnosis," *The Psychoanal. Quart.*, 1949, **18**, No. 4, 455–65

6. BRENMAN, M., and GILL, M. *Hypnotherapy*. New York: International Universities Press, Inc., 1947

7. EISSLER, K. R. "The Chicago Institute of Psychoanalysis and the Sixth Period of the Development of Psychoanalytic Technique," *J. Gen. Psych.*, 1950, **42**, 103–57

8. ELLIS, ALBERT. "An Introduction to the Principles of Scientific Psychoanalysis," *Genet. Psych. Monogr.*, 1950, **41**, 147–212

9. ERICKSON, M. H. "Experimental Demonstrations of the Psychopathology of Everyday Life," *Psychoanal. Quart.*, 1939, **8**, No. 3, 338–53

10. ———. "The Problem of the Definition and the Dynamic Values of Psychiatric Concepts," *Med. Rec.*, February 2, March 2, 1938

11. ERICKSON, M. H., and HILL, L. B. "Unconscious Mental Activity in Hypnosis —Psychoanalytic Implications," *Psychoanal. Quart.*, 1944, **13**, No. 1, 60–78

12. ERICKSON, M. H., and KUBIE, L. S. "The Permanent Relief of an Obsessional Phobia by Means of Communications with an Unsuspected Dual Personality," *Psychoananl. Quart.*, 1939, **8**, 471–509

13. ———. "The Successful Treatment of a Case of Acute Hysterical Depression

by a Return Under Hypnosis to a Critical Phase of Childhood," *Psychoanal. Quart.*, 1941, **10**, 583–609

14. ———. "The Translation of the Cryptic Automatic Writing of One Hypnotic Subject by Another in a Trance-Like Dissociated State," *Psychoanal. Quart.*, 1940, **9**, 51–63

15. ———. "The Use of Automatic Drawing in the Interpretation and Relief of a State of Acute Obsessional Depression," *Psychoanal. Quart.*, 1938, **7**, 443–66

16. FARBER, L. H., and FISHER, CHARLES. "An Experimental Approach to Dream Psychology Through the Use of Hypnosis," *Psychoanal. Quart.*, 1943, **12**, No. 2, 202–16

17. FINGER, F. W. "Experimental Behavior Disorders in the Rat," in HUNT, J. McV. (ed.), *Personality and the Behavior Disorders*. New York: The Ronald Press Company, 1944, **1**, 413

18. FRENCH, T. M. "Clinical Approach to the Dynamics of Behavior," in HUNT, J. McV. (ed.), *Personality and the Behavior Disorders*. New York: The Ronald Press Company, 1944, **1**, 255

19. FREUD, ANNA. *The Ego and the Mechanisms of Defence*. London: Hogarth Press, 1937

20. FREUD, S. *The Interpretation of Dreams*. London: Allen & Unwin, Ltd.; New York: The Macmillan Company, 1913. Revised printings through 1927

21. ———. *Psychopathology of Everyday Life*. New York: The Macmillan Company, 1913. Reprinted through 1930

22. GREGG, ALAN. *The Furtherance of Medical Research*. New Haven: Yale University Press, 1941

23. HARTMANN, H., and KRIS, E. "The Genetic Approach in Psychoanalysis," *Psychoanal. Study Child*. New York: International Universities Press, Inc., 1945, **1**

24. HARTMANN, H., KRIS, E., and LOEWENSTEIN, R. M. "Comments on the Formation of Psychic Structure," *Psychoanal. Study Child*. New York: International Universities Press, Inc., 1946, **2**

25. HUSTON, P. E., SHAKOW, D., and ERICKSON, M. H. "A Study of Hypnotically Induced Complexes by Means of the Luria Technique," *J. Gen. Psych.*, 1934, **11**, 65–97

26. JAMES, WILLIAM. *The Varieties of Religious Experience*. New York; Longmans, Green & Co., Inc., 1908. See especially pp. 387–93

27. JENNESS, A. "Hypnotism," in HUNT, J. McV. (ed.), *Personality and the Behavior Disorders*. New York: The Ronald Press Company, 1944, 1, 466

28. KEET, C. D. "Two Verbal Techniques in a Miniature Counselling Situation," *Psych. Monogr.*, 1948, **62**, No. 294

29. KRIS, ERNST. "The Nature of Psychoanalytic Propositions and Their Validation," *Freedom and Experience*. Essays presented to Horace M. Kallen. Ithaca: Cornell University Press, 1947

30. KUBIE, L. S. "Body Symbolization and the Development of Language," *Psychoanal. Quart.*, 1934, **3**, No. 3

31. ———. Discussion of paper, "The Behavior of the Stomach During Psychoanalysis," by Sydney Margolin, *Psychoanal. Quart.*, 1951, **20**, No. 3, 369–73

32. ———. "The Experimental Induction of Neurotic Reactions in Man," *Yale J. Biol. & Med.*, 1939, **2**, No. 5, 541–45

33. ———. "The Fallacious Use of Quantitative Concepts in Dynamic Psychology," *Psychoanal. Quart.*, 1947, **16**, No. 4, 507–18

34. ———. "Instincts and Homoeostasis," *Psychosom. Med.*, 1948, **10**, No. 1, 15–30

35. ———. *Practical and Theoretical Aspects of Psychoanalysis*. New York: International Universities Press, Inc., 1950

36. ———. "Psychiatric Implications of the Kinsey Report," *Psychosom. Med.*, 1948, **10**, No. 2, 95–106

37. ———. "Relation of the Conditioned Reflex to Psychoanalytic Technic," *Arch. Neur. & Psych.*, 1934, **32**, 1137–42

38. ———. "Research Project in Community Mental Hygiene: Fantasy," *Ment. Hyg.*, 1952 (in press)

39. ———. "Resolution of a Traffic Phobia in Conversations Between a Father and Son," *Psychoanal. Quart.*, 1937, **6**, 223–26

40. ———. Review of *Lectures on Conditioned Reflexes, Vol. II: Conditioned Reflexes and Psychiatry*, by I. P. Pavlov, translated and edited by W. Horsley Gantt [New York: International Publishers Co., Inc., 1941], *Psychoanal. Quart.*, 1942, **11**, No. 4, 565–70

41. ———. Review of *The Nature of Human Conflicts: An Objective Study of Disorganization and Control of Human Behavior*, by A. R. Luria, translated and edited by W. Horsley Gantt [New York: Liveright, Inc., 1932], *Psychoanal. Quart.*, 1933, **2**, 330–36

42. ———. Review of *Pavlov and His School*, by Y. P. Frolov [New York: Oxford University Press, 1937], *Psychoanal. Quart.*, 1941, **10**, No. 2, 329–39

43. ———. Review of "A Study of Hypnotically Induced Complexes by Means of the Luria Technique," by P. E. Huston, D. Shakow, and M. H. Erickson [*J. Gen. Psych.*, 1934, **11**], *Psychoanal. Quart.*, 1935, **4**, 347–49

44. ———. "The Use of Induced Hypnagogic Reveries in the Recovery of Repressed Anamnestic Data," *Bull. Menninger Clin.*, 1943, **7**, Nos. 5, 6, 172–82

45. ———. "The Value of Induced Dissociated States in the Therapeutic Process," *Proc. Roy. Soc. Med.*, 1945, **38**, No. 12, 681–83

46. KUBIE, L. S., BRENMAN, M. (chairman), *et al.* "Problems in Clinical Research" (Round Table, 1946), *Am. J. Orthopsychiat.*, 1947, **17**, No. 2, 196–230

47. ———. "Research in Psychotherapy" (Round Table, 1947), *Am. J. Orthopsychiat.*, 1948, **18**, No. 1, 92–118

48. KUBIE, L. S., BRENNER, A. F. (chairman), *et al.* "The Objective Evaluation of Psychotherapy" (Round Table, 1948), *Am. J. Orthopsychiat.*, 1949, **19**, No. 3, 463–91

49. KUBIE, L. S., and BRICKNER, R. M. "A Miniature Psychotic Storm Produced by a Superego Conflict over Simple Posthypnotic Suggestion," *Psychoanal. Quart.*, 1936, **5**, 467–87

50. KUBIE, L. S., and LEWIN, B. D. Footnotes to "An Endocrine Approach to Psychodynamics," by R. G. Hoskins, *Psychoanal. Quart.*, 1936, **5**, No. 1

51. KUBIE, L. S., and MARGOLIN, S. "An Apparatus for the Use of Breath Sounds as an Hypnagogic Stimulus," *Am. J. Psychiat.*, 1944, **100**, No. 5, 610

52. ———. "A Physiological Method for the Induction of States of Partial Sleep, and Securing Free Association and Early Memories in Such States," *Trans. Am. Neur. Assoc.*, 1942, 136–39

53. ———. "The Therapeutic Role of Drugs in the Process of Repression, Dissociation and Synthesis," *Psychosom. Med.*, 1945, 7, No. 3, 147–51

54. KUBIE, L. S., OBERNDORF, C. P., GREENACRE, P., *et al.* "Symposium on the Evaluation of Therapeutic Results," *Int. J. Psychoanal.*, 1948, 29, 7–33

55. LEVY, DAVID M. "Experiments on the Sucking Reflex and Social Behavior of Dogs," *Am. J. Orthopsychiat.*, 1934, 4, 203–24

56. ———. "On Instinct Satiation: An Experiment on the Pecking Behavior of Chickens," *J. Gen. Psych.*, 1938, 18, 327–48

57. LEWIN, BERTRAM D. *The Psychoanalysis of Elation*. New York: W. W. Norton & Company, Inc., 1950

58. LEWIN, KURT, DEMBO, T., FESTINGER, L., and SEARS, P. S. "Levels of Aspiration," in HUNT, J. McV. (ed.), *Personality and the Behavior Disorders*. New York: The Ronald Press Company, 1944, 1, 333

59. LIDDELL, H. S. "Conditioned Reflex Method and Experimental Neurosis," in HUNT, J. McV. (ed.), *Personality and the Behavior Disorders*. New York: The Ronald Press Company, 1944, 1, 389

60. LURIA, A. R. *The Nature of Human Conflicts*. Translated and edited by W. Horsley Gantt. New York: Liveright, Inc., 1932

61. MARCINOWSKI, J. "Gezeichnete Träume," *Zentr. Ps.-A.*, 1911–12, 2, 490–518

62. MARGOLIN, S. "The Behavior of the Stomach During Psychoanalysis: A Clinical Study," *Psychoanal. Quart.*, 1951, 20, No. 3, 349–69

63. MARGOLIN, S., and KUBIE, L. S. "An Acoustic Respirograph. A Method for the Study of Respiration Through the Graphic Recording of the Breath Sounds," *J. Clin. Investig.*, 1943, 22, No. 2, 221–24

64. McDOWELL, MEHL. "An Abrupt Cessation of Major Neurotic Symptoms Following an Hypnotically Induced Artificial Conflict," *Bull. Menninger Clin.*, 1948, 12, 168–77

65. McLean Hospital. "Dedicatory Exercise, May 17, 1946," *Psychiat. Res.* Cambridge, Mass.: Harvard University Press, 1947

66. MILLER, N. E. "Experimental Studies of Conflict," in HUNT, J. McV. (ed.), *Personality and the Behavior Disorders*. New York: The Ronald Press Company, 1944, 1, 431

67. NACHMANSOHN, M. "Über experimentell erzeugte Träume nebst kritischen Bemerkungen über die psychoanalytische Methodik (vorläufige Mitteilung)," *Ztschr. Neurol. Psychiat.*, 1925, 98, 556–86 (also see Reference 70, p. 257)

68. PIAGET, J. *The Language and Thought of the Child*. London: Kegan Paul, Trench, Trubner & Co., Ltd.; New York: Harcourt, Brace and Company, 1926

69. RAPAPORT, D. *Emotions and Memory*. Baltimore: The Williams & Wilkins Company, 1942

70. ———. *The Organization and Pathology of Thought*. Austen Riggs Foundation Monograph No. 1. New York: Columbia University Press, 1951

71. RICHET, CHARLES. *The Natural History of a Savant*. French original, 1923.

Translated by Sir Oliver Lodge. London-Toronto: J. M. Dent & Sons, Ltd., 1927

72. ROFFENSTEIN, G. "Experimentelle Symbolträume; ein Beitrage zur Diskussion über die Psychoanalyse," Ztschr. Neurol. Psychiat., 1923, 87, 362–71 (also see Reference 70, pp. 249–57)

73. ROSENZWEIG, SAUL. "An Outline of Frustration Theory," in HUNT, J. McV. (ed.), Personality and the Behavior Disorders. New York: The Ronald Press Company, 1944, I, 379

74. SAUL, L. J. "Physiological Effects of Emotional Tension," in HUNT, J. McV. (ed.), Personality and the Behavior Disorders. New York: The Ronald Press Company, 1944, I, 269

75. SCHRÖTTER, KARL. "Experimentelle Träume," Zentr. Ps.–A., 1912, 2, 639 (also see Reference 70, pp. 234–49)

76. SEARS, R. R. "Experimental Analysis of Psychoanalytic Phenomena," in HUNT, J. McV. (ed.), Personality and the Behavior Disorders. New York: The Ronald Press Company, 1944, I, 306

77. ——. "Survey of Objective Studies of Psychoanalytic Concepts. A Report Prepared for the Committee on Social Adjustment," Social Science Research Council, New York, Bulletin, 1943, 51

78. SIDIS, BORIS. "An Experimental Study of Sleep," J. Abnorm. Psych., 1908, 3, 1–32, 63–96, 170–207; An Experimental Study of Sleep. Boston: R. Badger, 1909

79. SILBERER, H. "Bericht über eine Methode, gewisse symbolische Halluzinationserscheinungen hervorzurufen und zu beobachten," Jahrb. psychoanalytische Forschungen, I, 513–25. Abstracted by L. Blumgart, Psychoanal. Rev., 1916, 3, 112. "Symbolik des Erwachens und Schwellensymbolik überhaupt," Jahrb. psychoanalytische Forschungen, 3, 621–60. Abstracted by L. Blumgart, Psychoanal. Rev., 1921, 8, 431–33 (also see Reference 70, pp. 195–234)

80. SPIEGEL, H., SHOR, JOEL, and FISHMAN, SIDNEY. "An Hypnotic Ablation Technique for the Study of Personality Development," Psychosom. Med., 1945, 7, 273–78

81. WOLFF, HAROLD, et al. "Life Situations, Emotions, and Nasal Disease," Psychosom. Med., 1951, 13, No. 2, 71–83

PUMPIAN-MINDLIN—*The Position of Psychoanalysis in Relation to the Biological and Social Sciences*

1. BENEDEK, THERESE, and RUBENSTEIN, B. B. "The Sexual Cycle in Women," Psychosom. Med. Monogr., First Series, Washington, D.C., 1942

2. BENJAMIN, J. D. "Methodological Considerations in the Validation and Elaboration of Psychoanalytic Personality Theory" (Approaches to a Dynamic Theory of Development, Round Table, 1949), Am. J. Orthopsychiat., 1950, 20, No. 1, 139–56

3. BLUM, G. S. "A Study of the Psychoanalytic Theory of Psychosexual Development," *Genet. Psych. Monogr.*, 1949, 39, 3–99
4. BREUER, J., and FREUD, S. *Studies in Hysteria* (1895). New York: Nervous and Mental Diseases Publishing Co., 1936
5. ELLIS, HAVELOCK. *Studies in the Psychology of Sex.* Philadelphia: F. A. Davis Co. (6 volumes), 1900–10
6. ESCALONA, S. K. "Discussion" (Approaches to a Dynamic Theory of Development, Round Table, 1949), *Am. J. Orthopsychiat.*, 1950, 20, No. 1, 157–60
7. FENICHEL, OTTO. *The Psychoanalytic Theory of Neurosis.* New York: W. W. Norton & Company, Inc., 1945, 83–84
8. FLIESS, ROBERT. *The Psychoanalytic Reader.* New York: International Universities Press, Inc., 1948, 1, 14 (footnote)
9. FRANKLIN, J. C., SCHIELE, B. C., *et al.* "Observations on Human Behavior in Experimental Semistarvation and Rehabilitation," *J. Clin. Psych.*, 1948, 4, No. 1, 28–44
10. FREUD, S. *Aus den Anfaengen der Psychoanalyse* (1887–1902). (Not yet translated into English.) London: Imago Publishing Co., 1950
11. ———. *Beyond the Pleasure Principle* (1920). London: Hogarth Press, 1948
12. ———. *The Defense Neuro-psychoses* (1894). London: Hogarth Press, 1940, Coll. Papers, 1
13. ———. *The Ego and the Id* (1923). London: Hogarth Press, 1947, 29
14. ———. *Fragment of an Analysis of a Case of Hysteria* (1905). London: Hogarth Press, 1933, Coll. Papers, 3, 139
15. ———. *My Views on the Part Played by Sexuality in the Aetiology of the Neuroses* (1905). London: Hogarth Press, 1940, Coll. Papers, 1, 277
16. ———. *New Introductory Lectures on Psychoanalysis* (1933). New York: W. W. Norton & Company, Inc., 1933, chap. v, "The Psychology of Women," 153–85
17. ———. *On the History of the Psychoanalytic Movement* (1914). London: Hogarth Press, 1940, Coll. Papers, 1, 289–90
18. *Ibid.*, 299–300
19. *Ibid.*, 298
20. *Ibid.*, 298
21. ———. *An Outline of Psychoanalysis* (1940). New York: W. W. Norton & Company, Inc.,1949, 14
22. ———. "Psychoanalysis: Freudian School," *Encyclopaedia Britannica* (14th ed.), 1926, 18, 674
23. ———. *Three Essays on the Theory of Sex* (1905). Translated by J. Strachey. London: Imago Publishing Co., 1949
24. ———. *The Unconscious* (1915). London: Hogarth Press, 1934, Coll. Papers, 4, 98–136
25. FRIEDMAN, PAUL. "Some Aspects of Concentration Camp Psychology," *Am. J. Psychiat.*, 1949, 105, No. 8, 601–5
26. GROTJAHN, MARTIN. "From and About Freud's Letters to Fliess" (read in mss.). Presented in honor of the ninety-fifth anniversary of Freud's birth at the Joint Meeting of the Los Angeles–San Francisco Psychoanalytic Societies,

October 1950. Re-presented at the Annual Meeting of the American Psycho-analytic Association, Cincinnati, Ohio, May 6, 1951

27. KEET, C. D. "Two Verbal Techniques in a Miniature Counselling Situation," *Psych. Monogr.*, 1948, **62**, 294

28. KINSEY, A. C., POMEROY, W. B., and MARTIN, C. E. *Sexual Behavior in the Human Male.* Philadelphia: W. B. Saunders Company, 1948

29. KRAFT-EBING, RICHARD VON. *Psychopathia Sexualis* (1892). Brooklyn: Physicians and Surgeons Book Co., 1932

30. KRIS, ERNST. "The Significance of Freud's Earliest Discoveries," *Int. J. Psychiat.*, 1950, **31**, 1–2, 108–16

31. KUBIE, L. S. "The Fallacious Use of Quantitative Concepts in Dynamic Psychology," *Psychoanal. Quart.*, 1947, **16**, No. 4, 507–18

32. ———. "Instincts and Homeostasis," *Psychosom. Med.*, 1948, **10**, No. 1, 16–30

33. LURIA, A . R. *The Nature of Human Conflicts.* Translated and edited by W. Horsley Gantt. New York: Liveright, Inc., 1932, 128–68 ("The Investigation of Complexes Produced During Hypnosis by Suggestion")

34. MASSERMAN, J. H. "Experimental Neuroses," *Sci. Am.*, 1950, **182**, No. 3, 38–43

35. RADO, SANDOR. "A Critical Examination of the Concept of Bisexuality," *Psychosom. Med.*, 1940, **2**, No. 4, 459–67

36. "Report of Committee on Evaluation of Psychoanalytic Therapy," *Bull. Am. Psychoanal. Assoc.*, 1950, **6**, No. 1, 17

37. SEARS, R. R. "Survey of Objective Studies of Psychoanalytic Concepts. A Report Prepared for the Committee on Social Adjustment," Social Science Research Council, New York, *Bulletin*, 1943, **51**

38. SPITZ, R. A. "Anxiety in Infancy: A Study of Its Manifestations in the First Year of Life," *Int. J. of Psychoanal.*, 1950, **31**, Nos. 1–2, 138–43

39. ———. "Hospitalism: An Inquiry into the Genesis of Psychiatric Conditions in Early Childhood," *Psychoanal. Study of Child*, 1945, **1**, 53–74. "Hospitalism: A Follow-up Report," *Psychoanal. Study of Child*, 1946, **2**, 113–17

40. ———. "The Smiling Response: A Contribution to the Ontogenesis of Social Relations," *Genet. Psych. Monogr.*, 1946, **34**, 57–125

41. STERBA, RICHARD. "Introduction to the Psychoanalytic Theory of the Libido," *Nerv. & Ment. Dis. Monogr.*, No. 68, 1947

42. THOMPSON, CLARA. " 'Penis Envy' in Women," *Psychiatry*, 1943, **6**, No. 2, 123–26

43. ZILBOORG, G. "Masculine and Feminine," *Psychiatry*, 1944, **7**, No. 3, 257–96

General References

BOHR, NIELS. "On the Notions of Causality and Complementarity," *Science*, 1950, **111**, 51–54

ERICKSON, E. H. *Childhood and Society.* New York: W. W. Norton & Company, Inc., 1950

KARDINER, ABRAM. *The Individual and His Society.* New York: Columbia University Press, 1939

MARMOR, JUDD. "Psychoanalysis," 317–39. In *Philosophy for the Future.* New
    York: The Macmillan Company, 1949

RADO, SANDOR. "Psychodynamics as a Basic Science," *Am. J. Orthopsychiat.,* 1946,
    16, No. 3, 405–9

————. "The Paths of Natural Science in the Light of Psychoanalysis," 1922,
    Psychoanal. Quart., 1932, 1, No. 4, 683–700

REINER, MARKUS. "Causality and Psychoanalysis," *Psychoanal. Quart.,* 1932, 1,
    No. 4, 701–14

Index